THE HISTORY AND THE FUTURE
OF THE
ROMAN LITURGY

DENIS CROUAN, S.T.D.

THE HISTORY AND THE FUTURE
OF THE
ROMAN LITURGY

Translated by Michael Miller, M.A. Theol.

IGNATIUS PRESS   SAN FRANCISCO

Original French edition:
Histoire et avenir de la liturgie romaine
© 2001 by Téqui, Paris

Cover art: Stained glass windows in the Church of Santa Croce,
Florence, Italy
© Royalty-Free/CORBIS

Cover design by Riz Boncan Marsella

CONTENTS

PREFACE

The manner in which the renewal of the Roman rite called for by the Second Vatican Council has been applied has given rise, within the bosom of the Church, to quarrels that pit those in favor of a liturgy that is ceaselessly revised according to the tastes and expectations of the parish communities against those who favor a liturgy of an unchanging character, which is considered the mark of its authenticity and sacredness.

But this is now producing a new situation: from now on there will be a dividing line that separates those believers who still have some ideas about liturgy from those who no longer have any notion at all. And this situation, almost unheard of in the history of the Church and of her liturgy, poses a crucial question: Is the Roman liturgy, with all the riches that it bears within it, in danger of disappearing eventually in the years to come? "In fact, it is threatened with destruction, if the necessary steps are not taken to stop these damaging influences", writes Cardinal Ratzinger.[1]

Fortunately, it seems that now there is a greater awareness of the problem. Faced with the precipitous decline of attendance at Sunday Mass, some bishops are beginning to discuss and denounce certain pastoral errors made in the course of the postconciliar years; some young priests, who are in the unenviable position of having to put up with a liturgical context that is hardly encouraging, spiritually and humanly speaking, denounce the mediocrity of the parish celebrations that they are obliged to carry out.

Still, it would be wrong to think that we can easily emerge from those years in a liturgical "no man's land" that so virulently marked the postconciliar years and that had origins well before Vatican II.

These pages were also written in the hope that they might be of some help to those who want to learn about the Roman liturgy

---

[1] Joseph Ratzinger, *The Spirit of the Liturgy* (San Francisco: Ignatius Press, 2000), Preface, p. 8.

and look forward to its full realization, both as to its exterior form and in its interior dimension. The purpose here is not to answer all the questions that might arise in the course of a study of the Roman liturgy, but rather to survey the long and rich history of the elaboration of a rite that the Church has always intended to preserve and maintain, despite the difficulties that she has met with in every age.

May these pages enlighten all believers who are no longer content with the way in which the liturgy is treated today; may they help all the pastors of the Catholic Church who are concerned about celebrating a truly Catholic liturgy, that is, a liturgy that is capable of transcending the limits of the community that is gathered for the Eucharist and of putting a stop to the dismantling and desacralization of the Roman rite.

I

RITE AND LITURGY

What is a liturgical rite?

On October 17, 1985, speaking to the members of the Congregation for Divine Worship, Pope John Paul II said,

> The liturgy! Everybody speaks about it, writes about it, and discusses the subject. It has been commented on, it has been praised, and it has been criticized. But who really knows the principles and norms by which it is to be put into practice?
>
> The Constitution *Sacrosanctum Concilium* referred to the liturgy as the "source" and the "summit" of the Church's life (no. 10); what is being done to make this sublime definition a reality?

Today everyone is interested in the liturgy: the number of studies that appear each day is proof of that. But if so many works are being published on the subject, is that not also a sign indicating that the present state of the liturgy poses serious problems?

Recently Cardinal Ratzinger ventured to speak of a "collapse of the liturgy": indeed, we can say that the liturgy is in ruins or, if you prefer, in an advanced state of dilapidation. It is enough to look at how, forty years after Vatican II, the liturgy is celebrated in certain churches to admit that something is not working: whereas the Church demands adherence to the official liturgical books that were published following the Council, which logically should lead to unity in the manner of celebrating the Eucharist, one discovers that there are as many ways of carrying out the liturgical rites as there are churches or celebrants. And it is enough to ask Catholics, "What is the liturgy? What is a rite?" to see that the answers are multifarious, sometimes incomplete, often contradictory.

We must therefore clarify things and reestablish true definitions for the elements that make up the liturgy. Let us begin, then, by asking the question, what is a rite?

A liturgical rite is a complex thing that is difficult to define in a few words. Let us say that a rite is normally a compulsory form of official worship rendered to God; this form is composed of elements that are harmoniously interrelated, having arisen from customs that are at first accepted by a specific community and then approved by the legitimate ecclesiastical authority.

Let us examine this definition in detail:

A rite is a compulsory form of worship. By these words we should understand that the form of the worship is obligatory for all believers, whatever their office in the Church may be. All baptized persons must respect the form of worship handed down by tradition and accepted by the Church—the Pope, the bishops, the priests, the deacons, and the lay faithful.

A rite is composed of elements that are harmoniously interrelated. The different parts of the rite are not added one to the other in an arbitrary fashion that is subjective or, perhaps, heterogeneous; they are grouped according to a logic that is determined by a theology that is fully guaranteed to be Catholic.

A rite is the product of customs that are accepted by a community. This clearly indicates that a rite is not composed of elements that are invented or imposed by one person or by a group of persons; rather, it arises from customs that have gradually and automatically prevailed in a community, the members of which are bound by the same Creed and therefore express their identity in these practices.

A rite must be approved by the ecclesiastical authority. It is the prerogative of the legitimate authority (the Holy See) to say whether the use of a particular rite involves any danger, either for the faith of each of the individuals who make up the community, or for the unity of the group itself. The authority, therefore, is responsible for determining whether a particular liturgical practice tends to lead to an ill-regulated religiosity.

The legitimate authority, therefore, can play the role of a moderator, without prejudice to the rite, to the extent that the authority itself is subject to it; the authority has the prerogative of saying whether a particular rite manifests certain shortcomings or whether some ritual practice may not be in danger of leading the faithful toward a spirituality that is not sound. If such is the case, it will be necessary to modify the rite or to suppress the element within it that could cause the faithful to deviate toward a too sentimental or too subjective belief, which, by that very fact, is detached from the common Creed.

The four components of the Eucharistic liturgy

The Constitution on the Sacred Liturgy of the Second Vatican Council teaches that every liturgical act is composed of two sorts of elements.

> For the liturgy is made up of unchangeable elements divinely instituted and of elements subject to change. These latter not only may be changed but ought to be changed with the passage of time, if they have suffered from the intrusion of anything out of harmony with the inner nature of the liturgy or have become less suitable (Sacrosanctum Concilium, no. 21; hereafter this document is abbreviated SC).

This excerpt from the Constitution *Sacrosanctum Concilium* shows that the liturgy has never been something that is hermetically sealed and immune to all deviation; over the centuries it has in fact been possible to introduce into it some elements that were ill suited to the intimate nature of the Church's official worship.

In order to frame the issues properly, we must learn to distinguish between the "unchangeable elements" of the liturgy and the "elements subject to change".

The unchangeable part of the liturgy or the "essential component":

In every liturgy there is an "essential component": without it, the liturgy is no longer possible. For example, in the Mass, the "essential component" consists of

- the offering of bread and wine,
- the Consecration,
- Communion.

If one of these elements is missing, there is no celebration of the Eucharist; there is nothing left but a simulation of the Mass.

The parts subject to change include

The "substantial" components:

Every liturgy includes a "substantial" part, which, in itself, is not necessary for the Eucharistic liturgy but which is found in more or less developed forms in all the Christian liturgies.

This part is made up of psalms (entrance antiphon, gradual or responsorial psalm, Communion antiphon) as well as readings from Sacred Scripture (Old Testament, Letters of the Apostles, Gospel). It also includes the use of incense, the vestments, posture, and gestures of the officiating ministers, the different prayers, and so forth.

The "modal" component:

This comprises the manner in which the "essential" and "substantial" components take place or are supposed to be carried out.

The "modal" component depends to a great extent on the traditions of the local churches. It determines the order of the ceremonies and thus allows us to distinguish between large families of rites (the Roman rite, the Ambrosian rite, the rite of Lyons, the Maronite rite, the rite of Saint John Chrysostom, etc.).

The "accessory" components:

Unlike the essential and substantial parts of the liturgy, the "accessory" component is not codified: it does not immediately concern the beliefs of the faithful and can therefore be left to the discretion of those who are responsible for conducting the liturgy.

The "accessory" component is used to enhance the elements of the three other components of the liturgy; it appeals to "good taste" and to "common sense" and thus includes everything that appeals directly to the senses in order to indicate the degree of solemnity of a celebration: candles, altar cloths, flowers, lighting, etc.[1]

It is through the "accessory" component that a liturgy can be adapted to the temperament and circumstances of different peoples, as the Council explains:

> Even in the liturgy the Church does not wish to impose a rigid uniformity in matters which do not involve the faith or the good of the whole community. Rather does she respect and foster the qualities and talents of the various races and nations. Anything in these peoples' way of life which is not indissolubly bound up with superstition and error she studies with sympathy, and, if possible, preserves intact. She sometimes even admits such things into the liturgy itself, provided they harmonize with its true and authentic spirit (SC 37).

Still, in order that the "accessory" may be introduced into the liturgy and yield its fruits, care must be taken to fulfill two conditions:

—that the "accessory" does not become something cumbersome or more important than what is "essential", "substantial", or "modal", and that it does not become, for example, an opportunity for entertaining the congregations that have gathered in the first place to participate in the Church's liturgy (recall the famous "collage" pastoral letter [of the French bishops], which now clutters our sanctuaries with brightly colored posters and felt banners that are supposed to testify to the so-called participation of children in the liturgy).

—that the "accessory" does not make us lose sight of the "noble simplicity" that the rites should have (cf. SC 34).

---

[1]Although we will place Gregorian chant in the modal part, since it is characteristic of the Roman rite and makes it possible to unify the essential and substantial parts of the liturgy, we will include the Latin language, considered in itself, in the accessory part of the liturgy, basing this decision on the teaching contained in the Preamble of the Roman Missal (section 12): "The Second Vatican Council, like that of Trent, examined in depth the didactic and pastoral nature of the liturgy. And since there is no Catholic who would deny that the rite carried out in the Latin language is legitimate and efficacious, it was able to concede ... that the use of the living [vernacular] language can often be very useful for the people, and it permitted its usage."

Did Jesus "invent" a Christian liturgy?

Christian liturgies, whatever their forms may be, have their origin in the words spoken by Christ on Holy Thursday: "Do this in memory of me." We too often forget that without this commandment, which is disarming in its simplicity, we would never have had a liturgy. Should these words of Jesus be considered unique, original, "revolutionary"? Must we see in them a regulation that obliges believers to depart from the religious framework of the Jewish era in order to invent something entirely new?

Not at all. In the time of Christ, indeed, all of the Jewish laws had become identified with liturgical regulations that Mary, Joseph, and then Jesus himself observed faithfully.[2] Now, in his teaching and in his conduct, Jesus always affirmed the necessity of observing the law "to the letter", without changing a single iota. Christ simply wanted to fulfill, to complete these commandments with a supreme law that summarized them all: the law of love. That was the novelty.

Jesus would have had plenty of reasons and occasions to rail against all the abuses, the exaggerations, and all the liturgical deviations of his day. However he never did so: at no point do the Gospels present him to us in the guise of a proponent of liturgical reform, much less of a new liturgy. To the Apostles who ask him how to pray, he does not reply by inventing a "new" prayer; he is content to take up again the main themes of daily prayers and of the psalms, which he prefaces with the traditional invocation "Our Father, who art in heaven".

Finally, when Jesus institutes what will become the heart of all Christian liturgical prayer, the Eucharist, he makes the institution of his Paschal Mystery coincide with the anniversary of the Passover of Moses, in order to underscore the fact that the sacrament of the New Covenant is the prolongation and fulfillment of the Old Covenant.

---

[2] Furthermore, it was in the area of liturgical observances, rather than that of his teaching, that the enemies of Christ sought at first to find fault with him.

The Apostles are faithful to the liturgical heritage

The Apostles, too, following the example of Jesus, did not create a new liturgy; in the Acts of the Apostles, we see them "day by day attending the temple together and breaking bread in their homes" (Acts 2:46).

This conjunction of two loyalties—fidelity to the Jewish liturgy on the one hand, and fidelity to Jesus' commandment ("Do this in memory of me") on the other—illustrates perfectly how compliance with a commandment just received is registered within the continuity of a liturgical prayer that is already venerable.

Over the course of the centuries this apostolic fidelity will find its expansion and its fulfillment in all the Christian liturgies, always proceeding by way of evolution and not by revolution.

The organization of the Christian liturgy and the progressive establishment of rites

Judeo-Christian in its origin, the newborn liturgical prayer of the Church will espouse cultural and therefore cultic forms of a more universal character as it gains non-Jewish neophytes, without thereby denying its Semitic and Old Testament origins.

At Jerusalem and then in Antioch, in Alexandria, in Rome, and later on in Byzantium, the same evangelical teaching, the same apostolic succession [*filiation*], and the same liturgical prayer unite all the Christian communities of the Empire, both in the eastern part and in the western part.

Although circumstances require that it be celebrated, during three centuries of persecution, in private dwellings or subterranean cemeteries, the unfolding of the principal liturgical act (the "breaking of the bread") is appreciably the same everywhere.

To the Eucharistic anaphora, which constitutes the "essential component" of the liturgy (the offertory, narrative of the Last Supper, Consecration, and Communion), other elements are gradually added: readings from the Letters of the Apostles, excerpts from the Gospel, prayers of intercession, processions, recitation of the Apostles' Creed and of the "Jesus prayer", and prayers of thanksgiving, etc., which will form the "substantial component" of the [particular] rite.

Liturgy and orthodoxy

In the fourth century, the end of the persecutions means for all of Christianity a new springtime and a flourishing, which is both theological and liturgical.

But the five mother churches (the apostolic Patriarchates of Jerusalem, Antioch, Alexandria, and Rome and, later, Constantinople) must now fight together against the first great heresies in order to preserve the true faith, or "orthodoxy". Reverence for the liturgy that has been handed down is what will guarantee fidelity to the true faith.

Thus, during the entire first millennium, unity of faith will be maintained along with unity of liturgical prayer.

Yet, even if the liturgical unity remains quite evident, it does not exclude legitimate differences, principally in the exterior forms and expressions of worship.

Indeed, the different cultures in which these churches take root and develop bring forth various cultic forms. So it is that in every liturgy the "accessory components", which are closely bound up with the local cultural contexts and associated with the "substantial components" of the worship as an expression of Christian prayer, give rise to different rites.

It is very important to recall here, in connection with the rest of our study, that the diversity of rites in the Church has never been the product of division among Christians, nor of any sort of anarchy, nor of a refusal to allow tradition to evolve; rather, it is the product of an "inculturation" willed by Christ himself, so that his Church might be at the same time "orthodox", faithful to her true beliefs and the true praise of God,[3] and also "catholic", faithful to her universal mission.[4]

---

[3] Cf. John Paul II, Letter *Orientale Lumen* ["Light of the East", May 2, 1995].

[4] The present chapter is to a great extent inspired by a conference given by Bishop Bernard Dupire at the *Pro Liturgia* Association, 79, rue du Général De Gaulle, 67560 Rosheim, France.

2

LITURGICAL RITE IN THE
CATHOLIC CHURCH

Often many people do not know the difference between the idea of "liturgy" and the idea of "rite". Yet these are two concepts that must be distinguished, even though they are closely connected, since there could be no liturgy without a rite.

Liturgy

According to its etymology, the word "liturgy" means "service", or, again, "work". Do we not speak of "worship services" and of the *opus Dei* (work of God) to designate cultic activities?

Yet in the official documents of the Church, the word "liturgy" scarcely ever appeared before the twentieth century. In the Middle Ages, instead of speaking about "liturgy", scholars preferred to use titles such as *"De divinis officiis"* or *"De ecclesiasticis officiis"* in their treatises.

From the sixteenth century on, the treatises were entitled *"De ritibus Ecclesiae"* or *"De sacris ritibus"* ["On the rites of the Church", "On the sacred rites"]. These new expressions that were used to designate liturgical celebrations indicate a change of mentality; henceforth it seems that more attention was paid to the ceremonial aspect of worship than to the deeper significance of carrying out the liturgy.

It was to counteract this reductive view of things that Pope Pius XII published the encyclical *Mediator Dei*[1] on November 20, 1947. In it the Supreme Pontiff states that the liturgy does not consist

---

[1] The texts of *Mediator Dei* and of *Sacrosanctum Concilium* are published in booklet form by the Daughters of St. Paul, Boston, Massachusetts. See also: Aidan Nichols, ed., *A Pope and a Council on the Sacred Liturgy* (Farnborough, Hants, UK: St. Michael's Abbey Press, 2002).

23

solely in the externals of the ceremonies; on the contrary, it is in the first place and essentially the exercise of the priestly ministry of Christ.

In December of 1963 the Second Vatican Council, in the Constitution *Sacrosanctum Concilium*, would complete the teaching of *Mediator Dei* by giving to the entire Church an even more perfect definition of the liturgy. The conciliar text declares:

> The liturgy, then, is rightly seen as an exercise of the priestly office of Jesus Christ. It involves the presentation of man's sanctification under the guise of signs perceptible by the senses and its accomplishment in ways appropriate to each of these signs.[2]

Like the Church herself, the liturgy in its entirety is a sign: a sacramental sign of the Lord's presence and at the same time of the action of the Holy Spirit.

It is understandable, then, that the connection between the Church and the Church's liturgy is so close that to impair the liturgy, to distort the form of it, whether deliberately or unwittingly, is to commit an offense against the Church herself: it is tantamount to injuring the Mystical Body of Christ and of needlessly tormenting the faithful by depriving them of the graces that accompany worship that is carried out correctly and truly.

Rite

The word "rite" comes from the Sanscrit word *riti* and denotes that which must be carried out in accordance with given norms.

A rite is an action that is stereotypical (which does not mean mechanical or thoughtless) that allows the assembled community to affirm its identity. Thus, in most religions, to perform a rite is to act like God and with God. Still, the founding act of the rite (in the case of the Eucharist: the Last Supper) is not confused with the subsequent rite, which proceeds rather in a stylized and symbolic way to evoke its source and its effective power.

[2] SC 7; see also 9 and 10.

One does not invent a ritual; by its very nature it is programmed in advance. In the Church, a rite is handed down as a sign of the liturgical family to which one belongs by Baptism.

The rite must allow priority to be given to what is said and what is done during the liturgical celebration, rather than to the person who is saying or doing those things. That is why the liturgical rite cannot tolerate didacticism, moralism, endless explanations, or subjective attitudes.[3] It simply lives its life, because its principal purpose is not to teach; it educates by imbuing, playing the role not so much of a school as of a womb in which the faithful are formed.[4]

The richness of the rite depends first of all on the fact that it does not only disclose a set of contents that are accessible to reason, but opens the horizons to the living faith that is being celebrated. When it is put into practice correctly and reverently, the rite effects in and of itself that which it expresses, presenting thus for our contemplation the faith inasmuch as it is a communal act, but also inasmuch as it is an act experienced individually by each believer. That is why it is appropriate to enter into the rite as one enters into a game: one expresses and involves oneself therein without seeking any practical benefit, but rather to discover a meaning in it.[5] One then discovers that the rite in itself cannot be identified with tradition, but that it contains and gives shape to the principle of the living tradition that nourishes the faith of the entire Church.

Rites and liturgical families

Finally, the rite makes it possible to identify different liturgical families that are found in the Church and that all have one common source.

In the East, the cradle of Christianity, the liturgies can be classified in two groups that correspond to the traditions of the two most ancient patriarchates: Antioch and Alexandria.

[3] Cf. Louis-Marie Chauvet, *Du symbolique au symbole* (Paris: Le Cerf, 1979).

[4] Romano Guardini, *The Spirit of the Liturgy*, trans. Ada Lane (London: Sheed and Ward, 1930).

[5] Cf. Marie-Laure Bourgueil, doctoral thesis (Sorbonne).

The group of Antiochene liturgies includes

- the Syrian rite of Antioch,
- the Maronite rite,
- the Byzantine rite,
- the Armenian rite,
- the Nestorian rite,
- the Chaldean rite,
- the Malabar rite.

The group of Alexandrian liturgies includes

- the Coptic rite and
- the Ethiopian rite.

In the West, also, there used to be several rites. However the ancient Gallican rites disappeared in the Carolingian period, and the Celtic rites fell into disuse with the Gregorian reform in the eleventh century, which put an end to the control of the secular powers over the Church. Certain religious orders likewise had their own rites: the Carthusians, the Dominicans, the Premonstratensians, the Cistercians, and so forth.

Today it is the Roman rite that has prevailed over all; and even if elements derived from other neighboring liturgies (for example, the Celtic liturgy) can be found within it, it has preserved its own character, which proceeds from the Latin genius: objectivity and noble simplicity.

Still in existence, besides the Roman rite, are the Ambrosian rite (in Milan), the Mozarabic rite (in certain diocese in Spain), and the Lyonnais rite (in Lyons, France).[6]

During the Second Vatican Council, the Church officially recognized that all of these venerable rites are of equal right and dignity; she declared that they are legitimate and wished that they should be preserved and fostered (cf. SC 4). Yet at the same time the Church desired to restore the Roman rite, to reexamine it thoroughly and carefully in the light of tradition, so as to restore it to vigor while taking into account present-day circumstances and needs (SC 3–4).

[6] *Droit canonique*, Précis Dalloz.

Everyone knows what would happen next: some Catholics—opposed to any change in the liturgy desired by the Church or hurt by the manner in which a modification of the liturgy was imposed on them, which in no instance could be identified with the renewal called for by Vatican II—have confused three very different things:

- the restored Roman rite according to the will of the Church today,
- the Mass as it was until the beginning of the Council and that goes back, roughly, to the restoration put into effect by Saint Pius V, but celebrated [in France] with a sort of decorum that owes much to a sensibility inherited from the nineteenth century, and
- the parish celebrations that have been reconstituted on the basis of supposedly pastoral letters that tend to drift farther and farther from what is required by the official liturgical books.

From these confusions or from these amalgams have arisen misunderstandings, divisions, errors, mutual condemnations—and even a schism.

This situation, which could be described as anarchical, means that today, forty years after Vatican II, the renewal of the Roman rite has not always been accomplished in the parishes. An increasing number of Catholics—clerics and lay people—do not know what the Roman rite is; they are no longer acquainted with its gestures, its chants, its prayers, because the Roman liturgy as defined subsequent to the conciliar studies has progressively been replaced by random celebrations that are so unsubstantial—one must admit—that they repel the faithful instead of attracting them.

It was in order to put an end to the "collapse"[7] of the liturgy that Pope John Paul II invited all the faithful on December 4, 1988, on the occasion of the twentieth anniversary of the Constitution *Sacrosanctum Concilium*, to rediscover the great inspiration that stirred up the Church during Vatican II and to ensure that the earthly liturgy is united with the heavenly liturgy, so that we might lift up with one voice the song of praise that the Church offers to the Father.[8]

---

[7] This term is used by Cardinal Ratzinger.

[8] Cf. the papal Letter *Vicesimus quintus annus*, art. 22–23.

THE BEGINNINGS OF THE LITURGY

Thus far, we have tried to understand what a rite is, we have determined the origin of our Eucharistic liturgy, we have recognized the roots common to all Christian liturgy, and we have shown how distinct liturgical families developed from these roots.

Finally, we have managed to discover the place that the "Roman rite" occupies today at the heart of these liturgical families. Isn't it time now to trace the history of this "Roman rite", to see how it developed over the centuries and came down to us in its present form?[1]

This history is often eventful and sometimes marred by periods of obscurity; the documents that remain from certain eras are often incomplete or else still have not been studied carefully enough. Then, too, it is a very long history! That is why we will divide it up into segments.

At the very beginning

In our libraries there is a lamentable lack of documents giving a detailed description of a Eucharistic celebration after the Resurrection of Christ! It would all be so simple if the Apostles had thought to write something on this subject. They did not consider it necessary to do so. Must we conclude that there was no liturgy in the first centuries [of the Christian era]? Should we conclude that everyone did as he liked when celebrating the Eucharist?

The most serious historical research allows us to give at least a partial answer to these questions.

We know that Christianity was born into a markedly religious context that was not without its liturgies and rituals. Indeed,

---

[1]Cf. Denis Crouan, *L'Histoire du missel romain* (Paris: Éd. Téqui, 1988).

from the revelation of God to Abraham, down to the coming of Christ, a monotheistic liturgy, which was codified during the time of Moses, prepared the way for the Christian liturgy. The characteristic traits of the latter can be found already in all of the preceding liturgies, those that we call "pagan" and those of the Jewish religion.

What are these principal traits? Let us note first the clear affirmation of a distinction between the sacred and the profane (places, objects, persons, times . . .); then the importance of sensible things (words, songs, gestures, objects . . .) as an expression of spiritual realities; then the sense of beauty and of celebration (ornaments, vestments, decorations . . .); likewise, the role of a hierarchy (sorcerers, levites . . .) whose authority can never be contested, not even by the "temporal" rulers; finally, and most significantly, the strict transmission, from generation to generation, of rituals and customs which are codified in minute detail. One finds examples of this concern for strict transmission throughout certain books of the Bible.

The Jewish liturgical prescriptions were faithfully observed by the Holy Family as well: the purification in the Temple, the custom of going up to Jerusalem each year, the sabbath observance, daily prayers, ritual washings, kosher food, etc.

This is why the Apostles, too, following their Master's example and faithful to their Jewish heritage, do not create a brand new liturgy. As we read in the Acts of the Apostles, they continue their custom of "day by day attending the temple together" while on the other hand "breaking bread in their homes" (Acts 2:46).[2]

Traces of a liturgy with clearly defined contours can likewise be found in the Book of Revelation (Rev 7:13). Saint John's vision strongly suggests a liturgical rite in which precise elements appear, such as the throne, white vestments, incense, a book, postures, and acclamations.

But can the liturgy be celebrated as it was during the first centuries? With difficulty. Indeed, in certain periods the early Christians experienced the trial of persecutions, and it is understandable that, in such circumstances, forced into hiding, it was not always possible for them to carry out in all its splendor the liturgy to which they aspired and of which they were simultaneously the heirs and the custodians.

---

[2] This is paraphrased from Bishop Bernard Dupire, *Quelle liturgie pour demain?* in *Actes du colloque de Solesmes* (Rosheim, France: *Pro Liturgia*).

Improvisation

The Church then enters a period of "improvisation" in the liturgy. We still must come to an understanding as to the meaning of the word "improvisation" in that long-gone era.

Today, when we speak of "improvisation", we think of "freedom of expression". Now in a society such as that of the first Christian centuries, in which liturgies (whether religious or civil) play a major role, it is unthinkable that improvisation in matters concerning worship could be synonymous with emancipation from ritual traditions.

For the early Christians, improvisation—necessitated by the difficulties of the era—means simply the exercise of a regulated freedom that allows one to adapt the liturgical schema to a particular circumstance, with a view to preserving it and handing it down. Improvisation, then, is neither independence nor freedom of expression—much less anarchy.[3]

We have trouble imagining or understanding what liturgical improvisation could have been in the first centuries of Christianity because this notion is foreign to our modern mentalities. We offer a musical example for clarification.

When Händel composed his concertos for organ and orchestra, he himself played the organ part. Therefore he felt no need to write down the notes that he played. Today Händel is no longer on earth—and the scores that he has bequeathed to us have gaps in them; organists who perform the concertos, therefore, are free to "improvise" the requisite number of measures. What are they supposed to do? Play contemporary music? That is unthinkable. Incorporate passages from similar works by Händel? That might not always sound right, and music lovers would quickly discover the deception. The best thing, therefore, is to remain within the framework set up by the master and to improvise "in the Baroque style". Now this is quite difficult: such an "improvisation" cannot be improvised, because it requires on the part of the performer-interpreter an ongoing effort to assimilate the style and the technique from the

---

[3] See Appendix V.

period of the composer, so as to remain within the framework determined by the time of the composition.

The readers will excuse this digression; it was offered only to help them to understand better the meaning that the word "improvisation" ought to have in the field of liturgy.

Be that as it may, improvisation—principally of the words related to the Eucharistic celebration—must have caused problems (the danger of doctrinal errors, awkwardness of style, etc.), because from the third century on Christian communities feel the need to have standardized texts.

In Rome, Saint Hippolytus (d. 235) gives this advice, which is both prudent and judicious:

> It is not necessary for the bishop to recite the formula exactly as given above, making an effort to repeat it by heart in the course of his Eucharistic prayer. If the bishop is truly capable of improvising in a suitable manner a long prayer in an elevated style, that is fine. But if, on the other hand, he prefers to pray only a set formula, no one should prevent him from doing so.[4]

This short paragraph demonstrates clearly

- that there are set formulas that the community is careful to hand down;
- that the option of improvising is allowed for only a small number because one must be "truly capable", one must improvise "in a suitable manner", and the prayer must be "in an elevated style".

In short, these requirements considerably limited the enthusiasm of those who, already in that age, may have had an immoderate taste (perhaps not shared by the faithful) for improvisation.

The formularies written in that age, and which remain faithful to the earliest tradition, will not all be lost or destroyed with the passage of time. They will constitute the earliest elements of a library: the *Scrinium* of the Lateran.

In studying the manuscripts that were conserved in this way, one finds that the liturgy already obeys well-established laws—so well

[4] Cf. *The Apostolic Tradition.*

established that they will withstand the subsequent efforts of compilation.

And so gradually, in an uninterrupted manner, a treasure is amassed that is both liturgical and literary, which will serve as a basis for those who will produce the first missals. Already, in its main lines, the profile of our Roman rite is being sketched, even though during these early centuries there is still no liturgical book that could be described as "Roman" in the strict sense of the word.

The first liturgical collections

What we call "the Mass" is, strictly speaking, the union or combination (which varies according to the rite) of two elements: the first is Eucharistic and the second is biblical.

This union becomes organized in a more coherent way after the Edict of Milan in A.D. 313, which guaranteed freedom of Christian worship.

Indeed, the onset of this period of peace gives rise to the desire to bring better order into the liturgy. But "putting things in order" implies "sorting things out". Starting with the fourth century, then, those ancient liturgical customs that are worth saving are preserved, and those of a lesser value are suppressed, missing parts are supplied, and those that are in need of improvement are perfected.

An important project is undertaken, chiefly during the pontificates of Saint Leo the Great (440–461) and of Gelasius I (492–496). This work of revision that resulted in the first liturgical books was accomplished in a traditional manner, respecting ancient usage and the ritual heritage; it was all the more necessary because certain bishops were using prayers composed by authors who were sometimes incompetent,[5] indeed, heretical, as Saint Augustine and others note. The urgent need for a stricter discipline is therefore evident.[6]

This ordering of liturgical prayer was done in an era that saw the convergence of two factors that cannot be overlooked: the transition from Greek to Latin and the setting of the sacred texts to music.

---

[5] In *De baptismo contra Donatistas*, PL 43, col. 213–14.
[6] A. G. Martimort, *L'Église en prière* (Paris: Éd. Desclée, 1961).

These two historical facts warrant the supposition that this initiative was as much a work of compilation as it was a work of creation: a compilation based on the documents already preserved in the *Scrinium* of the Lateran, and a creative effort that became necessary in order to adapt public worship to the setting of the first great basilicas and thus to give it a new solemnity in keeping with the aspirations of the Christian communities.

The history of sacred song perfectly illustrates the spirit in which the scholars of that era worked to bring order into the liturgy; we find, for example, that the existence of autonomous rites corresponding to definite geographical areas is indisputable. Thus there was a "chant of Benevento" for the liturgies of southern Italy, a "Roman" chant for the liturgies of Rome and the nearby territories, a "Milanese" chant for northern Italy, an "Hispanic" chant for the liturgies celebrated on either side of the Pyrenees Mountains, and finally "Gallican" chants in use in the regions of Roman Gaul.

In the fifth century the schola cantorum appears in Rome. A core group of specialists within this choir goes on to elaborate a new musical repertoire. In order to do that, they refurbish on the one hand the ancient repertoire, so that pieces formerly sung by a soloist can be performed by a schola, and on the other hand they create new pieces corresponding to the development that the liturgy is undergoing at that time.[7]

As we see—and this is a constant in our liturgy—when innovation [*une création*] becomes necessary, it is conceivable only within the framework of respect for tradition and fidelity to customs.

In 530 the *Liber Pontificalis* is published, in which are recorded the liturgical functions reserved to the bishop. At the same time *Libelli missarum* are created at the Roman chancery; these are like little anthologies containing the essential prayers for the Eucharistic liturgy.

The year 560 witnesses the promulgation of the *Leonine Sacramentary*. In this case we are dealing with a genuine liturgical book based on ancient texts that were preserved in the *Scrinium* of the Lateran and are generally attributed to the Popes Saint Leo the Great, Saint Gelasius I, and Vigilius. In this same period we also

---

[7] Dom Daniel Saulnier, O.S.B., *Le chant grégorien* (Solesmes: Abbaye Saint-Pierre, 1995).

find *florilegia* ["bouquets"] of prayers, that is, collections of selected prayers (containing series of Collects and Postcommunion prayers) that were drawn from ancient formularies.[8]

From this period on, the development of the liturgy in the East will differ increasingly from the evolution of the liturgy in the West, because in the West the influence of the Roman Pontiffs makes itself felt more than in the East; as a result, the Eastern churches will preserve a greater diversity of rites, whereas the liturgies in the Western churches will submit to varying degrees to the direct influence of the liturgy that is practiced in Rome.

We must note also that these centuries, during which the primitive liturgy is put into order and new liturgical prayers are created, are considered to be the most beautiful and the richest, in that they allow the attainment of an equilibrium that, later on, the Church would always be trying to retrieve, using different methods and with varied results: an equilibrium between creativity and organic development in the liturgy (an idea that recurs many centuries later in articles 21, 22, and 23 of the conciliar Constitution *Sacrosanctum Concilium*), between *the law of subsidiarity*—which requires that each participant in the liturgy (celebrant, deacon, lector) perform only his own office (which is reiterated in article 28 of the conciliar Constitution)—and *the law of interiority*, which means that genuine participation in the sacraments is necessarily a personal matter (a concept found recently in article 11 of the conciliar Constitution as well as in the references that John Paul II has made to this subject).[9]

The ancestors of our "Roman Missal": The sacramentaries

The creation of "Mass books" leads gradually to the composition of the first sacramentaries.

In the seventh century a work appears that was written for the priests who ministered in the parishes of Rome: the "Old Gelasian

---

[8] The *Rotulus* [in French, *Rouleau*] of Ravenna is said to be one of the oldest *florilegia*, which was purportedly composed in part by Peter Chrysologus (d. 450).

[9] See the apostolic Letter *Vicesimus quintus annus*, written for the twenty-fifth anniversary of the Constitution on the Sacred Liturgy.

Sacramentary".[10] It is made up of three books: the first contains the Temporal Cycle; the second, the Sanctoral Cycle (the feasts of the saints that are included allow us to determine in which Roman parishes this sacramentary was in use); and the third, a series of supplements showing that the work was also used in the monasteries that were immediately subject to [the diocese of] Rome.

It is interesting to note that at the beginning of the third century we find the rubric *Incipit Canon actionis* (the beginning of the Canon). This rubric comes before the *Sursum corda* ("Lift up your hearts") from the dialogue of the Preface, the Preface itself ("It is fitting indeed and just, etc."), the *Sanctus*, and the Canon that corresponds to our present Eucharistic Prayer I, although nowadays the Preface and the *Sanctus* are no longer considered as part of the Eucharistic Prayer, strictly speaking.[11]

Dating from this same period as well is a Roman *Ordo* that is very precious, in that it records for us in detail the rituals of a Mass celebrated by the Pope in the Basilica of Saint Mary Major on Easter morning. We will describe this liturgy in the next chapter.

Finally, the first half of the eighth century witnesses the diffusion, in Gaul, of a series of works for use in the local rites that, however, are already more or less inspired by the Roman liturgy. Only one of these collections remains typically Gallican; it provides us with a series of seven Masses that were probably transcribed at the beginning of the seventh century.

[10] This was incorrectly attributed to Pope Gelasius as a result of an error going back to the ninth century, which was uncritically repeated in the seventeenth century.

[11] A form of the liturgy that was in use at Rome (can one speak in this case of a "Roman liturgy"?) would be introduced in England after 664, following the council of Whitby.

4

THE "ROMAN" LITURGY

The Roman liturgy spread throughout Gaul

Until the beginning of the eighth century, liturgies continued to vary from one region to the next. Nevertheless, the liturgical rituals that were in use in Rome gradually spread and influenced the local liturgies to varying degrees, and certain historical events favored this trend. Let us examine how this evolution took place, which would culminate in the establishment of what we still call today the "Roman rite".

During the eighth century, many churches in Gaul were destabilized by invasions; every French schoolchild remembers the history lesson in which the teacher explained that "in 732 Charles Martel stopped the Arabs at Poitiers."

But the Saracens were not the only ones to make the churches totter: after them came the conquerors, the Franks, who had no scruples about plundering the Christian communities.

In those troubled times, Christian worship had much to endure; the liturgy was no longer celebrated regularly, and when it was still possible, it was done in a very disorderly fashion.

It fell to the members of the Carolingian dynasty—and to Pepin the Short in the first place—to put the Christian liturgy at the heart of the program for restoring and unifying the Frankish kingdom. And so the order was given to a monk from Burgundy (who was probably stationed at Flavigny) to compose a liturgical book that could serve as the basis for the restoration and unification of Christian worship.[1]

---

[1] Emmanuel Bourque, *Étude sur les sacramentaires romains, 2ᵉ partie: les textes remaniés. Tome 1: le Gélasien du VIIIᵉ siècle.* (Bibliothèque théologique de Laval, Québec, PUL, 1952); see also the review of this book written by Dom Paul Lannurien, *Revue Grégorienne*, no. 5 (Solesmes, 1955).

To complete this work, the monk used a sacramentary of the Roman type (the "Old Gelasian", which was discussed in the preceding chapter and which had arrived in Gaul probably as early as the end of the seventh century), as well as Gallican sacramentaries, with which he was well acquainted, being accustomed himself to the Gallican liturgy.

At about the same time, Pepin the Short asked Pope Paul I to send him some books that were being used in Rome so that he could make copies of them. He received from the Supreme Pontiff an "antiphonary" containing the chants of the Mass and a "responsorial" containing the responses of the Divine Office.

Around 750, the Roman *Ordo* (in which we find the description of the Mass celebrated by the Pope at Saint Mary Major) made its departure from Rome; it was sent to the kingdom of Pepin the Short.

It is difficult to summarize in a few lines a history as complex as that of our liturgy [in France]. We will recall, however, that in the eighth century, at the prompting of the first Carolingian kings, there is a new project of liturgical restoration and compilation that accompanies the diffusion of the books originating in Rome.

This confluence of various currents is the source of our so-called "Roman" liturgy. This liturgy, it is well understood, was not created such as it is today; it is the product of exchanges, amalgams, of works of compilation carried out on the basis of different ritual customs, which all had a common source that is to be found in the tradition received from the Lord and faithfully handed down by the first churches that were founded in apostolic times.

The time of Pepin the Short provided a definite geographic area and an historic context that can be described as favorable, in which were found all the "ingredients" needed for the creation of a liturgical book that would be called "Roman" because its sources were at Rome, but which, in reality, would be more "Romano-Frankish", since it is the result of a work of compilation carried out under the influence of two different liturgical traditions.

This fact is confirmed by what we call today "Gregorian chant", which is in reality the result of a fusion of two musical traditions: the Roman and the Frankish. We will return later to this question of liturgical chant.

It is no less true that the "Roman-Frankish" *Ordo*—which is produced in this way and which incorporates the essentials of the papal Mass described in the Roman *Ordo*—serves as a point of departure and of reference for our present Roman Missal. The liturgy described in the "Romano-Frankish Sacramentary" will serve, over the centuries, as the initial model for all the Masses of the Roman rite, as we shall see.

The papal Mass described in the Roman *Ordo* and incorporated in the "Roman-Frankish" *Ordo*

Thus far we have mentioned many times the liturgy celebrated by the Pope on Easter morning at Saint Mary Major. It is high time to describe it, to see how it unfolds. The attentive reader will be astonished to discover in it the features of our present liturgy, when it is celebrated in keeping with the official books published following Vatican II.[2]

Upon arriving at the basilica, the Pope goes to the *secretarium* (the ancestor of our present-day sacristies) to put on the liturgical vestments and to inquire about the ministers who are appointed to sing or to recite the readings.

When everyone is ready, the celebration begins: while the schola sings the designated *Introit* (the entrance hymn of the day), the procession makes its way to the altar. The acolytes walk at the head, carrying smoking censers and candles. The Pope is the last one in the procession; he is flanked by two deacons who assist him.

When they reach the altar, the group of acolytes divides in two so as to allow the Pope to pass; he prostrates himself for a silent prayer. Then he rises, venerates the altar, makes the Sign of the Cross, says, "Peace be with you" to the ministers who are present, and goes to his throne.[3] During this time, the acolytes have placed the candlesticks on the ground beside the altar, and the schola has

---

[2] Cf. A. G. Martimort, *L'Église en prière* (Paris: Desclée, 1961); Dom Guy-Marie Oury, *La messe romaine et le peuple de Dieu dans l'histoire* (édition de l'Abbaye de Solesmes, 1981).

[3] The reader will note the absence of any "prayers at the foot of the altar", which were introduced rather late into the Roman liturgy. Of course, the celebrant says prayers in preparation for the Mass, but these do not form part of the liturgy as such; they remain an act of private devotion.

finished singing the *Introit* and has intoned the chant for the *Kyrie eleison*.

When the singing of the *Kyrie* is over, the Pope intones from his throne the *Gloria in excelsis Deo*. When the hymn is finished, the Pope turns to the people and says, *"Pax vobis"* (Peace be with you), before singing the opening prayer.

After the prayer, all sit down for the Liturgy of the Word of God. Between the readings, one or more soloists perform the chants designated by the liturgy. Then the deacon appointed to proclaim the Gospel goes to stand before the Supreme Pontiff; he kisses his feet (a sign of respect common in that era), receives his blessing, and goes in procession to the ambo, escorted by acolytes, carrying candles and incense.

When the reading of the Gospel is finished, the deacon presents the Gospel book to be kissed by the Pope; he then puts the precious artifact back into its case so as to carry it back to the Lateran.

During this period it is not yet customary to recite the *Credo* at Mass.[4]

Now it is time for the offertory procession. The Pope and the bishops who are present approach the faithful to receive the gifts; these are arranged in a cloth that is held by the deacons. Then the acolytes prepare the altar for the offertory rites: they place upon it a corporal the size of an altar cloth and set the bread and the wine upon it. During this time, the Pope has returned to his seat where—according to specifications in certain manuscripts—he washes his hands.

When everything is ready, the deacons invite the Pope to go to the altar; the Pontiff adds to the offerings already arranged upon the altar his own offering of bread. All during this rather long interval, the schola is chanting the offertory antiphon. When these rituals are completed, the Pope makes a sign to the choir members to finish their singing. Then the Pontiff says the prayer that ends with the traditional formula *"Per omnia saecula saeculorum"*.

---

[4] In 747 the council of Cloveshove [Clyff, England] decreed that the *Credo* and the *Pater noster* be recited in the language of the people in England. In 813 the council of Tours would decree that sermons should no longer be given in Latin but rather in the common language.

This is the beginning of the Eucharistic Prayer, properly so called: the Pope sings the Preface dialogue and the Preface itself. When the latter is over, the subdeacons who are standing at the entrance to the sanctuary, facing the altar (therefore with their backs to the people), bow and sing the *Sanctus*. They will remain thus, bowing, during the entire Canon (i.e., the Eucharistic Prayer).

There is no such thing as a Canon recited in a low voice; on the contrary, according to the ancient liturgical tradition, it is sung in its entirety.[5] It ends with a gesture of offering (the elevation of the Bread and Wine) at the recitation of the final doxology.

At the beginning of the Canon, an acolyte brings the paten; it is placed inside a cloth sack tied around his neck because it is large and quite heavy. This paten is held reverently during the entire time of the Canon[6] since it will then be used at the fraction or breaking of the Bread.

After the Canon, the Pope sings the *Pater noster* with its embolism [conclusion] *quia tuum est regnum* ... (For the kingdom, the power, and the glory are yours ...); then he gives the kiss of peace, which is passed on to the members of the clergy and then to the people, and takes a particle of Bread that was consecrated at an earlier Mass and places it in the chalice. It is specified that the Pontiff

> begins the fraction at the altar and returns to his seat; the archdeacon himself makes the other necessary preparations in order to continue the ritual; indeed, to avoid the loss of particles, the loaves are placed in small linen bags held by the acolytes, who take them to the bishops and the priests; the latter break them through the cloth.[7]

During this time the *Agnus Dei* is sung, a chant introduced into the liturgy by Pope Sergius I (687–701); the invocation is repeated as many times as necessary while the ritual of the fraction takes place.

---

[5] The present liturgy provides for the singing of the Eucharistic Prayer.

[6] Before the Council, this gesture had been preserved in High Masses, although it had long since lost its meaning: during the entire Canon the subdeacon was supposed to hold the paten concealed under a veil. It was a rare Catholic who could have explained the origin of this gesture, which, in itself, did not even have a symbolic meaning.

[7] Dom Guy-Marie Oury, *La messe.*

The Pope takes Communion at his seat, according to a rather complicated ritual that had been preserved until the time of the Second Vatican Council only in papal Masses. The faithful communicate in turn, following a well-established protocol.

During Communion, the schola sings the Communion antiphon with verses from a psalm; as with the entrance hymn, the antiphon itself serves as a refrain repeated between the psalm verses.

After Communion, the Pope returns to his seat to wash his hands. Then he goes to the altar to recite the final prayer (the Postcommunion). Then a deacon intones the *Ite missa est*. The response is *Deo gratias*.

This final dialogue, which signals the end of the Mass, is sung to a brief melody; it is an error to sing the *Ite missa est* to an elaborate melody that reiterates the theme of the *Kyrie*, since, logically speaking, this formula is not a prayer but rather a command.[8]

Immediately the procession lines up again, as at the beginning of the Mass, so as to leave the sanctuary and go back to the sacristy. You will note that there is no "closing hymn", since the habit of singing "another" hymn "after" Mass has never been part of the Roman rite.

Such is the Roman rite in the eighth century: it is sober, dignified, logical, devoid of anything that could seem affected or ponderous. The orderly sequence [*ordonnancement*] of the ceremonies, as it appears in this era, combined with the use of candles, incense, and a genuinely liturgical chant, lends to the celebration of the Eucharist an extraordinary dignity, which should be perceptible to all the faithful.

We will return later to the question of chant, which, as performed in this period during the celebration of the liturgy described here, is a novelty that will have a profound influence on all of Western music.

---

[8] Fortunately, this error was corrected by the liturgical restoration that followed Vatican II. Today there are only two melodies for the *Ite missa est*: one for the Paschal season, in which only the two *Alleluia*'s are ornamented (*Ite missa est, alleluia, alleluia* . . .), the other for the rest of the liturgical year.

A BRIEF HISTORY OF THE CHURCH
BUILDING AND THE ALTAR

In the eighth century, the liturgical rite used in Rome is, so to speak, established. Yet one question remains: In what sorts of places is it celebrated? in what buildings and upon what altars?

The first places of worship

The Acts of the Apostles tell us that the first Christians in Jerusalem went to the Temple regularly. But all the evidence indicates that that was not where they celebrated the liturgy that was specifically their own. Thus, during the early years of Christianity, there was a twofold worship: Jewish in the Temple and Christian in other places. These other places where the faithful gathered for the "breaking of the bread" were nothing more than houses equipped with at least one rather large and well-furnished room, similar to the one that had served as the Cenacle.

Gradually, as the early Christian communities became important enough to declare their autonomy with regard to the Temple, Christians started to build the first "churches", large halls constructed according to the local architectural traditions.

Whenever possible, the room for the early Christian assembly consisted of a rectangular hall divided into naves by rows of columns, headed by a narthex and extended by a semicircular apse. These buildings, of modest dimensions, did not need to be concealed because, more often than not, the waves of persecution knew nothing about them.

The Catacombs

It has often been taught that during the first few centuries Christians were obliged to flee to the Catacombs in order to escape the persecutions. What is the truth of the matter? What role did the Catacombs play in the liturgy?

In ancient Rome the cult of the dead was one of the rare social activities that could be carried on with complete freedom. Citizens had the right to form associations with a view to these practices. Christian believers, also, made use of this freedom of association as much as possible in order to legalize their community life and thus have the right to own buildings.

Therefore it was the cult of the dead and the pursuit of the "advantages" that accompanied it that impelled the Christians, so to speak, to gather on cemetery grounds or in passageways that had been carved out. But the Catacombs were never conventional places of worship, much less a refuge unknown to the Roman authorities; people went there for funerals or to pray on the anniversary of the death of a loved one. The Catacombs were not considered ordinary places of worship; indeed the liturgical use of them ceased—without the least bit of nostalgia, it seems—as soon as peace was granted by the Edict of Milan in A.D. 313.

Only one custom was preserved, which was derived from the Christian practice of praying near the altar of the Popes or the martyrs entombed in the Catacombs: the custom of placing relics in altars so as to demonstrate the connection between professing the faith and the Eucharist.

The peace of Constantine

At the beginning of the fourth century, the freedom of worship granted to the Christians by Constantine involved the construction of new sanctuaries: these are the "basilicas", a term that indicates less the size of the building than its architectural type. The "basilica", in the original meaning of the word, was a large meeting hall that was found in Roman villas, having a design that was reminiscent of public buildings by the same name.

The first Christian basilicas, therefore, followed the plan of these meeting places: hall, narthex, and apse. They added, however, a rich interior decoration that often took up motifs from the Christian paintings that decorated the Catacombs.

Indeed, the Constantinian basilicas provide the archetypal blueprint for Christian church buildings in the West: a plan that subsequently will manage to continue through all the major styles (Romanesque, Gothic, flamboyant, classical, Baroque, etc.) without losing its identity. It is only during the latter years of the twentieth century that the attempt was made to depart from the traditional plan so as to adapt new church buildings to what was thought to be the architectural environment of future centuries. The very least that one can say is that contemporary architecture is far from having left us nothing but masterpieces.

The altar

Symbolically, the altar is at once the cross of the sacrifice and the table of the meal: it is the place upon which Christ makes himself present, and for this reason it is the center around which the entire liturgy is organized.

Although it is the center of the liturgy, the altar is not the only place where the liturgy is celebrated, for it is not the "center" in the geometric sense of the word. It is complemented, as it were, by the ambo (the place for the proclamation of the Word of God) and by the celebrant's chair or the bishop's throne (the place for presiding). One could also add the stalls that are found in monasteries or collegial churches [i.e., churches with a chapter of canons] (a place for the choral recitation of the Divine Office) or the choir loft (the place where the singers perform their particular ministry):[1] these different places are so many "poles" where competent ministers, who are delegated by the Church, put into practice one of the components of the liturgy.

Over the centuries the altar has had various forms and orientations. Originally it was a movable wooden table. From the fourth or fifth century on it is gradually transformed into a stone table on

[1]Cf. SC 29.

account of the obvious biblical symbolism: it recalls the rock from which Moses made water spring, prefiguring Christ (1 Cor 10:4), as well as the cornerstone supporting the entire Church (Acts 4:11; Mt 21:42; Eph 2:20, for example). Furthermore the stone altar, which has its origin in the Book of Genesis (Gen 28:18), becomes the subject of precise legislation in the Book of Deuteronomy (Deut 27:5–7).

Finally, in the New Covenant, Christ, the stone rejected by the builders, becomes the sole altar and the one temple. That is why, when a new altar is consecrated, five crosses are engraved in the stone, which recall the wounds of Christ. Moreover, the altar is anointed, just like Christ after he sacrificed himself and died.

The sanctuary today: What the Second Vatican Council says

Contrary to what is sometimes supposed, liturgical tradition has always required that the altar be separate from the wall of the church so that it can be in a position of prominence [*mis en valeur*]. It was not until the medieval period that the custom began of providing the altar with a backing or "reredos", thereby making it impossible to walk around it. Then gradually, in parish churches on a smaller scale, the altar was moved toward the back of the apse and, from the fifteenth century on, a tabernacle was added for the reservation of the Blessed Sacrament.

According to the tradition of the Church, the altar should be devoid of all ornamentation; it is sufficient unto itself by virtue of its symbolism and its function. Besides the cloth that covers it and the candles that can be placed upon it during the course of a liturgical celebration, nothing should be put on the altar: no Bible, no posters, or other notices advertising this or that parish group. Even the microphone should be as discreet as possible; it is not a liturgical object, and the Lord has no need of audio equipment in order to hear our prayers. As for bouquets of flowers, they should never be placed directly upon the altar; it is better to save them for decorating the sanctuary,[2]

---

[2] By "sanctuary" is meant the "choir" (*presbyterium*) of the church, and not the entire church building.

that is, the clearly defined[3] sacred space in which the liturgical rites are carried out.

One of the great benefits of the Second Vatican Council was that it promoted the rediscovery of the real meaning and importance of the altar. That is why, in our churches, the main altar should be designed in relation to all the other features of the sanctuary in which it is located; it has to be the "center" toward which everything converges and to which the congregation's attention is spontaneously drawn.[4]

However, as we saw earlier, this idea of "center" is of the psychological rather than the geometric sort; indeed, the altar should "impress" the assembly by its form, by the place that it occupies, by the lighting that enhances it, and by its elevation.[5]

The liturgical experiments that have been conducted in recent years have shown that placing a small, worthless altar near the nave is no solution to the problem of emphasizing the liturgical space and of allowing the rites to be carried out. Indeed, it is not appropriate to place a "mini-altar" at the intersection of the transept, in front of a cavernous sanctuary,[6] which from then on would remain empty:[7] the importance of the altar can be understood only to the extent that one realizes first the functional role of the sanctuary, the place in which the rituals must be carried out and where all their richness of expression can be manifested.

It is good for the altar to be built separate from the wall so that, in keeping with ancient liturgical tradition, one can easily incense it while walking all around it, and so that it is also pos-

---

[3] The Second Vatican Council never required the removal of the "Communion rails" that mark off the sacred space in church buildings.

[4] [French] Bishops Commission on the Liturgy, *Directives pratiques pour le renouveau liturgique et la disposition des églises* [Guidelines for the liturgical renewal and the furnishing of churches], July 20, 1965; published in *La liturgie* (Paris: Édition du centurion, 1966), I.A., 1–2.

[5] Ibid., 2a.

[6] Ibid., 2b: "The sanctuary is intended ... to be the place in which the liturgical rites are carried out, and not an additional nave." Therefore pastors should discontinue the practice of using the sanctuary as a weekday chapel and of placing chairs and a little altar in it.

[7] Ibid., 2b. The sanctuary is reserved for those who carry out liturgical functions. It is a sacred space into which no one else should enter.

sible for the priest to celebrate the Eucharist while facing the congregation.[8]

As for the size of the altar, the Church makes no specifications. She simply requires that its massiveness be dependent upon the size of the building and that its dimensions be in harmony with the symbolic function that the altar serves; the dimensions that were common from the sixteenth century on, which have left us a heritage of altars on a monumental scale, are no longer relevant.[9] Indeed, from the Council of Trent (sixteenth century) until the Second Vatican Council, the altar was thought of as the sole place where the rites of the Eucharistic celebration could be carried out; its volume had to furnish the entire sanctuary by itself, and its dimensions had been considerably augmented by the fact that, ever since the late Middle Ages, the priest had to stand there during the entire Mass at three distinct places.[10] Now, by returning to the [historical] sources of the liturgy, the renewal of the Roman rite called for by Vatican II provided that the celebrant would stand at the altar only for the Liturgy of the Eucharist, properly so called (that is, from the offertory until the end of Communion), and the chair and the ambo became the other essential poles of the celebration.

During every liturgical function it is required that a sufficiently large cross with an image of Christ crucified be placed upon the altar, as well as with candles. However, for practical and aesthetic reasons, it is also permitted today to place the cross beside the altar and to put candles on either side of the altar,[11] right on the floor, if decorum demands it.[12]

---

[8] This is not so that he can look at the congregation in front of him, but so that the faithful can see the rituals that are taking place at the altar. Recall that neither the Second Vatican Council nor the official liturgical books require the priest to celebrate "facing the people".

[9] *Directives pratiques*, I.B., 2.

[10] The three places were in the center for the "prayers at the foot of the altar", at the right from the end of the "prayers at the foot of the altar" to the *Alleluia* following the Epistle, at the left for the Gospel (the reading for the day as well as the "Last Gospel"), and in the center again from the *Credo* until the final blessing.

[11] *Directives pratiques*, I.D., 1–2.

[12] Placing candles directly upon the floor around the altar is nothing new; as we have seen, this was the usual practice in the Roman liturgy, at least since the eighth century.

One thing, though, should be avoided: grouping several candles on one corner of the altar, as one very often sees it done nowadays. Besides the fact that this arrangement betrays a propensity to be the slave of every thoughtless novelty, it causes a disequilibrium, a break in symmetry; the liturgy at all time seeks to avoid this, in that every voluntary lack of harmony in the external forms of worship runs the risk, either of revealing a lack of psychological maturity on the part of those who are responsible for carrying out the liturgy or else of gradually leading to questionable behavior among those who participate in the liturgical actions.

One altar or two?

The altar and the sanctuary have gone through an evolution with the result that today, in most of our churches, we find two altars: the one on which the priest celebrated Mass until Vatican II, and the more recent one upon which the Eucharist is celebrated today.

It must be acknowledged that the little altars "facing the people" that are used everywhere today are rarely masterpieces of artistry and good taste. Who has not been shocked to find, in some churches, a cheap construction made of a few boards assembled more or less correctly? What impression does it make when the liturgy is celebrated on such "altars"—if they deserve the name? Does it not show a lack of respect for the Lord? Doesn't this subterfuge initiate a process of desacralization that will end up causing a certain casualness in the comportment and attitude of Catholic clergymen and lay people?

A recent and unfortunately little-known official document [of the French bishops] gives precise and very instructive guidelines as to the meaning of the altar and the place that it should occupy:

> The Eucharist is at the same time the sign and the cause of communion.... Ecclesial communion is, ultimately, Eucharistic communion, and the entire cause of ecumenism is focused on the possibility of achieving that communion: participating in the same Eucharist, approaching one and the same altar.... St. Ignatius of Antioch had already exhorted the faithful to do this. I emphasize the statement of St. Ignatius about *one altar*; this is important from the symbolic and educational perspective; but this is a difficult issue with regard to the present-day arrange-

ments in our cathedrals and, in general, in our churches, when the clergy want to celebrate facing the people.

We must try to solve this problem; there are solutions, certainly, but they cannot yield in a facile way to the temptation of setting up an almost insignificant table in order to celebrate facing the people, while leaving behind it the old altar with the cross, the candelabras, and the flowers, as if one wanted to celebrate Mass on two altars.[13]

What can be done concretely to settle in an intelligent and definitive way this question about the one altar? On June 30, 1965, Cardinal Lercaro, President of the *Consilium* for the Liturgy, explained:

> There is a general enthusiasm for celebrating facing the people.... But this enthusiasm, good in itself, has also given rise to solutions in bad taste which are sometimes illogical or contrived.... In any case, we must emphasize that celebrating the entire Mass facing the people is not absolutely indispensable for effective pastoral results. The entire Liturgy of the Word, which involves to the greatest extent the participation of the faithful through dialogue and singing, is already celebrated while facing the congregation.... It is certainly to be hoped that the Liturgy of the Eucharist, too, might be celebrated facing the people so that the faithful can follow the entire ritual in a more immediate way, and thus participate in it with greater awareness. But this must not lead to a ... sometimes thoughtless renovation of pre-existing churches and altars which irreparably destroys other values which should be safeguarded, too.[14]

Is it not time to return to having one altar in our churches, so as to give back to the liturgy, as it has been restored following the Council, its fullest dimension and its true meaning? Learning to

[13] *Bulletin du secrétariat de la conférence des évêques de France* [Bulletin of the secretariat of the French Bishops Conference], no. 5 (March 1995): a conference given by Bishop Garriga Pere Tena during the colloquium of the Sacred Art Committee of Rheims.

[14] Recall that the Constitution on the Liturgy of Vatican II does not require celebrating Mass "facing the people"; this question is not even raised by the Council, as Cardinal Ratzinger recalled in a conference given on the occasion of the tenth anniversary of the Motu Proprio *Ecclesia Dei adflicta* (archived at www.ewtn.com). Similarly, neither the Roman Missal nor the Bishops Ceremonial obliges priests to turn toward the congregation in order to celebrate the Eucharist. Whatever the arrangement in a church, it must be kept in mind that pastoral considerations are subject to the truth of the liturgical celebration, and not the other way around.

use the old altars more, instead of abandoning them in order to celebrate facing the people at all costs, could enable the faithful to rediscover a love for Eucharistic adoration.

A return to the one altar would acquire the proper significance if all of the specifically Eucharistic part of the liturgy (from the offertory to the end of Communion) were to be carried out there, whereas the Liturgy of the Word and the recitation of the [opening and concluding] prayers by the celebrant would take place respectively at the ambo and at the presider's chair, both of which are situated toward the front of the sanctuary.

The liturgy will not regain its full significance unless, instead of worrying only about the position of the altar, we also take into account the entire space that surrounds the celebration and that allows the rituals to take on their proper aesthetic and symbolic dimensions.

6

THE ORIGINS OF THE CHANT
OF THE ROMAN LITURGY

As we have seen previously, in the eighth century the Roman liturgy is already established, so to speak: it is the result of a harmonious fusion of the Roman rite with some Frankish customs. While this rite was developing, Christians were building places of worship, thus the Eucharistic liturgy was carried out in sanctuaries and upon worthy altars. But we have seen also that the normal form of the liturgy is the sung form; anything other than a chanted liturgy is inconceivable.[1] Hence the twofold question: What is sung? How is it sung?

Gregorian chant: The chant "specially suited to the Roman liturgy"

Many people like to listen to the sacred chants of religions from far-off lands; they find them admirable, even if they do not grasp their meaning. Today there is a marked preference for what is "mysterious", "exotic", for anything that can set the spirit sailing toward arcane horizons.

Yet often these same people, when they happen to go to church, completely forget that our Roman liturgy, too, possesses a sacred chant, the eminent role of which at the heart of liturgical ceremonies has been acknowledged and emphasized by the Church. Indeed, does not article 116 of the conciliar Constitution on the Liturgy teach, "The Church recognizes Gregorian chant as being specially suited to the Roman liturgy. Therefore, other things being equal, it should be given pride of place in liturgical services"?

---

[1] "Low Masses", which are merely "read", can be described as a late invention.

How did this chant come to be called "Gregorian"?[2] Where did we get all of these melodies, some of which have become so popular that advertisement firms (which rarely err when it is a question of appealing to the public!) use them on television to showcase such and such a variety of cheese or of some other delicacy?

From the origins to the Edict of Milan (313)

Not much is known about how they sang or what they sang in the Christian Church of the early centuries; Saint Paul simply tells us that Christians sang "hymns", a general term that comprises psalms, canticles, and readings followed by a chant.[3]

Since the first Christians were Jews, everything leads us to suppose that psalmody must have made up the essential part of liturgical chant. The text of a psalm was sung by a cantor, who now and then punctuated the musical phrase with the help of a cadence that was easy to memorize, because it was composed on the basis of a traditional pattern.[4] During this time the assembly remained mute, so to speak: its "active participation" consisted first and foremost in keeping themselves in the presence of God and in listening to his Word—an attitude that seems to be essential in liturgy and that we would often do well to rediscover.

It was not until the third or the fourth century that the faithful were invited to sing. At that time, the ceremonies were performed in the basilicas that were built following the Edict of Milan, and the liturgy abandoned Greek for Latin, the language of the people.

From the fourth to the eighth century

Liturgical chant—the primary role of which is to be at the service of the liturgy—follows an evolution parallel to that of the liturgy.

---

[2] For a simple history of Gregorian chant, see Denis Crouan, *Le chant grégorien, son histoire et son actualité* (Paris: Édition F. X. de Guibert, n.d.).

[3] In the office of the Easter Vigil we find faint traces of this chant that follows a reading; every Old Testament reading is succeeded by a canticle that forms part of the reading and has a melody that is nothing more than ornamented psalmody.

[4] Here we find the remote origin of the *iubilus* of the *Alleluia* (that is, the melisma or long melodic development that is sung to the final vowel "a" of the word "alleluia").

Since at that time there was a great variety of rites corresponding to specific cultural areas, it follows that there was also a diversity of musical repertoires: every region in the Christian West had
a local repertoire. Everyone used the same language (Latin), but
the texts and the melodies varied from one church to the next:

> We are certain today that there existed: a chant of Benevento for South-
> ern Italy, a "Roman" chant for the city of Rome and the territories
> subject to it, a "Milanese" chant in Northern Italy, an "Hispanic" chant
> on either side of the Pyrenees Mountains, and a "Gallican" chant (or
> several?) in the lands of Roman Gaul.[5]

What should be learned from history is that a diversity of musical
repertoires corresponded to the diversity of liturgies. The so-called
"Roman" liturgy was associated with a "Roman" chant; we should
also take note that this "liturgy-chant" pairing was prevalent only
in a very restricted geographical area.

What was the Roman chant like? We do not know, because it
was dependent upon oral tradition. On the other hand, studies show
that its composition dates from the fifth and sixth centuries.

How did this musical composition come about? We have seen
that, originally, chant was reserved for a soloist, the "cantor" [*"psalm-
iste"*]. But as soon as the liturgy was deployed in basilicas of considerable proportions, two new imperatives appeared: it became
necessary to replace the soloist by a group of singers and to create
new pieces to meet the requirements of the worship services.

The schola cantorum (the school that trains singers) gradually
replaces the soloist(s); at the same time, "masters" [*magistri*] are
ordered to develop a repertoire in accordance with the new liturgical forms such as, for example, the processions (entrance, offertory, Communion). This work proceeds along two lines: on the
one hand, the composition of new pieces, on the other hand, the
adaptation of ancient melodies that formerly were reserved to
the soloist(s); this is true in the case of the "Gradual", which is
sung upon the steps (*gradus*) leading up to the ambo, between the
proclamation of the sacred texts (the Epistle, the Gospel).

---

[5] Dom Daniel Saulnier, O.S.B., *Le chant grégorien* (Solesmes: Abbaye Saint-Pierre, 1995).

In the midst of these new compositions the repertoire of the celebrant is maintained. Since he is not necessarily an expert singer, the repertoire is kept simpler for him, closer to the simple declamatory style. Sometimes the melodies are a bit more ornate, mainly for the sake of solemnity on a feast or of emphasizing an important moment in the liturgy.

The liturgical repertoire

Specialists in Gregorian chant are of the view that the liturgical repertoire was nearly established toward the end of the fourth century; what the composers of that period intended was, not to introduce entertaining music or pleasant tunes into the liturgy, but to make it possible for the liturgy itself to be sung. The music that they composed, therefore, was not of just any sort; a kind of chant was developed that was directly inspired by the rituals and the sacred texts of the liturgy, a chant that first and foremost should be suited to proclaiming the holiness of the Lord, touching the hearts of the faithful, and eliciting praise by fostering contemplation.

This chant—which would later be called "Gregorian"—corresponds exactly to the definition of liturgical chant given by the Popes: this chant is closely connected to the sacred texts, so closely connected with these words that, without them, it no longer exists and is little more than an uninteresting series of tones. As John Paul II emphasized in his address to the American bishops who had come for their *ad limina* visit in October 1998, the Gregorian melodies are superbly adapted to the genius of the Roman rite.

In this sense one can say that, like the liturgy that is its source and its basis, the chant that later on would become the official chant of the Roman liturgy is a school of spirituality, praise, and contemplation (SC 2). To keep alive this specifically liturgical chant in our Eucharistic celebrations,[6] as the Second Vatican Council (SC 114) and the bishops expressly demand, is to allow the faithful to participate in an earthly liturgy that is truly a reflection of the heavenly liturgy (SC 8).

---

[6] Not as chant that is one "pleasant" or "interesting" sort of music among others, but rather as a chant that is an essential constituent of our liturgy.

From the ninth to the twelfth century: The "Golden Age"

Gregorian chant, born of the fusion of two liturgical repertoires—Roman and Frankish—appears as a genuine innovation with respect to the older repertoires.

Given that Pepin the Short and then Charlemagne participated actively in the work of unifying the "Romano-Frankish" liturgy—which we will now refer to by the name of the "Roman liturgy"—the musical repertoire itself would be unified, that is to say, transformed:

> There are indeed at the source of Gregorian chant two different traditions, which met and underwent a sort of hybridization.
>
> Gregorian chant has, first, a Roman origin. From Rome, indeed, and from the Roman liturgy came the texts for the Gregorian melodies. And Roman tradition is always a guarantee of security, of doctrinal soundness, of realism, of sobriety, and thus of a priestly character. The texts are always drawn from Sacred Scripture (the official book); they have been chosen with the greatest possible care and marvelously express the meaning of each feast. Of course, the other side of the coin is sometimes a formal conservatism which is rather strict and, let us admit it, somewhat lacking in imagination. It should be acknowledged that, as far as we know, the music of the old Roman chant was hardly attractive. It was, instead, poor, monotonous and therefore gloomy.
>
> And then there is the tradition of the Gauls. Almost as ancient as that of Rome, but quite different. For Gaul had been evangelized directly by the Eastern Christians, and not by Rome. The Churches of Marseilles, of Lyons, of the Rhône Valley and many others besides were founded by Christians from Asia Minor, notably from Syria. And so the old Gallic chant had a rather oriental side to it. A lot of poetry in the texts, with a slight risk of doctrinal deviance. A certain prolixity. And absolutely opulent, sumptuous, florid music which was positively enchanting. To get some idea of it, it is enough to listen to the chant of the Eastern liturgies that are still alive today. The Gallic tradition thus provided the essential elements of the Gregorian melodies.
>
> The Gregorian repertoire, therefore, is the product of the encounter between what was better in the Roman tradition—the texts of the chants—and what was better in the Gallic tradition—the music.[7]

---

[7] From a conference given by Dom Daniel Saulnier on July 25, 1996, as part of an international training course in Gregorian chant in Fontevraud.

Now in a period when all new repertoire necessarily must be learned by heart—since musical notation does not yet exist—this poses a certain number of problems. We know that it is easier to make a choir use new hymnals than it is to change the brain of a singer! But in the ninth century there were no hymnals.

The singers therefore had to memorize a repertoire that was completely new to them. And the idea did occur to directors to use a notation that could assist a sometimes failing memory: the entire Gregorian repertoire would be very faithfully transcribed with the help of signs, the main purpose of which was to transcribe onto parchment all of the signals that the choir master gives to his singers by means of appropriate gestures, indicating an ascending or descending melody line. Thus arose the so-called "neumes", a practical notation that served as a sort of "musical stenography". Certain monasteries then became centers of neumatic notation; in the manuscripts the copyists gave the necessary indications by means of signs placed above the liturgical texts. This nascent musical notation almost never specifies the pitch of the notes; it is used primarily to recall the nuances of the chant as well as the fine points of interpretation that make a good performance of it possible.

In the eleventh century, the Italian monk Guglielmo d'Arezzo would revolutionize the neumatic musical notation: he placed each musical sign on lines that were drawn to indicate musical pitch. Thus were born the musical staff (or "stave") and *diastematia*. The system of *diastematia* involves arranging notes on a staff so as to establish a visual connection with the height or depth of the tone.

The musical staff—what a great invention! Well, scholars are not so sure about that. Now that singers were able to write down a melody, they would not hesitate to do so, thus assigning more importance to the figured music on the parchment than to the melody that was preserved and transmitted by a still-living liturgical memory. The musical staff would have two effects: on the one hand it would fix the Gregorian repertoire, and on the other hand it gave rise to the desire to compose melodies inspired by Gregorian chant, but which were no longer Gregorian.

That is, in summary form, the history of the chant belonging to our Roman liturgy: an art "which was capable of surpassing local particularities so as to create a masterpiece worthy of entering into the cultural patrimony of all humanity".[8]

From decadence to restoration

From the thirteenth century on, Gregorian chant would enter into a period of decadence that would reach its nadir during the Renaissance.

We must look ahead to the nineteenth century in order to witness the start of a Gregorian chant revival; this work of restoration, which is still being pursued to this day, thanks especially to the studies carried out under the aegis of the Benedictine monks of the Abbey of Solesmes, has in a way been crowned by the fact that the Church has solemnly described Gregorian chant as "specially suited to the Roman liturgy".[9] Echoing this declaration of Vatican II, the bishops of France acknowledge that Gregorian chant fosters prayer and the authentic participation of the faithful in the liturgical prayer of the Church.[10]

Today we can only hope, therefore, with all our hearts, that choirs specializing in Gregorian chant will be formed and that centers for the further study and propagation of the chant of the Roman liturgy might be established. Although we can rejoice to learn that in many countries the bishops have encouraged such initiatives, it is nonetheless astonishing to see that in France, the cradle of Gregorian chant, the enthusiasm is still far from remarkable.[11]

---

[8] Ibid.

[9] Vatican II, Constitution on the Sacred Liturgy [116].

[10] *Directives de l'épiscopat français sur la musique sacrée* [Directives of the French bishops on sacred music], dated May 6, 1964.

[11] Paul VI and then John Paul II sent to the bishops of the whole world a little book entitled *Iubilate Deo* containing the minimum Gregorian repertoire that should be known by the faithful throughout the world; the bishops were asked to circulate this work in all the dioceses. This circulation, unfortunately, has never been carried out in the dioceses of France. A copy of *Iubilate Deo* can be obtained from éditions Téqui, 82 rue Bonaparte, 75006 Paris.

7

THE ROMAN LITURGY
IN THE MIDDLE AGES

We have seen that, in the form in which it is found during the Middle Ages, our liturgy is the product of a compilation of Roman rituals and Frankish rituals. It is impossible to insist enough upon this point: the essential components of what we call today the "Roman rite" are Romano-Frankish. Well, then, why describe this liturgy as "Roman"?

We offer an example: if I draw water from the Seine River in the city of Rouen, I have very little chance, really, of getting exclusively that water from the Seine that runs off from the land on the plateau of Langres. Nevertheless, I am certain that what I draw at Rouen is indeed water from the Seine.

It is the same with the liturgy: in the form that it has attained in the Middle Ages, the rite is truly "Roman" because it has its source in Rome.

A liturgy determined once and for all?

Will this Roman liturgy remain stable over the course of the medieval period? Absolutely not. Quite to the contrary, it will be modified in a relatively simple process: its basic structure remains, but elements are added to it that are derived essentially from prayers taken from private devotions.

Why these additions? It is generally believed that they are the result of a convergence of three historical facts that will influence the medieval mentality and, in turn, the liturgical expression of the Christian faith:

1. From the tenth century on, the Church goes through a somber period. Its institutional structures are in the hands of powerful laymen who give orders to the bishops and the parish priests; the

inevitable result is spiritual, intellectual, and moral decadence among the clergy, which Gregory VII (1073–1085) will have to face. The restoration will be achieved on the basis of a genuine reeducation of the clerics, an education that will inevitably lead to a new spirituality.

2. Wars have caused many deaths. We witness then the multiplication of Masses for the deceased, and the priest becomes the man of intercessory prayer; he becomes in a way the man whose choice of a consecrated life is truly realized only at the altar. As time goes on, the priest becomes completely identified with the Mass, to the point that the man who has received priestly ordination has to fulfill by himself all the liturgical functions; thus, in the course of the same Mass, the priest will have to be in turn the celebrant, the lector, the cantor, and so forth.

3. The Middle Ages are fond of everything that is expressive. Therefore the simple liturgical word no longer suffices; the believer demands that it be accompanied by a gesture that lends weight to it and somehow confirms it. Conversely, the silent gesture is no longer sufficient; more and more it will be complemented by a prayer enabling the lay faithful and the celebrants—who are sometimes poorly instructed—to discover the meaning of the actions that they are supposed to carry out.[1]

A new spirituality, the monopolizing of functions by the priest, and the addition of gestures and prayers: to these three elements, which will warp the form of the Roman liturgy, a new custom will be added. The latter, which is completely foreign to any authentic liturgical tradition, consists of multiplying "Low Masses", that is to say, Masses during which nothing is chanted because everything is said in a low voice by the priest. We will return later to this point.

The prayers added during the Middle Ages

The prayers "before" the Mass: Psalm 42

During the liturgy on Good Friday, the priest walks toward the altar and prostrates himself for a few moments. This is how the

---

[1]Cf. Dom Guy-Marie Oury, *La messe romaine et le peuple de Dieu dans l'histoire* [The Roman Mass and the people of God in history] (édition de Solesmes, 1981), p. 105.

Roman liturgy started, originally.[2] There is one difference, though: during the prostration of the celebrant, the schola sing the entrance antiphon of the day (the *Introit*), which is not the case on Good Friday, when all this is done in silence.

Before the liturgical celebration started in this manner, priests were expected to prepare themselves by saying prayers; this preparation for Mass was left to the personal devotion of each one, however, as no precise indication was given in the oldest Roman liturgical books. To be sure, some prayers exist and are recommended, but the priest says them privately, most often while putting on the liturgical vestments[3] or while walking to the altar.[4] In certain churches it became the custom, from the ninth century on, to recite Psalm 43 [42] (*Iudica me Deus et discerne causam meam . . .*),[5] framed by the antiphon *"Introibo ad altare Dei . . ."*,[6] a text that is perfectly suited to preparing oneself to celebrate Mass.[7]

The Confiteor

Although it does not constitute part of the Eucharistic celebration, strictly speaking, the public confession of sins appears in various forms in all the ancient liturgies. Originally the formula for the confession was left to the inspiration of the celebrant; later on, in certain places, we observe the appearance of fixed formulas, some of which are drawn from Psalm 118 [117].

---

[2] See the description of the Roman Mass in the eighth century in the preceding pages of this book.

[3] This is the case in Rheims, for example, whereas in Tours, at the tomb of Saint Martin, the celebrant says the prayers in a particular chapel.

[4] This seems to have been the case in Soissons.

[5] The psalm begins, in English, "Vindicate me, O God, and defend my cause against an ungodly people."

[6] "I will go in to the altar of God, to God who giveth joy to my youth . . ." [Douay-Rheims].

[7] It is interesting to note here that although Psalm 43 [42] is inserted into the Roman rite from the sixteenth century on (quite late, then, following the work of the Council of Trent), it will nevertheless not be introduced either into Masses during Passiontide or into the Masses for the deceased, since these two liturgies have preserved a more primitive form that is closer to the authentic Roman rite.

Thus we find, in the liturgical books of the Abbey of Cluny, a prayer closely resembling the *Confiteor* ("I confess to almighty God ...") that we use today in our liturgy; it is remarkable for its brevity and for its avoidance of redundant formulas. Here is the text of it: *Confiteor Deo et omnibus sanctis eius, et vobis Pater, quia peccavi in cogitatione, locutione et operatione. Mea culpa. Precor vos, orate pro me.* [I confess to God and to all his saints, and to you, Father (i.e., the celebrant), that I have sinned in thought, word, and deed. Through my fault. I beg you, pray for me.]

Later on, the Carthusians and the Dominicans would have a similar *Confiteor*; they would simply interpolate the mention of the Virgin Mary.[8]

Gradually, the devotions of the Middle Ages led to the interpolation of the names of certain saints into this prayer, starting with those whose relics were preserved in the parish church. That brings us to the end of the twelfth century and, to a certain extent, we are departing more and more from the original Roman traditions and their characteristic sobriety.

The prayer Oramus te

Immediately after the *Confiteor*, the celebrant recites a prayer that begins with the words *"Oramus te"*, in which he asks pardon for his own sins.

This short prayer appears in the eleventh century and does not become widespread until the twelfth century. In keeping with a custom of the late Middle Ages, the prayer is added to a gesture that was sufficient in itself: the veneration of the altar with a kiss. It is not difficult to see that this new prayer is a useless repetition of the *Confiteor*, which is recited beforehand.

As time goes on, all of these prayers, which originally were only acts of private devotion enabling the priest to prepare himself

---

[8] The current text of the *Confiteor* of the Roman liturgy reads: "*Confiteor Deo omnipotenti et vobis, fratres, quia peccavi nimis cogitatione, verbo, opere et omissione. Mea culpa, mea culpa, mea maxima culpa. Ideo precor beatam Mariam semper Virginem, omnes Angelos et Sanctos, et vos, fratres, orare pro me ad Dominum Deum nostrum.*"

better for the celebration of the Eucharist, will be included in the liturgy; it reaches the point where, from the fourteenth century on, the Roman rite becomes inconceivable without the recitation of these psalms and prayers; by then they would form a unit that would later be called the "prayers at the foot of the altar".[9]

But it must be said once more: with the exception of the confession of sins, these different prayers are not a part of the primitive Roman liturgy, which, as we have seen, began with a procession of the ministers during the entrance hymn (*Introit*), followed by a prostration of the celebrant.

The new prayers of the offertory

It is not only the preparation for Mass (the "prayers before Mass") that will be augmented by numerous prayers; the offertory rite of the Roman liturgy, in turn, will undergo several transformations during the Middle Ages as well.

We have seen that in the oldest form of the Roman liturgy that is known, the offertory rite began with an impressive procession with the offerings, during which the bread and wine needed for the Eucharistic sacrifice were brought to the altar. An initial change took place in the ninth century: during that period, the Roman liturgy adopted the use of unleavened bread, whereas until then it simply used leavened bread.

But medieval spirituality and sensibilities would bring many new modifications in their train. From the twelfth century on, the bread used at Mass takes on the round form that we recognize today. Still later, in the fourteenth century, white wine would be used instead of red wine. To be sure, red wine was a better symbol of the blood of Christ, but it had the disadvantage of being very thick and of making stains on the linens or the vestments.

That same fourteenth century also witnesses the multiplication of the prayers that accompany the gestures of offering that were originally performed in silence or, more precisely, performed dur-

---

[9] Called this because these prayers would be recited by the priest before the steps leading up to the altar.

ing the offertory chant sung by the schola cantorum.[10] This need to add prayer to gestures, which hitherto were sufficient unto themselves, seems to be so urgent that prayers of private devotion that have no connection whatsoever with the liturgy would be introduced into the Roman rite.[11]

Little by little, the offertory prayers end up repeating those of the Eucharistic Prayer. Then, until quite recently, scholars would attempt to justify the parallel set up between the rites of offering and the rites of Consecration; this would be done by means of dubious theological commentaries that were sometimes even erroneous—not to mention those that bordered on heresy.

Another novelty introduced into the liturgy at about the same period was the incensing of the offerings, the celebrant, and the people.[12] Until the twelfth century, the Roman rite seems unaware of such a practice.

Finally, although the washing of the hands is a typically Roman liturgical act mentioned in the books of the eighth century, this gesture tends to disappear from the eleventh century on, along with the offertory procession. The washing of the hands would not regain its place, as a gesture symbolizing the celebrant's need for interior purification, until the fourteenth century.

In passing, let us note that this gesture is essential to the offertory rites, and for that reason it is still obligatory in the current liturgy.

Other additions

The liturgy undergoes still other modifications. For the record, we note

---

[10] The original offertory chant had a musical form that is scarcely ever found nowadays except in the present offertory antiphon in the Mass for the deceased (*Domine Jesu Christe*), which is striking in its melodic simplicity.

[11] Thus a prayer taken straight from the personal prayer book of Charles the Bald would be introduced into the offertory of the Mass; eventually this prayer would be suppressed in the liturgical restoration called for by Vatican II.

[12] It seems that swinging the censer is a Frankish custom, which was itself the distant descendant of an Eastern practice. In the Roman liturgy, incensing is done simply by elevating the censer, noiselessly, as a sign of offering.

- that from the twelfth century on, the Host is raised immediately after the Consecration[13] (the chalice, however, is raised
  from the fourteenth century on);[14]
- that from the thirteenth century on, the use of colors for the
  liturgical vestments is systematized;
- that from the fifteenth century on, the material in the liturgical vestments becomes so heavy as a result of the rich embroi-
  deries that enhance them, that it becomes necessary to cut
  out the chasubles beneath the arms, so that the celebrant can
  make gestures more easily. Thus, by the seventeenth century,
  one finds so-called "fiddleback" chasubles, which are made
  so flat and stiff that they are only distantly related to the traditional chasubles that are depicted in ancient manuscripts[15]
  or [in sculptures] on top of the columns in certain Romanesque
  churches;[16]
- that the celebrant becomes accustomed to reciting aloud, at
  the altar, after Mass, the prologue to the Gospel according to
  Saint John, which originally he recited in a low voice, as a
  private devotion, while returning to the sanctuary.

Nevertheless, in this late medieval period, some very ancient liturgical practices remain; but they will be lost by the sixteenth century, swamped by the sheer number of new customs, and they will
not be recovered until the twentieth century, thanks to the Second
Vatican Council. An example of a traditional practice that would
disappear after the Council of Trent: the celebrant does not recite
privately the texts that are sung by the schola or by a cantor, and
he reads the Canon[17] aloud,[18] so that the faithful can join [men-
tally] in the prayer of the priest.

---

[13] This rite was introduced by Hugues de Sulloy, the Bishop of Paris.

[14] This was ordered by Clement V, Pope of Avignon.

[15] For example, see the Pontifical of [the Diocese of] Sens.

[16] Very interesting capitals [i.e., the sculpted tops of columns] can be found in [the churches of] Vezelay and Saint-Dié.

[17] That is, what we call today the "Eucharistic Prayer No. 1".

[18] This is done although the practice already is tending to disappear at this period, which elicits calls to order on the part of certain bishops.

The first printed Roman Missal[19]

The liturgy, modified in this way over the course of the Middle Ages, becomes the norm of the Roman rite. Still, for a time, this Roman rite would include variants, inasmuch as the books that describe it—the missals—are not all copied from the same original and with complete accuracy.

With the appearance of printing, however, things change: in order to promulgate a Roman Missal that is intended to be "reliable", they would take the manuscript missal that is deemed the best and, after making a few corrections, they would propose it as the model. On the basis of this model the form of the first printed Roman Missal would be established; it appeared in 1474. At that moment a new episode in the history of our Roman liturgy began.

It has often been remarked that the liturgy has been amplified at certain points in its history; either gestures were added to make a prayer more expressive, or prayers were added to lend greater force to a gesture. Now, such phenomena often result when the meaning of the liturgy becomes obscure, causing the people to lose their sense of the rituals and the symbols; this rule is borne out impressively during the entire late Middle Ages:

All the gestures which were formerly silent are [now] accompanied by words that help the priests, who often have had little formation in private prayer, to avoid routine, to rediscover the profound significance of what they are doing. And all the words of the liturgy call for corresponding gestures, due to a need to involve the body fully in the movement of the prayer.[20]

This phenomenon can still be observed today: at the outset of the twenty-first century, when the sense of the liturgy has been dulled for a great number of the faithful—in the West perhaps more than in the East—we see that many celebrants feel the need to comment on and explain everything that they do, which results in weighing down the ceremonies, tiring the congregation, emptying the

[19] See Appendix I.
[20] Dom Guy-Marie Oury, *La messe.*

rites of their symbolic meaning, and polluting liturgical celebrations with useless verbiage.[21]

Was it not, after all, to avoid "encumbering" our liturgy in this way, that the Second Vatican Council very appropriately recalled that "[t]he rites should be distinguished by a noble simplicity. They should be short, clear, and free from useless repetitions. They should be within the people's powers of comprehension, and normally should not require much explanation"?[22]

---

[21] A symbol that is explained ceases to be a symbol and becomes nothing more than an arbitrary sign. (See *Le symbolisme*, published in the series "Que sais-je".)

[22] Constitution on the Liturgy, art. 34.

8

THE ROMAN LITURGY AT THE TIME
OF THE COUNCIL OF TRENT

From the beginning of the Renaissance, during the pontificate of Leo X, a genuine need was felt within the bosom of the Church to restore the liturgy defined by the Roman Missal that was printed in 1474. This need became even more urgent with the appearance of the theological currents that heralded the Protestant Reformation, currents that compelled the liturgy to be a rampart against the crisis that was assailing Christianity, to be a factor that would unify the Church around the Apostolic See, and the act by which the true faith was professed.

Now during that same time the Roman liturgy was encumbered with subjective gestures and private prayers, which meant in practice that the Eucharist was celebrated in ways that varied greatly from one church to another, from one diocese to the next: a variety—one might say anarchy—that was not without danger to the unity of the faith.

Furthermore, as of the fifteenth century, a restoration of the liturgy was imperative. But it was conceivable only with respect to two principles:

- the celebration of the Eucharist must be the same everywhere so as to manifest the unity of the Church;
- the symbols and the rites to be performed in the course of a liturgical celebration must be defined by the Magisterium and completely codified so as to allow no room for doubt or subjectivity in what pertains to the Catholic faith.

We can say, then, that the restoration of the liturgy envisaged at that time would be more apologetic than pastoral in scope.[1]

[1] By the time of Vatican II the circumstances will have changed, and the restoration of the liturgy will be subject to a pastoral concern rather than to apologetic preoccupations.

The Ceremonial

We have seen that, especially during the thirteenth and fourteenth centuries, the liturgy had been augmented by gestures, postures, and prayers that were not part of the original Roman rite. During this period, which is marked by profound changes in mentality (the Middle Ages are ending, debates about the Church's authority are beginning, mercantile cities are gaining prestige, the temporal realm takes the upper hand over the spiritual, Romanesque art yields to Gothic art, etc.), there is a love for everything that is expressive, anything that is capable of conveying human emotions or feelings.

The liturgical gesture, therefore, will tend to be detached from the natural and practical significance that it had to begin with and to become a symbol invested with meanings that are often conventional. But slippage of this sort is not without risks: the liturgical gesture will tend at times to become artificial or even mechanical.

All of these modifications would perhaps have been less momentous if the liturgy had been part of the exclusively private domain. Yet by its very essence it is part of the public and collective domain. Therefore the Church will have to legislate; she will codify the gestures, the postures, the movements of the liturgy, so that the celebrants will not fall victim to their own capriciousness and so that the decorum found in the society of the kings and princes of that era might likewise be safeguarded in the sacred rites. That is how the Ceremonial developed, in which ways of organizing the liturgy are described: ways that will rapidly become obligatory because they are considered to be the only correct methods of attaining the goal to which the celebration of the sacrament itself is ordered.

How to go about "restoring" the Roman liturgy?

One must first analyze the problem that one is dealing with. What is at stake?

It is a matter of restoring to the Roman rite its original balance as well as its initial meaning, by ridding it of late additions—those subsequent to the thirteenth century—in order to make it a reliable instrument in the service of the faith and of Church unity.

But at the same time one must also take into account the Ceremonial, which prescribes the best way of performing liturgical actions in the light of traditions and practices that have been handed down.

It is understandable that all this is not going to make the job of restoring the liturgy any easier. For it is not enough merely to want to restore a medieval equilibrium; one must also succeed in finding a style of celebration that, while respecting tradition, is capable of synthesizing Christian values with the new historical situation of the day.[2] Then, too, opinions often differ, and among the groups of scholars bent over the task at hand, three major trends appear.

A "humanist" trend

The "humanists" are of the opinion that the chief defect of the Roman liturgy, in the form in which it existed then, was in the use of the Latin language: a barbarous language, they said. Their desire, therefore, was to use Greek for the recitation of the Divine Office and Hebrew in chanting the psalms.[3]

A "radical" trend

Those in favor of this approach want the liturgy to be completely recast: they have to start from scratch, they say, because what has been passed down by tradition has been so corrupted and confused that it is useless to try to save anything that might still be of value.[4]

---

[2] On this subject see Evangelista Vilanova, *Histoire des théologies Chrétiennes*, in the series *"initiations"*, 3 vols. (Paris: Le Cerf, 1997).

[3] Among the members of this group we note Pietro Bembo, the cardinal secretary of Leo X; Zaccaria Ferreri, a Benedictine monk who had become the papal legate to Poland; John Bessarion, a monk from Constantinople who had become the Bishop of Nicea; and Pierre Pomponazzi, a philosopher who would be condemned by the Church for his statements about the soul and about miracles.

[4] In this group we find Francisco Quignonez, a Spanish Franciscan who would become a cardinal and then a bishop; Reginald Pole, who would flee England for Rome at the time of the schism in 1534, but would return to his native land as Bishop of Canterbury; and Jacopo Sadoleto, apostolic secretary during the pontificates of Leo X and Clement VII, then Bishop of Carpentras.

A "wise" trend

This group includes those who have no illusions as to the qualities and the defects of the liturgy, but who think that, instead of throwing everything overboard, it is better to highlight what is worthwhile and to provide a proper formation for those who will have to use the liturgical books in the future. Clearly, there will have to be a reform, they say; it should be concerned with the serious formation of priests instead of undertaking the huge task of rewriting all the books—the results of which are far from certain.[5]

The restoration of the Roman liturgy at the Council of Trent

We must not imagine the liturgical restoration as a monolithic work resulting all at once from the Council of Trent or the will of Pope Saint Pius V. The restoration of the Roman rite, in the sixteenth century, took place in fits and starts, with fortunate and unfortunate results, with successes in certain areas and failures in others, the progress—especially in the domain of the liturgy—never having a definitive character.

Everything started, one might say, when Leo X (1513–1521) called upon Zaccaria Ferreri—a "humanist" in his approach—to revise the Hymnal, that is, the book containing the hymns that must be sung as part of the Divine Office. The final product was an almost brand-new book that preserved only a few verses vaguely reminiscent of the old Roman Hymnal. This episode, which marked the beginning of the liturgical reform, also shows that a certain anarchy prevailed on the eve of the Council of Trent: indeed, the particular churches were still free, in that period, to organize their liturgy as they saw fit.

The fundamental questions pertaining to a liturgical reform that was desired by numerous regional synods or councils were mentioned in the first period of the Council of Trent (1545–1547); they were put on the agenda during the second period (1547–

---

[5] In this group we find Enea Silvio Piccolomini, Bishop of Siena and later Pope with the name of Pius II; Antonio Carafa, who would become cardinal during the pontificate of Saint Pius V; and Jean Burchard of Strasbourg, who would become master of pontifical ceremonies and then chaplain of Innocent VIII and Alexander VI.

1552), but were not dealt with directly until the final conciliar sessions that were held from 1562 to 1563.

However, by late 1563, not much progress had been made. One new development, though, is worth emphasizing: the specialists and the researchers no longer form three groups, but two, which clarifies the situation somewhat. The first group favors complete uniformity in the liturgy, whereas the second group desires the preservation of local privileges that would allow the continuance of particular diocesan rites.

At the very least one can say, therefore, that the Roman liturgy as such seems merely to be keeping afloat, as best it can, in the midst of a motley fleet of sometimes contradictory ideas. Will it be possible, under such conditions, to establish a connection between the "traditional Roman liturgy" and the "Tridentine rite", as some people still think they can do today? Will they be able to say that the liturgy resulting from the labors of the Council of Trent is truly the Roman liturgy handed down by the most ancient tradition? Strictly speaking, nothing could be less certain, one must admit.

Fortunately, the work of liturgical restoration would take a turn for the better, thanks to Pope Pius V and his close collaborator: Cardinal Sirleto.

The work of Saint Pius V

Before Pius V, there was Pius IV. It is fitting that we should speak of this Pope who, although often forgotten, played a not insignificant part in this question of the liturgy.

Indeed, it was Pius IV who reopened the Council of Trent in order to confirm its decisions. Wishing to complete the work of restoring our liturgy, he called together a Commission that went to work in 1564, then suspended its efforts, and finally resumed the work in 1566.

Pius V enlarged the Commission appointed by his predecessor, Pius IV, by adding to it several brilliant personages whose outstanding talents had been noted during the Council of Trent. One of these personages was Cardinal Guglielmo Sirleto; being in charge of the Vatican Library, he was able to furnish the working group with the best available documents concerning the Roman liturgy.

Very quickly Cardinal Sirleto became the soul of the Commission responsible for the liturgical restoration; his method of working was the opposite of what had been done until then under the influence of Cardinal Quignonez, a prelate who wished to innovate at any cost.

Cardinal Sirleto, indeed, demanded that nothing essential to the liturgy as it existed then should be suppressed; yet on the other hand he wanted to bring that liturgy, as much as possible, back to what it had been originally, taking into account the development of the Roman rite over the centuries.

We note in passing that this is exactly the same task that was proposed, four centuries later, by the Second Vatican Council:

> In order that the Christian people may more certainly derive an abundance of graces from the sacred liturgy, holy Mother Church desires to undertake with great care a general restoration of the liturgy itself. For the liturgy is made up of unchangeable elements divinely instituted, and of elements subject to change.[6] These latter not only may be changed but ought to be changed with the passage of time, if they have suffered from the intrusion of anything out of harmony with the inner nature of the liturgy or have become less suitable. . . .
>
> In order that sound tradition be retained, and yet the way remain open to legitimate progress, a careful investigation—theological, historical, and pastoral—should always be made into each part of the liturgy which is to be revised. Furthermore the general laws governing the structure and meaning of the liturgy must be studied in conjunction with the experience derived from recent liturgical reforms and from the indults granted to various places.[7]

That is what the Council Fathers declared at Vatican II; during the sixteenth century, no doubt, Cardinal Sirleto could have made these words his own.

A difficult task

Several difficulties in bringing the work to its successful completion arose. They were principally of two sorts:

[6] See pages 17–19: "The four components of the liturgy".
[7] Vatican II, Constitution on the Sacred Liturgy, articles 21, 23. ["22" is a misprint.]

First, the specialists in charge of restoring the liturgy in the sixteenth century did not have at their disposal scholarly tools as sophisticated as the ones that we have available today, which limited their investigations; their work of classifying, comparing, and researching documents was not made any easier. As a result, many areas in the history of the Roman liturgy remained obscure.[8]

Second, they would very often amalgamate the elements of the Roman rite with the directions given in the Ceremonial. This amalgam would give rise to confusions: many of the faithful (to this very day) would no longer be able to distinguish between certain gestures and postures that originated in the most elementary sense of decorum, and those gestures and postures that are truly essential to the Roman rite.

An illustration: the Ceremonial shows priests, for example, what is the best way—the "fitting" manner, let us say—in which to put on the liturgical vestments for Mass. The same Ceremonial also gives rules of etiquette: one must not turn one's back on distinguished persons, and so, when the acolytes are about to leave the altar with the priest, they should make sure to turn toward him. Similarly, in carrying out the rituals, one should maintain symmetry in gestures or postures (when walking two by two in procession, each pair should be of the same height; if they are carrying candles, they must be held toward the outside of the procession, etc.) and take care not to get in each other's way.

These details are so much a part of basic common sense that originally they were not recorded in the liturgical books. Now, they would henceforth be strictly codified and introduced into the Roman rite, as revised in the sixteenth century, as though they were an integral part of the liturgy inherited from ancient Rome.

Thus, in the Roman Missal edited following the work of the Council of Trent, we find an incredible number of rubrics describing in detail the smallest gesture, the slightest movement of every participant in the liturgy. We cite here, as an example, the rather amusing rubric concerning the way in which the celebrant should vest before Mass:

---

[8] At that time certain ancient documents had not yet been discovered or else still had not been studied in depth.

First of all, [the celebrant] takes the amice by the ends of the cords, kisses it in the center, where a cross is embroidered, places it over his head and allows it to fall to his neck to cover it; he passes the cords under his arms, then around his back, and then again to his chest, where he makes a knot. Then he puts on the alb: to do this he puts his head through [the opening provided for this purpose], then slides his right arm through the right sleeve and finally his left arm through the left sleeve.[9]

The Roman Missal, codified in this way, is the one that would remain in use until the Second Vatican Council and which, for convenience, would be called the "Tridentine Missal" or else the "Missal of Saint Pius V", even though, as the history of the liturgy shows us, these names are scarcely fitting.[10]

The publication of the revised Roman Missal will not elicit the deep reverence for the liturgy that one rightly expects; on the one hand, many dioceses, especially in the eighteenth century, would deviate from it in favor of neo-Gallican liturgical books. On the other hand, it would be modified or augmented several times by the Popes who would succeed Saint Pius V.[11]

What exactly did Saint Pius V do that is so often at issue when the liturgy is discussed nowadays? He simply made it obligatory to use the Roman Missal that resulted from the labors of the Fathers

---

[9] Cf. *Missale Romanum ex decreto Sacrosancti Concilii Tridentini restitutum summorum Pontificum Cura recognitum*, 1962 edition, *Ritus servandus in celebratione missae, I. De preparatione sacerdotis celebraturi*, article 3.

[10] Cf. Denis Crouan, *The Liturgy Betrayed* (San Francisco: Ignatius Press, 2000), pp. 31–36.

[11] Given a missal that is so strictly codified, we might do well to ask another question. It is obvious that celebrating the liturgy has always demanded more than a scrupulous respect for the rituals and the rubrics. The preliminary requirement is a veritable education on two levels: one level that is both human and psychological, and another level that is both spiritual and doctrinal. Now, wasn't this education forgotten the moment that it was supposed that scrupulously following the strict rubrics could constitute, in certain extreme cases, the essential concern in the religious and spiritual universe of the priest? The manner of celebrating the Roman liturgy, as it was inherited from the Council of Trent, would undeniably bring about some progress in the Church; but we must realize that it would not be without its risks for weak or scrupulous minds, especially when it would take place within a social context where the spirituality is tinged with Romanticism and Jansenism, as would be the case in the nineteenth century, and where the emphasis is placed more on the juridical aspect of worship than on the genuinely traditional element.

of the Council of Trent. The exact title of this restored missal is: "The Roman Missal, corrected in virtue of a decision by the Council of Trent and published by order of the Supreme Pontiff Pius V".

What do we find in this new Roman Missal?

- a new calendar,
- some general rubrics,
- an exact description of the rituals of the Eucharistic celebration,
- a chapter on the "accidents" that can occur in the course of a Mass.

Take note: the Roman Missal includes no description of Solemn Mass. This would not be given until thirty years later, in the "Bishops' Ceremonial" published in 1600 during the pontificate of Clement VIII.

The Bull *Quo primum tempore*

Pius V makes the new missal obligatory for all the churches of the Latin rite that celebrate according to the Roman rite,[12] except for the local churches having a particular rite that is at least two hundred years old.

Why two hundred years? Basically it is quite easy to understand. The aim of Pius V was to eliminate the customs that had been introduced in liturgical celebrations from around 1350 on, because in that period the root causes were already developing of what would later become the Protestant Reformation. Now the Pope knew that these root causes had allowed doctrinal errors to circulate throughout the Christian West and even to leave traces in liturgical practices as well as in the missals used at that time.

Therefore, if Saint Pius V rejected across the board all the local liturgies that had come to light from the fourteenth century on, it was primarily because he knew that the ideas of nascent Protestantism had spread and because he realized that sorting out the customs that could be described as "orthodox" from those that were more dubious—or even downright heretical—was much too difficult a task to be feasible.

---

[12] From this moment on, "Latin" will become the synonym of "Roman", whereas we have seen in the course of our study that there are Latin rites that are not Roman.

The Bull *Quo primum tempore*, dated July 14, 1570, which promulgated the new Roman Missal, is often used by those who claim
today that the Mass said to be "of Saint Pius V" is forever valid and
that no Pope can suppress it or forbid it. In good faith, what should
we think of this opinion?

Is it even thinkable that Pius V could have forbidden his successors, until the end of the ages, to touch his arrangement of the
Roman liturgy? Indeed, if we read carefully the text of this Bull,
which is printed at the front of the missal published following the
Council of Trent, we see that Pius V forbids every person having
authority in the Church to modify on his own authority the liturgy that he had codified; the Pope even takes great care to specify
who these persons are who hold authority: from the cardinals down
to the simple curate who serves as administrator of a parish, including the bishops, the canons, the prelates, etc. Only one dignitary is
not mentioned: the Pope. Thus Saint Pius V, being an excellent
pastor and theologian, prudently refrains from limiting the powers
of the Popes who will be, in the ages to come, entrusted with the
same mission in the Church as he.

After all, none of the Popes who would succeed Saint Pius V
would be mistaken as to the real import of the Bull *Quo primum
tempore*. That is why, over the centuries, the Roman liturgy would
in fact be modified again by the Supreme Pontiffs:

- On July 14, 1600, Clement VIII determined the rituals of
  the Mass celebrated by a bishop. The reader will note that
  this solemn liturgy is closer to the ancient Roman liturgy
  than the ordinary Mass described in the missal promulgated
  by Pius V.
- In 1604, Clement VIII corrected the Roman Missal issued by
  Pius V and made modifications in the sung sections of the Mass.
- In 1634, Urban VII modified the rubrics issued by Pius V.
- During the sixteenth century, under the influence of the
  Counter-Reformation, tabernacles appeared on the altars,
  which had not been foreseen at all by Pius V and which would
  necessitate the addition of new rituals.

We will have to study, now, the way in which the Roman liturgy
is presented in the missal published by the authority of Saint Pius V.

9

THE ROMAN MASS IN THE MISSAL
PROMULGATED BY SAINT PIUS V

As we find it in the Roman Missal restored following the Council of Trent and promulgated by Saint Pius V, our liturgy, the heir to the rites that were in use in Rome during the first centuries of the Church, has lost its original simplicity: it has become a composite, having been transformed by some additions, some suppressions, and also by some confusions.

Some additions and suppressions

The first thing that you notice, when you compare the "Tridentine" Roman liturgy with that of the early Church, is the addition of private prayers at the beginning, during, and at the end of the Mass.

These prayers, which already existed several centuries before but were said by the celebrant privately, are now included in the liturgy defined by the new missal; they are essentially the "prayers at the foot of the altar", several offertory prayers, and finally some prayers added after the dismissal of the faithful (that is, after the *Ite missa est*).

What you notice then is the suppression of certain ancient rites such as the "general intercessions"[1] and the offertory procession.

Some confusions

As we have seen in the preceding pages, the mentality of the sixteenth century has often led to confusions between what belongs

[1] In fact, not one of these very ancient prayers remains except the *Oremus*, said by the celebrant at the beginning of the offertory: an invitation to prayer that is not followed by any prayer.

to the ceremonial order and what belongs to the liturgical order. Thus, gestures that were codified solely to guarantee that they would be carried out well, gradually become—at least in the minds of some believers—constitutive elements of the Roman rite.

But most of all, an entirely new element makes its appearance: whereas one should never celebrate the liturgy without musical support, the missal published by the Tridentine reform now conceives of the Mass as a prayer that is read, spoken, and recited in a low voice. Already the late Middle Ages had seen the development of a tendency to make of the liturgy a private act of the celebrant, an act performed in a low voice at altars that recede farther and farther back into the apses. But during that period the bishops had repeatedly called the clergy to order and had specified that the celebrant's prayer had to be heard by the faithful.

But now, what would be called "Low Mass" seems to be firmly ensconced. It is enough to glance through the Roman Missal promulgated by Saint Pius V to see that the rituals are arranged in such a way that a celebrant can perform all the liturgical functions alone and celebrate Mass without raising his voice, almost as if the presence of the faithful were something secondary. This practice, it must be noted, is a novelty in the history of the Church; even today it is totally unknown in the Eastern liturgies that, having preserved their ancient customs, exist only in their sung form (even though this form is simplified in the smaller parishes).

The consequences of the "Low Mass"

The multiplication of "Low Masses" (which are "read") would have several consequences on the liturgical level as well as on the pastoral level:

First, when it comes to celebrating a Solemn Mass—that is, one that is sung—it will be necessary in some way to "combine" the "Low Mass" given in the Roman Missal promulgated by Saint Pius V with the requirements of the chant.

Thus the sung Mass—the "normal" form of the liturgy—is presented, from the sixteenth century on, as a "Low" Mass, upon which have been superimposed the Gregorian melodies belonging to the Roman liturgy; the schola cantorum sings the pieces from the Proper and the *Kyriale*, which the celebrant recites in a low voice at the altar.

Since there is necessarily a time lag between the words recited by the celebrant and the singing performed by the choir, the Ceremonial (and not the "liturgy", as such) foresees a system whereby the singing can "catch up" with the rituals (gestures and actions) that are to be performed. Thus, for example, the celebrant intones the *Gloria in excelsis Deo*, but he goes on to recite the hymn in a low voice while the choir members continue the chant. When the priest finishes "his" *Gloria*, it is expected that he goes to sit down, while waiting for the music to end. In smaller parishes, he joins his voice with those of the singers to help them, which means that the celebrant says a good number of the prayers of the Mass twice: once alone, and once with the congregation.

Then, because many parts of the Mass are recited by the celebrant in a low voice in the liturgy that has come down from the Tridentine reform, it becomes necessary to provide something to "keep the congregation busy" during the moments of silence. Two means will be employed to accomplish this: either one adds so-called "sacred" music (i.e., music that is nonliturgical) during the course of the liturgical action or else one encourages the faithful to say private prayers, which will often be the case in the smaller parishes that have no instrumentalists available and where "Low Masses" are celebrated.

"Sacred" music and private prayers in the Tridentine Roman liturgy

"Sacred" music

The introduction into the Roman Mass of music other than the genuinely liturgical singing (the "Gregorian chant") dates from the Middle Ages,[2] at the moment when a system of musical notation has been established that allows melodies to be recorded with more

---

[2] "Tropes" are composed from the eleventh century on, the "organum" in the twelfth century, along with the "motet", which most likely is derived from the "organum".

precision.[3] This new music, which is described as "sacred", really gains impetus in the thirteenth century, in the period when the priest starts to say certain parts of the liturgy inaudibly: the blocks of silence allow the musicians to give free rein to their talent and their inspiration.

At the same time that the art of music is developing, the first organs are introduced in the churches. These instruments, modest at first, will serve to double the voices of the singers, whereas the characteristic chant of the Roman liturgy is meant to be performed *a capella*, that is, without accompaniment. Later, as they are gradually perfected, organs will play the role of a solo instrument in dialogue with the schola.

But it is above all the sacred "motet" that will carve out a great spot for itself in the liturgy; along with it, various instruments make their appearance in the churches: viols, horns, sackbuts [a medieval trombone], oboes—and later on, better-equipped ensembles that prefigure the orchestras of the nineteenth century.

Given the codification of the liturgy after the Council of Trent, and especially the Ceremonial that specifies how Solemn Masses are to be celebrated, the musicians have at their disposal moments of silence that allow them to show off their skill while the liturgical functions are being carried out. The introduction into Christian worship of an art that does not proceed directly from the liturgy means that, from the seventeenth century on, "the Church willingly keeps pace with all the other institutions, subject to the orders of the powerful men of this world." [4]

Here, nevertheless, is how Pierre Perrin, a seventeenth-century composer, explains the incorporation of motets into the liturgy handed down by the Tridentine reform: "I composed the major motets to be of such length that they can last a quarter of an hour ... and cover from the beginning of the Mass until the elevation. The motets for the elevation are smaller and can last until the Post-Communion, which begins with the *Domine*." [5]

---

[3] See chapter 6: "The Origins of the Chant of the Roman Liturgy."

[4] According to James R. Anthony, *French Baroque Music* (Pompton Plains, N.J.: Amadeus Press, 1974).

[5] He means the motet *Domine salvum fac Regem*, which is started at the prayer after Communion and continued until the end of Mass; ibid.

All this seems so far removed from the ideal of the Roman liturgy that Trent hoped to attain, that some pastors would say, "Nowadays the people attend concerts accompanied by Mass." Yet this form taken by the liturgy is the one that the faithful will be accustomed to for a long time: the ceremonies, arranged in such a manner and decked out with a pomp that is sometimes imposing, please the faithful, who are generally uneducated, inasmuch as they are more sensitive to what appeals to their senses or arouses their emotions than to the elements of the liturgy that convey balance and truth.

In places where there are no groups of musicians, the organ is expected to "set the tone". As far as France is concerned, musicologists agree that Normandy was the province where an original style of sacred music was born and developed. In the city of Rouen, Jehan Titelouze (born in 1563, that is, at the very moment when the Council of Trent was concluded) composed pieces based on melodic themes from the hymns of the great feasts of the liturgical year. The composer specifies that, in order to perform these brilliant pieces, one must play on the full stops of the instrument, while emphasizing the Gregorian melody by using a trumpet stop on the pedals.

This procedure, adopted by all the organists who followed Titelouze, would eventually mean that the Gregorian themes were relegated to the background, so that the listeners heard only the virtuosity of the accompaniments or the ornamentation.

Private devotions

When high-quality music is not available, when it is not possible to have qualified musicians, the faithful are kept busy with private devotions. Thus Bossuet himself declares that one can "obey the precept of hearing Mass while spending the whole time on other readings and prayers".[6]

Thus liturgical practice, little by little, favors a conformist or even legalistic frame of mind. Indeed, it ends up being tainted by an

---

[6] Quoted by Evangelista Vilanova, O.S.B., *Histoire des théologies Chrétiennes*, in the series *"initiations"*, 3 vols. (Paris: Le Cerf, 1997).

anthropocentrism that at first glance is not noticeable but which is nevertheless there. Then, in imitation of what is being celebrated, the preaching will become moralizing and dogmatic.

Are these not the potential ingredients for a religion consisting purely of façade, which has less and less to do with the complexity of life?

Do we not find here the seeds of a crisis that the Church will have to overcome in the nineteenth century and that will have repercussions until the late twentieth century?

The weaknesses in the restoration of the Roman Missal

As for what concerns the liturgy per se, it must be admitted that from the seventeenth century on, two weaknesses appear in the restoration of the Roman Mass, as it was carried out by the Council of Trent and by Saint Pius V: a lack of historical criticism on the one hand, and, on the other hand, the impossibility of harmonizing the ferial cycle[7] with the sanctoral cycle.[8]

Unity and observance of the rituals

Trent provided that the celebrant would say a large number of prayers in a low voice. Now, such a practice has its risks: won't certain priests take advantage of this to rattle off the prayers as quickly as possible, without always paying attention to the meaning of what they are supposed to say and do?

In 1561 the Bishop of Paris addressed his curates in the following terms: "We order all the priests who must celebrate Mass to read [the prayers] with respect, piety, modesty and attention, in a voice that is clear, distinct and understandable, until the Canon,

---

[7] Ferial: having to do with a "feria", a liturgical day without a proper office of a saint or of a feast.

[8] Sanctoral cycle: the feasts of the saints celebrated over the course of the year following the order of the calendar. The immediate successors of Saint Pius V—Gregory XIII (1572–1585), Sixtus V (1585–1590), and Clement VIII (1592–1605)—would be quick to modify the missal said to be "of Saint Pius V" by restoring several feast days that had been abolished following the Council of Trent. Dom André Malet, *La liturgie cistercienne* (Abbaye de Sainte-Marie-du-Désert, 1921).

which they will recite in a lower voice." [9] The council of Rheims issued identical directives in 1583.

Cassander, however, the great liturgist of the sixteenth century, had already recalled that, according to the Roman tradition, the Canon of the Mass should be read aloud so that the faithful can hear it and respond, "Amen", to the grace-filled action that the celebrant is performing.

As for Saint Vincent de Paul (1581–1660), a witness of the implementation of the Tridentine directives, he writes:

> If you had seen the diversity in the ceremonies of the Mass forty years ago, [10] it would have made you feel ashamed; it seems to me that there was nothing more ugly in the world than the various manners in which it was celebrated; some began the Mass with the *Pater noster*; others took the chasuble in their hands and recited the *Introibo*, [11] and then they put on the chasuble. Once I was at [the church of] Saint-Germain-en-Laye, where I observed seven or eight priests who were all saying Mass differently; one did it one way, another in some other way; it was a lamentable variety. [12]

We know that this variety would only increase over the following years.

Fidelity to Catholic doctrine

Does the fact that a priest scrupulously observes the rubrics given in a missal guarantee the transmission and the preservation of Catholic doctrine? This is a question that one could ask of every age and about all the liturgical rites, both Eastern and Western.

[9] M. Baudoin, *Apologie des cérémonies de l'Église expliquées dans le sens naturel et littéral par Dom Claude de Vert* [Apologia for the ceremonies of the Church, explained in the natural and literal sense by Dom Claude de Vert], 1712. Quoted by Dom Guy-Marie Oury, *La messe Romaine et le peuple de Dieu dans l'histoire* (édition de l'Abbaye de Solesmes, 1981).

[10] That is, about thirty years after the publication of the Roman Missal by Saint Pius V.

[11] *Introibo ad altare Dei*, the opening words of the celebrant's private prayers that are called "the prayers at the foot of the altar", which were introduced into the Roman liturgy by Saint Pius V and then suppressed again by the Vatican II reform (see the preceding chapters of this book).

[12] Saint Vincent de Paul, *Oeuvres* [Complete works] (Paris: Édition Coste, 1924); quoted by Dom Guy-Marie Oury, *La messe*.

One can reply that observance of the liturgies that are presented by the Church, acting in her capacity as guardian of the authentic tradition, assures the validity of the sacrament as well as the preservation and transmission of Christian doctrine. But this observance does not automatically assure the correct reception of the doctrine by every believer.

So it would happen that the Roman rite as reformed by the Council of Trent would be used by communities or particular churches that were no longer in communion with the Catholic Church: in the Lutheran churches of Scandinavia, for example, they would continue to use the Tridentine Roman Missal after the Reformation (which goes to prove that the faithful are less sensitive to changes affecting the content of their religion than they are to modifications in the ceremonies, the customs, or the singing).

Even today, certain churches that have broken with the Apostolic See observe in their entirety the liturgical ceremonies handed down by Trent.[13]

Since performing the rituals does not guarantee that each believer will receive and benefit from the doctrine of the faith celebrated by the liturgy, the Council of Trent insists that priests give sermons during their Masses and teach the faithful about the truths of Christianity that they are supposed to believe. Thus the liturgical reform is complemented by the publication of a catechism and by a program of opening seminaries designed for the doctrinal and spiritual formation of future priests.

It is interesting to note that, several centuries after Trent, Vatican II would insist on the same points: even the best liturgical reform (says the Constitution *Sacrosanctum Concilium*) will produce no fruit unless the faithful—first and foremost the priests—receive a formation enabling them to understand thoroughly what it is that they accomplish in the sacred functions that are carried out at the altar.[14]

After Trent, then, the liturgical problems are not all solved. New questions arise: What is the authentic liturgical tradition?[15] What

---

[13] For example, the Gallican church of Saint Rita in Paris.

[14] Constitution on the Sacred Liturgy, articles 15 through 18.

[15] This is the question that Pope John Paul II asks all the faithful in his Motu Proprio *Ecclesia Dei adflicta*, which was published after the schism of Archbishop Lefebvre.

elements should make up a reform so as to arrive at a synthesis between permanent liturgical values and the historical situations that unceasingly confront the Church? Cannot a liturgical reform be the product of decisions aimed at rearranging gestures and words? Should it not be spiritual in the first place, rather than administrative[16] (provided, of course, that spirituality is not reduced to a menu selection)?[17]

These are the same questions that the Church will ask at Vatican II, proof that in our earthly liturgy things are never perfect or definitive.[18]

---

[16] Speaking of the replacement of the Tridentine Roman Missal by the Roman Missal as revised after Vatican II, Cardinal Ratzinger notes: "But more than this now happened [i.e., things went further than anyone had expected]: the old building was demolished, and another was built, to be sure largely using materials from the previous one and even using the old building plans. There is no doubt that this new missal in many respects brought with it a real improvement and enrichment; but setting it as a new construction over against what had grown historically, forbidding the results of this historical growth, thereby makes the liturgy appear to be no longer a living development but the product of erudite work and juridical authority; this has caused us enormous harm. For then the impression had to emerge that liturgy is something 'made' [i.e., 'fabricated'], not something given in advance but something lying within our own power of decision" (Cardinal Joseph Ratzinger, *Milestones: Memoirs 1927–1977* [San Francisco: Ignatius Press, 1998], p. 148).

[17] This is the danger in certain contemporary communities that set about conducting their own "liturgical reforms" by mixing rituals derived from different cults and cultures.

[18] See Appendices I and II.

10

A PARTICULAR CASE:
THE DOMINICAN LITURGY

The study of the history of the Roman liturgy leads to a very delicate question that fuels impassioned debates even today: Is the liturgy defined by the missal that was promulgated by Saint Pius V more "Roman" and "traditional" than the one promulgated by Paul VI following Vatican II?

In our historical survey of the Roman liturgy we have seen that, after promulgating the revised missal following the studies conducted by the Council of Trent, Pope Pius V wished that certain particular liturgies should be preserved, namely, those that in his day were at least two hundred years old, i.e., that went back to the middle of the fourteenth century or before.

Besides the liturgy of Roman origin, the rituals of which are specified in the missal promulgated by Pius V, several other ancient liturgies would therefore continue in existence, both monastic (such as Carthusian and Benedictine) and diocesan (Milan and Lyons). Of these we will examine in particular the liturgy of the Friars Preachers (commonly called the "Dominicans"): this study will shed some light on the history of the Roman rite.

The origins of the Dominican liturgy

In December of 1216 the Order of Friars Preachers was recognized and approved by the Apostolic See. At that time the sons of Saint Dominic adopted the Rule of Saint Augustine, which they modified somewhat, following the customs of the Premonstratensians so as to adapt the rule to their way of life.

Now in August 1217, when Saint Dominic sent out the first friars, the new Order knew only the liturgical rites in use during that period: rites of Roman origin for the most part that, however, did not always have a fixed form. This gave rise to a certain "liturgical variety" that is mentioned by Humbert de Romans, the fifth Master General of the Friars Preachers, among others.

In itself, such a variety was not at all surprising at that time. For the Friars Preachers, however, it caused several difficulties. Indeed, since the Dominicans are itinerant by vocation, they have a strongly centralized Order; it would therefore be worthwhile for them to have the same liturgy everywhere, so that every friar who stays in one of the different houses of the Order can feel at ease in praying the official prayer of the Church, without having to adapt all the time to local rites, which would be impractical.

That is why in 1245 four Dominican friars were ordered to determine a more stable form of the liturgy than the Roman liturgy as it was then celebrated in the parishes. In order to do this they went to work under the guidance of Humbert de Romans, then the Provincial of the Order in France. In 1256 they produced a missal that would be approved in 1287 by Pope Clement IV.

What elements went into the making of this "Dominican missal"? Was it fabricated from whole cloth? Was it a brand-new book that broke with the Roman tradition? These are legitimate questions.

Examination of the "Dominican missal" shows that the liturgy is not new. It was copied from a liturgy that offered the stability that they were looking for: the one in use in the Roman basilicas. Thus, curiously enough, the Dominican liturgy devised in the thirteenth century contains "Roman" elements unknown in the parish liturgies of the same period.

Some particular features of the Dominican liturgy

What are the principal features found in the Dominican liturgy that are truly Roman and yet were not retained in the Roman Missal promulgated by Saint Pius V?

From its Roman sources, the Dominican liturgy has retained, above all, an air of "noble simplicity".[1] This trait would not always

---

[1] This is an expression used by Paul VI to describe the liturgy as it was reformed after Vatican II.

be evident in the Roman liturgy beginning in the seventeenth century and during the eighteenth century, once it became subject to the demands of an increasingly complex ceremonial that sometimes confused genuine "solemnity" with "triumphalism".[2]

Furthermore, like the original Roman rite, there are no "prayers at the foot of the altar", strictly speaking. The celebration of the Mass begins with the singing of the *Introit*;[3] the altar is not incensed during the singing of the *Kyrie*;[4] after the first prayer (Collect), the priest goes to sit down for the Liturgy of the Word until it is time to proclaim the Gospel;[5] the offertory prayers of the Dominican rite are simplified.

The old Dominican rite helps us to understand the form of the Roman liturgy as revised after Vatican II

The form of the Roman rite defined by the missal that Saint Pius V promulgated would remain in use in the Church until 1969. In that year a reformed Roman Missal was promulgated that changed the arrangement of the Eucharistic rite to which the faithful are accustomed.

To this day, some Catholics suspect that the Roman Missal promulgated by Paul VI foisted upon them a "newly fabricated" rite that had broken with two millennia of liturgical tradition in the Roman Church.

The history of the Dominican liturgy, however, shows that there is no reason for such suspicions. If we carefully compare the old Dominican missal with the current missal promulgated after the

---

[2] Cardinal Joseph Ratzinger, *The Ratzinger Report* (San Francisco: Ignatius Press, 1985), pp. 130–32.

[3] This manner of beginning the celebration of Mass would not be preserved in the missal promulgated by Saint Pius V, which indicates that the entrance hymn is sung while the celebrant, having arrived at the steps of the altar, recites private prayers.

[4] In the Roman rite as codified by Saint Pius V, it is incensed.

[5] In the missal promulgated by Saint Pius V, the priest remains at the altar, except when he has to wait for the schola to finish singing the *Kyrie*, the *Gloria*, or the *Credo*, in which case he can go sit down.

last Council, we see that the rites contained in these two volumes are very similar. The current missal published after Vatican II, therefore, does not consist, strictly speaking, of a new liturgy made up of new rituals. On the contrary, the missal promulgated by Paul VI can only be regarded as a truly "Roman" work:[6] one finds in it very old, thoroughly traditional elements that, for various historical reasons, had been omitted in the missal reformed by Trent.[7]

Therefore it will be readily admitted that, over the course of a turbulent history, our "Roman" liturgy has been capable of existing in various forms.

Choosing "one's own" rite?

For various reasons, every Catholic may prefer one legitimate form of the liturgy over another; the Church allows for many possibilities in this domain. Nevertheless it belongs to legitimate ecclesiastical authority to determine, in matters concerning the liturgy, whether personal choices and tastes[8] can take the place of theological reasoning to justify one type of celebration rather than another, this rite rather than some other.

[6] At the beginning of his Letter on the twenty-fifth anniversary of the Constitution on the Liturgy of Vatican II, Pope John Paul II notes that the work of revising the Roman Missal was carried out according to the conciliar principle of "fidelity to tradition and openness to legitimate development. [A]nd so it is possible to say that the reform of the liturgy is strictly traditional and in accordance with the ancient usage of the Holy Fathers [*ad normam Sanctorum Patrum*]."

[7] "A careful investigation—theological, historical, and pastoral—should always be made into each part of the liturgy which is to be revised. Furthermore, the general laws governing the structure and meaning of the liturgy must be studied in conjunction with the experience derived from recent liturgical reforms and from the indults granted to various places. Finally, there must be no innovations unless the good of the Church genuinely and certainly requires them, and care must be taken that any new forms adopted should in some way grow organically from forms already existing" (Vatican II, Constitution on the Liturgy, article 23).

[8] These choices and tastes are often guided by uncontrolled emotions or by fads that unfortunately can inhibit the true "*sensus Ecclesiae*".

Shouldn't this question[9]—still a painful one for many Catholics[10]—be asked calmly in the light of all that is taught by the rich history of our liturgical patrimony, acknowledging that the authentic Tradition of the Church, of which the liturgy is the highest expression, can be interpreted authentically only in conjunction with the councils, from Nicea to Vatican II?[11]

[9] This is of even greater present interest since the liturgy intended by the Church is generally not observed in the parish churches, which divides and deeply upsets the faithful.

[10] See, for example, Huguette Perol, *Les sans-papiers de l'Église* [The people in the Church who have no identification papers] (Paris: Édition de Guibert, 1996).

[11] John Paul II, Motu Proprio *Ecclesia Dei adflicta*, July 2, 1988.

THE ROMAN LITURGY IN FRANCE
IN THE BAROQUE PERIOD

Until the Council of Trent, the rites of the Roman liturgy presented a certain variety. Saint Pius V implied this, since he wished to remedy the "variations in the rites" by imposing a unification of the Roman liturgy.

The Tridentine reform and sung Mass

In order to curb a tendency toward the fragmentation of the Roman rite, due to the way in which it was transmitted in the sixteenth century, the Council of Trent regulated the celebration of the Mass which, at that time, for lack of printed missals, took on different forms from one place to another. But Trent was concerned above all with the "Low Mass" (that is, with a liturgy that was recited and not sung), which had become the ordinary form of the Eucharistic celebration in the parishes.

That is why the Roman Missal revised after the Council of Trent appears as a work that defines, above all, the rituals of "Low Mass" or the "private Mass".

From then on, the sung Mass, the normal form of the Roman liturgy, would appear as a "Low Mass", to which were added chants that, beginning in the fourteenth and fifteenth centuries, often had only a distant connection to the original Gregorian chant, to the point where they were usually replaced by motets. One of the peculiarities of the Roman liturgy described as "Tridentine" is that the texts for the Proper and the Ordinary of the Mass are pronounced twice: once in a low voice by the celebrant, who is "saying" a "Low Mass", and once aloud by the choir members, who sing antiphonally with the congregation.

The Mass: Public worship of the Church or an act of private devotion?

The reform of Saint Pius V owed much to the climate of contro-versy in which it was carried out, and it was enclosed within a social context where the *sensus Ecclesiae* was sometimes lost and an individualism was emerging that was rooted in the *Devotio mod-erna*.[1] This reform, despite the unquestionable progress that it brought about, remained in certain respects distant from the intended return "to the norms of the Church Fathers".

Thus, in giving priority to the "Low Mass", the Tridentine reform would progressively develop a practice of making the Eucharistic celebration an act of private devotion by the priest, whereas the faithful were simply invited to attend the Mass and to unite their prayers with it as sincerely as possible.

From the seventeenth to the eighteenth century: A difficult period for the liturgy

Already confronted with theological and historical problems that were often thorny, the "Tridentine" Roman liturgy is then plunged into a social context that is hardly favorable to it: in the seven-teenth and eighteenth centuries, indeed, Jansenism[2] and Gallican-ism developed.

---

[1] "This term designates the spiritual movement originating in the Netherlands at the end of the fourteenth century at the instigation of Gerard Grote and the Brothers of the Common Life (who later became the canons of Windesheim). Among the best-known spiritual authors of this movement we must mention Thomas a Kempis, now proved to be the author of *The Imitation of Christ*. Thanks especially to this last-mentioned spiritual anthology, the *Devotio Moderna* exercised a considerable influence on the spirituality of the West at the end of the Middle Ages and during the modern period. *Devotio Moderna* was characterized both by the desire to reform the clergy and the faithful and by a return to simple and practical evangelical ideas in spiritual matters" (*Dictionnaire de la foi Chrétienne* [Dictionary of the Christian faith] [Paris: Édition du Cerf, 1989]).

[2] On this subject see Fabian Gastellier, *Angélique Arnaud* (Paris: Édition Fayard, 1998). Also Jacques Attali, *Blaise Pascal ou le génie Français* [Blaise Pascal or the French genius] (Paris: Édition Fayard, 2000).

At first a simple theological current, Jansenism[3] was gradually transformed into a spirituality having a political connotation. Does the religious independence that the Jansenists always preached not sound like a prelude to that independence of man with regard to all legitimate institutions, the independence that would be demanded in 1789 in the name of individual liberty?[4]

As for Gallicanism, this appeared as a current in French politics that flatly asserted the independence of the national Church with

---

[3] Jansenism is "a doctrine that denies free will in man and the possibility for man to refuse the grace and the universality of salvation in the death of Jesus Christ" (*Dictionnaire des mots de la foi Chrétienne* [Dictionary of terms used in the Christian faith] [Paris: Édition du Cerf, 1989]).

[4] The Jansenists would play an increasingly important role in politics. Joseph Barry notes that at the time of Louis XV "thirty large cities in France made it a point of honor to have their own parliament, the one in Paris being the most important. The role of these assemblies was more juridical than legislative. Their leaders were descended from the nobility of the [judicial] robe and had a marked Jansenist tendency. Opposing it was the older, profoundly different nobility of the sword, which was in solidarity with the king, the court, and the Jesuits. Relations were strained. The parliamentarians that we are speaking of were, in fact, ennobled members of the bourgeoisie, men of the law who had the ambition of replacing the clergy in the government of the country. These men of money looked with disdain upon the Church as it chose the side of the landed aristocrats, out of contempt for those who derived their revenues from interest, which is to say from usury. The parliament gained popularity proportionally as the people lost faith in the clergy. D'Argenson noted that the priests could scarcely appear in the streets 'without being booed. Minds are turning to discontent and disobedience, and everything is leading toward a great revolution in religion and in government.'

"In 1753 Louis XV said to the Duke of Gontaut: 'The *Grandes Robes* [men who wear long judicial robes] and the clergy are always at each other with daggers drawn; their quarrels leave me desolate, but I detest the *Grandes Robes* much more. My clergy, at heart, is devoted to me and faithful; the others would like to keep me under their thumb.' Gontaut did not take the matter seriously; these 'little lawyers' were not powerful enough to disturb the State. The King went on: 'You do not know what they do and what they think; the assembly is full of republicans. Enough of that, anyhow: things as they are now will last as long as I do.'

"During that period the Archbishop of Paris, applying the papal bull *Unigenitus* literally, had given the order to refuse the sacraments to the Jansenists. The parliament retaliated by ordering the arrest and imprisonment of the priests who obeyed the Archbishop. The King then forbade the judicial courts to become involved in these matters. But the parliament took no notice and the King had to institute proceedings against their leader" (Quoted from *Versailles, passions et politique* [Paris: Édition du Seuil, 1987], pp. 204–5).

respect to the Holy See.[5] Gradually the idea became common that the decrees and the acts of the Roman Pontiff had no validity for the faithful unless they were confirmed by the civil authority.

To these two currents we should add a third belonging to the artistic realm: the Baroque style, with its love of theatricality. A popular art par excellence and the vehicle for an expressive spirituality, the Baroque style prevailed throughout Europe and, thanks to the missionaries, in Latin America. In the tiniest chapels as well as in important abbey churches, enthusiasm for the Baroque introduced a style that transformed sanctuaries into expanses of scenery, allowing the liturgy to take on the charms and pageantry of a classical ballet.

In this context, which was both spiritual and artistic, a new element appeared upon the main altar in the churches: the tabernacle. Now, since during this period the emphasis was upon Eucharistic adoration (thanks to the Counter-Reformation), the tabernacle very quickly became the principal component of the altar; the celebration of the Eucharist, strictly speaking, became secondary in importance.

Then, by topping off the altars with reredos decorated with symbols pertaining to Eucharistic adoration, and by installing tabernacles on a grand scale, the Baroque period transformed sanctuaries into religious dioramas,[6] designed to unveil or express the whole pathos of the Eucharist. From then on, the spectacular, of which the seventeenth and eighteenth centuries were so fond, was no longer found only on the street, in the court of Versailles, or in the theater; in a certain way it came to the churches as well through the liturgy.

The Baroque style, therefore, is not a neutral art; its purpose is to strike the imagination in order to captivate and convince. In the

---

[5] See the 1682 Declaration of the Gallican Church. Already at the beginning of the seventeenth century, Eustache de Caurroy (assistant choirmaster of Henry IV) composed a *Missa pro defunctis* [funeral Mass] that followed the Parisian rite rather than the Roman rite. The *Caeremoniale* published by the authority of Clement VIII and promulgated throughout Europe in 1600, therefore, was not accepted in the French dioceses that wanted to retain their privileges and assert their independence vis-à-vis the Holy See. (Cf. Eustache du Caurroy, *Requiem des Rois de France*, CD Astrée/Audivis E8660.)

[6] Gérard de Cortanze, *Le Baroque* [The Baroque style] (Paris: MA Éditions, 1987).

seventeenth and eighteenth centuries it would swiftly become an "art of propaganda", in which elements derived from the secular world encounter and mix with elements inspired by the spiritual realm.[7] It would thus provide to the State a unique opportunity to compromise with the Church. This would have consequences for the Roman liturgy at the moment when Jansenism and Gallicanism emerged.

The influences of the Baroque style upon the Roman liturgy codified following the Council of Trent

In seeking to be theatrical, the liturgy offers to the faithful the possibility of developing a personal sort of piety that takes its inspiration directly from their feelings. Consequently one "attends" Mass as a spectator; that is why the liturgical celebrations of the seventeenth and eighteenth centuries aim more at arousing emotions or expressing the feelings of the believer than at eliciting a genuine act of faith.

That being the case, whenever possible, the believer will prefer to go to a church where "the Mass is beautifully done", that is to say, where there is beautiful music, where you get to hear the great motets of composers, such as Campra, Lully, Lalande, Marchand, Couperin, Grigny, and so forth. The liturgy is almost obliged to be a reflection of the worldly vanities of the age.

As for Gregorian chant, which Vatican II would describe as being "specially suited to the Roman liturgy", it remains the forgotten art. The Council of Trent did not succeed in restoring its original beauty, which the fifteenth and sixteenth centuries had marred, and it is replaced—in France, at least—by rhythmic plainchant and by the "royal Masses" of Du Mont.[8]

The behavior of the clerics and lay people

The testimonies that we have from this period are instructive; they allow us to understand that the liturgy then was far from having all the advantages that we would like to attribute to it today.

[7] Ibid.

[8] James R. Anthony, *French Baroque Music* (Pompton Plains, N.J.: Amadeus Press, 1974).

Saint John Eudes shows us that, during the reign of Louis XIV, in the churches one used to find "people who converse during Mass, or else children or poor people making noise, and dogs or laymen who come too close to the altar".[9] In his *Traité historique de la liturgie sacrée* [Historical treatise on the sacred liturgy], published in 1701, Bocquillot speaks of "impious individuals" who look for a "Low Mass" so as to avoid having to attend the "grand Mass". Another author describes the many Catholics who are content to hear a "Low Mass" in a domestic chapel.[10]

In 1769 some missionaries received instructions that reveal the rather strange notion of participation in the liturgy that was prevalent at the end of the eighteenth century: "The prayers that the faithful are allowed to say in the vernacular during Mass must not be the same as the ones that the celebrant is reciting in Latin."[11] Was it the intention to encourage a certain discrepancy between what was going on in the pews and what was being celebrated at the altar?[12]

Be that as it may, the celebration of the Eucharist ends up being sequestered on a sort of "reservation" from which the layman must keep his distance, so as to contemplate with due reverence a work of art that is exclusively sacerdotal.

As for the celebrants, it is required of them, above all, to follow scrupulously the rubrics of the missal: rubrics that have become extremely detailed, given that the liturgical rite promulgated by Trent is considered first and foremost to be a rampart that must protect and express the Catholic faith. The celebration of the Mass, therefore, must leave no room for the private initiative of the priests,

---

[9] Ibid., p. 279.

[10] M. P. C. (Collot), *Instruction sur le Dimanche et les festes en général* [Instruction concerning Sunday and feast days in general] (Paris 1777), p. 5. Quoted by Dom G. M. Oury, *La messe Romaine et le peuple de Dieu dans l'histoire* [The Roman Mass and the people of God in history] (édition de Solesmes, 1981).

[11] Lionel de Thorey, *Histoire de la messe de Grégoire-le-Grand à nos jours* [History of the Mass from Gregory the Great to the present] (Paris: Édition Perrin, 1994), pp. 260 ff.

[12] However, in 1609 the council of Narbonne permits the faithful to say in French [i.e., the vernacular] the prayer that begins, "Lord, I am not worthy" (*Domine, non sum dignus ut intres sub tectum meum*), a "novelty" that would be reproved in 1612 by Saint Francis de Sales.

who in that period are not always excellent theologians or pious practitioners of their faith.

Thus, even though the Church was not very particular about the conduct of the lay faithful during the liturgies, she made up for this by not tolerating the slightest irregularity on the part of the priest. The *Ritus servandus in celebratione Missae* [Ritual to be observed in celebrating Mass] is very enlightening on this point. Here, in anecdotal form, is what it requires the celebrant to do at the moment when he is saying the first prayer of the Mass:

> The celebrant places his hands, palms down, upon the altar, on either side of the corporal, bows to kiss it in the middle, stands up straight and joins his hands again. Then, turning to the people by way of the Epistle side,[13] without leaving the middle of the altar, he says in a loud voice, while separating his hands and joining them again immediately, without raising or lowering them (he must hold his head erect with the eyes lowered modestly and not extend his hands until he has completely turned around toward the people, and he must join his hands before turning back; in this double movement he should not describe a full quarter-circle with his hands; finally, he should step away from the altar a bit so as not to rumple the chasuble): *Dominus vobiscum! R. / Et cum spiritu tuo!* Immediately after these words he makes a quarter turn toward the same Epistle side and, with his hands still joined, goes to the missal to read the Collect. He always begins by saying *Oremus*, accompanying this word with the four gestures that follow: he turns slightly toward the Cross, extends his hands, but not beyond the width of his body, joins them again while bowing his head (the wording of the rubric allows him to join his hands again either before saying *Oremus*, or after saying it. The only prescription is to bow his head at the same time that he says *Oremus*.) He then faces the missal again to read the prayers.[14]

Might one ask, what room is left here for prayer?

Be that as it may, in spite of the extreme precision of these rubrics, certain celebrants seem to have no scruples about ignoring the

---

[13] We should note that this is the right side of the altar, where the celebrant reads the Epistle, whereas the Gospel is read at the left side.

[14] René Dubosq, *Le guide de l'autel, directoire pour bien célébrer la messe* [Guide for the altar, directions for celebrating Mass correctly] (Paris: Desclée, 1938); *Missale Romanum*, editio XXVII (Ratisbonne: Pustet, 1950).

instructions recorded in the missal. One even encounters country curates who are past masters in the art of adapting the liturgy to their own tastes:

> One often sees priests, in the villages as well as in the rural areas who, in order to shorten the duration of the high Masses that they celebrate, offer the bread and wine before proclaiming the Gospel, while the choir is singing the Gradual, Alleluia, the Tract or the Sequence, or after having read the Gospel in a low voice while the choir is singing the *Credo*.[15]

[15] J. B. Thiers, *Traité des superstitions* [Treatise on superstitions] 3:444; quoted by Dom G. M. Oury, *La messe*.

12

SOME ERRORS ORIGINATING IN THE RENAISSANCE ARE STILL FOUND IN THE SEVENTEENTH AND EIGHTEENTH CENTURIES

As the Council of Trent worked to codify the Roman liturgy, all of the errors to which the Renaissance gave rise did not simply disappear. Certain ones would resurface in the seventeenth and eighteenth centuries.

The heritage of the Renaissance

While intending to exalt man, the Humanism of the sixteenth century had caused him to lose, in his own estimation, part of his divine likeness. Now the immediate consequence of such a loss was to enslave individual human beings to merely natural needs. We may suppose that the Renaissance signaled a break with the past on an anthropological order, the consequences of which were still very much alive at the time of the Council of Trent; indeed, they would extend into the seventeenth and eighteenth centuries and even into our modern times. This rupture would explain, at least in part, the religious crisis of contemporary societies.[1]

It cannot be denied that we find repercussions of this rupture in the Roman liturgy: overly apologetic and mainly concerned with guarding the faithful against the currents of thought produced by the Reformation, the liturgy has sometimes been in danger of confusing the "principle of rituality" (that is, the natural relation of man to the things that express the sacred) with an extremely codified

---

[1] Jean Brun, *Philosophie de l'histoire* [Philosophy of history] (Paris: Édition Stock, 1990).

ritual. The result is that every liturgical action is confined in a self-enclosed universe of rituals.

Misunderstandings in the implementation of the Roman Missal handed down by the Council of Trent?

Beginning with the Council of Trent, the implementation of the liturgical rite is sometimes confused with the scrupulous obser-vance of the rubrics contained in the Roman Missal.

Once the art of printing had given to books—as a material aid—an unprecedented status, people ended up attributing more impor-tance to the tome containing the rules for celebrating the Eucha-rist than to a proper understanding of the signs that are to be implemented, according to the liturgical tradition received from the Church.

Consequently, people began to lose sight of the fact that the liturgy is not a complex system of printed rules that one must fol-low to the letter, but rather an inexhaustible wealth of accurate signs[2] and of exact symbols selected by tradition[3] and safeguarded by the Church, which must be implemented with a view to reveal-ing and faithfully transmitting a message that has been handed down.[4]

With the Roman Missal of Saint Pius V, people end up thinking that the book is the best "tool" for defining and permanently set-ting the liturgical tradition; instead of tradition guaranteeing the missal, the missal becomes the guarantee for the tradition. Doesn't that reverse their respective importance? Isn't that forgetting that the liturgical tradition is principally made up of what is experi-enced and handed down by *homo ritualis*, "ritual man", that is, by the one whose comportment is informed and shaped by the man-ner in which the Church herself experiences and celebrates her relationship to Christ and her faith in God?

---

[2] That is, signs that leave no room for ambiguity.

[3] During Vatican I, when the question was whether to define papal infallibility, one group of bishops opposed to the promulgation of the dogma asked whether it was not necessary first to inquire into the tradition concerning this question. Pius IX replied, "*La Tradition, c'est moi.*" ["*I* am the Tradition."]

[4] Cf. Rev. Bruce Harbert, *Two Coronations and a Funeral*, bulletin no. 107 (The Associ-ation for Latin Liturgy, Bristol, Great Britain).

The missal and liturgical tradition

The missal—as a book—contains nothing more than reliable reference points that allow someone to say what is and what is not part of the Church's liturgy. Guaranteed by the Magisterium, it is a sure guide that makes it possible to correct someone who might be inclined to depart from tradition or who might have a tendency to hand it on incorrectly. These reference points, given in the form of rules (the "rubrics"), recall the practices (gestures, words, symbols) that best show forth a proper and right relation with what is divine and sacred.[5]

From the Renaissance on, however, a certain distance that intervenes between *homo ritualis* and the liturgical rite itself fosters the emergence of popular religious customs that tend to become more and more confused. These will increasingly appear to be a means of compensating for the "frustration" felt by the lay faithful, who are obliged to take part in ceremonies that are becoming ever more "clericalized", more and more foreign to their religious sentiments.[6] Hence, in the West, after the Renaissance one can say that there is a constant tension between what is "popular" and what is "official", between "rituals" and the need to express oneself more spontaneously at the heart of the Church's prayer.[7]

[5] On this very rich subject, see the Letter of John Paul II to all the bishops of the Church, "On the Mystery and Worship of the Holy Eucharist", February 24, 1980 (Boston: Daughters of St. Paul, 1980).

[6] This has been addressed by John Paul II in his apostolic Letter *Vicesimus quintus annus* (December 4, 1988) and *Dies Domini* (May 31, 1998).

We emphasize that these popular practices can be found again in the Sulpician art of the nineteenth century, in the hymns of the nineteenth and twentieth centuries, and, in what is perhaps an even more abrupt fashion, in a process of *desacralization* that we see being carried out after Vatican II, but which existed already in embryonic form well before the Council.

[7] It seems that there was no such tension in the Eastern Churches, which have succeeded much better in preserving the principle of rituality by assigning a very discreet place to the liturgical books during the celebrations and by fostering the role of the collective memory as the locus of the liturgical tradition. That is why the liturgies of the Eastern churches show, even today, a great ability to engage the human person in his totality. They are capable of enriching [*valoriser*] man in an integral way, in all his faculties, both rational and emotional. (Cf. John Paul II, Letter *Orientale Lumen*.)

Today many lay faithful still believe that they are entitled to change the liturgy to suit their own likes and dislikes. Pope John Paul II has emphasized the dangers of manipulating what is sacred in that way.

The need to study the "Tridentine" Roman liturgy

The study of the Tridentine liturgy should continue today to have great relevance, inasmuch as it helps us to understand better what is genuinely at stake in the present-day liturgy, as well as to have a better sense of tradition, which John Paul II has invited us to discover, in his apostolic Letter *Orientale Lumen*, of May 2, 1995.[8]

The Roman liturgy as "recodified" by Trent and promulgated by Saint Pius V is, therefore, one stage in the history of the Roman rite; it invites us to find a "traditional" and worthy manner of celebrating the liturgy that the Church is giving us today.[9]

A liturgy that has collapsed

In principle, the Roman Missal revised following the Council of Trent was supposed to safeguard the faithful against liturgical innovations by certain celebrants and against regional decisions made by bishops; presented as a "norm", the so-called "Missal of Saint Pius V" was to be untouchable.

The reality is quite different; as early as 1667, Nicolas Pavillon, Bishop of Alet but an avowed Jansenist, would publish a ritual "corrected" according to the spirituality of Port-Royal. The following year this new work was condemned by Clement IX. But the papal Brief remained a dead letter; Gallican France already seemed to pay no more attention to warnings from Rome.

Others emulate Nicolas Pavillon

Ignoring the calls to order coming from the Holy See, Nicolas Pavillon spread his new ritual throughout his diocese. Almost imme-

---

[8] See also the Motu Proprio *Ecclesia Dei adflicta* of July 2, 1988 [available in the library archives of www.ewtn.com].

[9] We note here that two associations aim in particular to realize this objective in specific ways: the Association *Pro Liturgia* (APL), Rosheim, France; and the *Centre International d'Études Liturgiques* (CIEL), Montrouge, France. The APL is a member of the *Fédération Internationale des Associations pour la Liturgie Romaine* [International Federation of Associations for the Roman Liturgy], an umbrella group for the movements in France, England, the Netherlands, and the United States.

diately, twenty-nine other French bishops officially declared their approval of the "ritual of Alet" and launched, one after the other, into a revision of the liturgical books.

In 1677 Bishop Le Tellier published a ritual for the Diocese of Rheims and, two years later, it was the turn of the Bishop of Vienne, Henri de Villars, to publish a breviary that, this time, was not simply a "correction" but a complete and utter recasting of the volume.

The collapse of the Roman liturgy as codified by the Council of Trent

Paris, though, was the seed-bed for the movement that would swiftly reduce the Tridentine Roman liturgy to anarchy.

In 1680 the Archbishop of Paris, François de Harlay, published a "Parisian breviary" strongly tainted with Gallicanism. We recognize, nevertheless, that this new work was not without its good points: several apocryphal homilies were suppressed, along with some legends and anything that smacked of Jansenism. But the real problem resulted from the fact that the commission assigned to compile the new Parisian breviary was not content with that; in its enthusiasm, it attacked the Roman Missal, taking as its point of departure the principle that all texts that are not from Sacred Scripture must be eliminated.

The result was astonishing—and destructive. Many beautifully composed Gregorian antiphons disappeared: *Gaudeamus* (the entrance antiphon for the feasts of the Assumption and All Saints), *Salve sancta Parens* (the *Introit* for feasts of the Blessed Virgin), *Benedicta et venerabilis es* (the Gradual of the Common of the Virgin Mary), and many others as well.

Then the itch for change struck the liturgy once more: citing the principle that the priest recites the Divine Office alone and that, in that case, the plural is not appropriate, the traditional *Dominus vobiscum* ["The Lord be with you"] was eliminated and systematically replaced with *Domine, exaudi orationem meam* ["Lord, hear my prayer"]. Furthermore, since this period was a high-water mark for Gallicanism, all the prayers in the Office on behalf of the Supreme Pontiff are suppressed: *Tu es Petrus* ["Thou art Peter"], *Tu es pastor ovium* ["Thou art the pastor of the sheep"], *Dum esset*

summus Pontifex ["When Christ appeared as a high priest"; cf. Heb
9:11].

Following François de Harlay, two other Parisian bishops attacked
what remained of the Roman Missal: first Cardinal de Noailles,
then Bishop de Vintimille. In 1706 Cardinal de Noailles issued a
new edition of the "Parisian Missal" that, in reality, was not that
different from the one by François de Harlay. But it was Bishop de
Vintimille, in particular, who took the most questionable initiative,
by entrusting to three notorious Jansenists the task of revising once
more the "Missal of Paris", which had gradually replaced the Tridentine Roman Missal. In 1738 the umpteenth edition of the *"Missale parisiensis"* was published, which would be adopted by around
fifty dioceses in France.

What remained of the Roman liturgy as restored by Saint Pius V?
According to one testimony from that period,

> every one sets himself up as a master and claims for himself the author-
> ity to revise, to change at will in his church the ceremonies that the
> universal Church has prescribed or handed down. We have seen some
> bold enough to undertake to administer [the sacraments] in the ver-
> nacular and to have the canonical office sung solemnly in French in
> their church.[10]

The features of the new "French" missals

The missals printed during the eighteenth century in the French
dioceses have several characteristics in common that, one might
say, betray a "Gallican" mentality. What are they?

First, the lengthening of the prayers: comments on the prayers
were added to make them more personal. Modified in this way
were the Prefaces, the Collects, the Secrets, and the Postcommunion prayers.

---

[10] J. Languet, *Du véritable esprit de l'Église dans l'usage des cérémonies ou réfutation du traité
de Dom Claude Vert* [On the authentic spirit of the Church in performing the ceremonies,
or: A refutation of the treatise by Dom Claude Vert] (Paris, 1715), pp. 458–59. (Dom
Claude Vert—also known as "le Vert"—a monk of Cluny, had been ordered by his Abbot
to refashion the liturgy at Cluny after the Parisian model.)

Then, the arrangement of the prayers and chants: the changeable prayers and musical compositions were chosen according to the main idea in the Gospel of the day so as to produce a sort of "thematic Mass".

Finally, in keeping with an idea going back to the sixteenth century and spread through the churches that resulted from the Lutheran Reformation, a simplified liturgy was promoted, one without too much mystery, and preferably celebrated in the popular language so as to be immediately comprehensible.

Consequences of the collapse of the Roman liturgy

The Roman liturgy [in France] seems to have become the plaything of numerous currents of thought, sometimes hostile to one another, sometimes complementary (e.g., Jansenism, Pietism, Gallicanism, and mysticism), which created a genuine mental block. To hope once again for a true restoration of the liturgy in such a situation would be utopian thinking, since it would be necessary first to tackle a mountain of prejudices, habits, and privileges, of which the beneficiaries and the particulars often can be hardly discerned anymore. Then, too, the bishops who would try again to clarify and unify the liturgy would run into such great difficulties that they would very quickly have to back down and abandon any reasonable project:

> The curates—and not only the ones in Paris, whose lack of discipline has become a tradition—would defend liturgical privileges and customs while hoping at the same time to purify and, as needed, to limit the power of the bishops. These antagonistic forces would result in an irreparable inertia that would only be overcome by the French Revolution and its consequences.[11]

The collapse of the Roman liturgy would reach its nadir in Austria—where the Emperor Joseph II meddled in liturgical reform just as he meddled abusively in all sorts of ecclesiastical matters—and in

---

[11] See Lionel de Thorey, *Histoire de la messe de Grégoire-le-Grand à nos jours* [History of the Mass from Gregory the Great to the present] (Paris: Édition Perrin, 1994).

Italy with the Synod of Pistoia, which adopts and exaggerates certain ideas of the innovative French clergy.

The attitude of the Popes

What did the Popes do (from Innocent XIII to Clement XIII) while the controversies over the liturgy were developing and spreading? Mainly preoccupied with pursuing the work of liturgical restoration begun at Trent at the instigation of Saint Pius V, they first settled upon the task of revising and editing the Martyrology and the Pontifical [Ceremonial for Bishops]. The interventions by Rome had no effect, inasmuch as the few bishops in France who were fighting against the abusive liturgical changes were still Gallicans, through and through; therefore they rarely made an appeal to the Pope.

There was rarely any doubt, however, as to the thinking of the Supreme Pontiffs; it would be expressed vehemently in 1794 when Pius VI, in his Bull *Auctorem fidei*, would condemn the Synod of Pistoia because of its erroneous doctrine, which led it to change the liturgical rituals.

13

THE SYNOD OF PISTOIA

Jansenism and Gallicanism, which developed during the seventeenth and eighteenth centuries, came to a head at the Synod of Pistoia. In that Italian city in Tuscany a certain number of decisions were made with regard to the liturgy and doctrine.

The origin of the Synod of Pistoia

In 1763 the Grand Duke of Tuscany, Pierre-Léopold, the brother of Joseph II of Austria, decided to take religious affairs into his own hands. In January 1780 he sent, therefore, to the bishops of his duchy a circular letter consisting of thirty-one articles dealing with, among other things, priestly ordinations, the selection of curates, the government of parishes, ecclesiastical tribunals, and, finally, religious devotions. Then, with a view to implementing the various points of his circular letter, Léopold called on the good offices of Scipione de Ricci, whom he appointed to the combined episcopal sees of Prato and Pistoia.

No sooner was he installed than the new bishop began proposing to the Grand Duke of Tuscany a series of circular letters that legislated on liturgical questions. Shortly thereafter these circulars were put into effect in the Diocese of Pistoia and Prato. The liturgical ceremonies were modified, then, at the same time that the writings of the French Jansenists were reissued in a series of anthologies—once again on the orders of Scipione de Ricci.

These anthologies taught the faithful that the Pope is not infallible and that the Congregations of the Roman Curia had no power. Singled out for special criticism were Pope Clement XI, who had condemned Jansenism in his Bull *Unigenitus*, as well as the position of Rome vis-à-vis the church of Utrecht, which had itself been won over to the ideas of Jansen. But it was in volume 7 of the anthology that the question of the Mass was raised most openly. Scipione de Ricci began by maintaining that the Communion of the faithful who attend Mass is as much a constitutive part of the Eucharistic liturgy as the celebrant's Communion is, and he continued by affirming that the practice of daily Mass for the priest is opposed to the most ancient tradition.

From 1781 on, Ricci attacked devotion to the Sacred Heart, the Stations of the Cross, the invocation of the saints, and various confraternities. According to him, these were "superstitions", pure and simple, that had to be suppressed in order to promote a return to a pristine religion, such as it was practiced by the first Christians.

In April of 1783 the curates of Prato and Pistoia received a letter signed by the Archbishop of Salzburg, accompanied by a message from the Grand Duke of Tuscany. This document permitted Scipione de Ricci to broach the question of the liturgy. From then on splendid ceremonies would have to be suppressed; it was forbidden to light more than fourteen candles in a church; only one altar could remain in any given church; the religious orders had to close their churches on Sundays and feast days so as to compel the faithful to attend Mass in their respective parishes; at the end of Mass the priest had to give benediction with the ciborium [and not with the Blessed Sacrament exposed in a monstrance]; certain parts of the singing had to be performed in the language of the people.

Ricci's work reached its apogee in January 1786, when the Grand Duke of Tuscany wrote a letter to the eighteen bishops on his estates. The letter concerns preparations for a national council aimed at bringing about a perfect unity of doctrine and religious discipline. The new ideas aroused genuine enthusiasm in a good number of the clergy: there was talk of stripping the churches as much as possible so that only one altar and one crucifix remained, of abolishing processions, of saying the entire Mass slowly and in a loud voice, so as to promote better participation by the faithful.

The Synod of Pistoia

For the sake of greater conformity to the directives issued by the Grand Duke of Tuscany, Ricci convoked a diocesan synod; it opened at Pistoia on September 18, 1786. In the very first session it was demanded that the powers "usurped by the Bishop of Rome" be restored to the diocesan bishops, and it was noted that the power of Rome was born of ignorance and was nourished only by pomp, adulation, and self-interest.

A few words say it all: the bishops gathered in synod were confronted with a program prepared by the Grand Duke of Tuscany and by Scipione de Ricci, aiming to limit the power of the Apostolic See so as to introduce the Jansenist theses more easily into the heart of the Catholic Church.

In addressing questions concerning the celebration of the Eucharist, the Synod of Pistoia provided many details with regard to the liturgy itself: the organ must keep silence from the offertory until the Prayer after Communion; vestments that are too ornate and might therefore distract the faithful may not be used; the rituals must be simplified and certain prayers must be recited in the language of the people; the faithful must receive Communion every time that they attend Mass; Communion is to be administered with Hosts consecrated at the Mass, and not with Hosts consecrated at an earlier Mass and then reserved in a tabernacle; flowers are no longer allowed upon the altars, and the reliquaries must be concealed.

Reactions to the decisions of the Synod of Pistoia

It would be a mistake to believe that the decisions made at Pistoia met with the approval of the faithful. In May of 1788 the Catholics of Prato invaded the cathedral in order to protect the sumptuous altar and the relics that were in it. Then they seized the episcopal throne of Scipione de Ricci and burned it on the public square while sounding the alarm.

The day after this riot, the inhabitants of neighboring villages, who had heard the bells tolling all through the night, came to Prato, in turn. Their first act—to the great embarrassment of the "reforming" clergy—consisted of venerating the saints whose relics were preserved in the cathedral.

In light of this popular uprising, Scipione de Ricci asked that the Acts of the Synod of Pistoia be propagated rapidly and offered his resignation. The Acts would be published, but the resignation of the Archbishop of Pistoia and Prato was refused by the Duke of Tuscany.

In 1790 the Grand Duke Pierre-Léopold of Tuscany succeeded his brother, Joseph II of Austria, taking the name of Leopold II. As he was leaving his duchy, he seemed convinced that his decisions and his program for reforming the Church would not make quite as vivid an impression as expected. Indeed, several bishops no longer followed his ideas, and Scipione de Ricci himself abandoned his episcopal ministry.

The Acts of the Synod were published anyway. Plainly Jansenist in their orientation, their only purpose was to rehabilitate Jansen,[1] Quesnel,[2] and their followers at Port-Royal.

As for Scipione de Ricci, now that he had become the object of attacks, he attempted to defend himself against them. Appealing directly to Pope Pius VI, he reminded him that the Pope had the duty to come to the defense of a bishop who was unjustly calumniated, because he had done nothing but restore the true spirit of Catholicism in his diocese by removing from the churches and from the liturgy anything that suggested luxury, worldliness, or error.

A response from Rome

On August 28, 1794, the feast of Saint Augustine, Pope Pius VI published the Bull *Auctorem fidei*. This magisterial document did not judge the intentions of Scipione de Ricci; it merely returned to the Acts of the Synod of Pistoia in order to condemn the error contained in each of its propositions.

Hence, as to what is directly concerned with the celebration of the Eucharist and the liturgical rituals, the Bull makes six clarifi-

---

[1] Born in 1585, Jansenius studied at Louvain and then at Paris. He became involved in the disputes that pitted the Thomists against the Molinists on the subject of grace, predestination, and free will. Nevertheless he became Bishop of Ypres in 1636. His most famous work, the *Augustinum*, the basis of Jansenism, which would be popularized especially by the circle at Port-Royal, would be published after his death in 1638.

[2] Pasquier Quesnel (1634–1719) became a priest of the Oratory. A disciple of Mother Angélique Arnauld, the Abbess of the Convent in Port-Royal, he tenaciously defended Jansenism. His teaching was condemned in 1713 by the Bull *Unigenitus* of Clement XI.

cations that go against what the Synod of Pistoia had affirmed. Thus it recalled the following:

- The Eucharist celebrated by a priest alone retains all of its sacramental efficacy.
- The Consecration brings about transubstantiation, whereby the entire substance of the bread is changed into the Body of Christ and the entire substance of the wine is changed into the Blood of Christ, in accordance with what is taught by the Council of Trent and defined as a dogma.
- The Eucharistic sacrifice can be offered for a particular intention.
- In every church there can be several altars, in keeping with ancient Christian tradition.[3]
- Altars can be embellished with reliquaries and flowers.
- Everything concerning the liturgy depends upon the authority of the Church, which is faithful to tradition, and not upon the decisions of a synod.

The reception of the papal Bull

The Bull of Pius VI appeared right in the middle of the political turmoil that was troubling Europe, in general, and France, in particular. And so it often went unnoticed.

The Synod of Pistoia, then, marked the high point of a movement that, together with Gallicanism and Josephism, had affected France, Italy, Austria, Holland, and Germany and contained the germ of the idea of man's independence, as it would later be taught and spread by the French Revolution.

Just as Luther had placed, between the Word of God and the believer, the possibility of judging matters of faith and religion by means of subjective impressions, so too the Synod of Pistoia had tried to place a particular or local church between the universal Church and the believer. For Scipione de Ricci it was a question of bringing about a transfer of authority from the universal to the

[3] After the Second Vatican Council, however, it would be specified that multiple altars must be avoided, not in the churches themselves, but in the same liturgical space (*presbyterium*) in a church.

particular, which is not in keeping with the divine constitution of the Church.

The Synod of Pistoia shows that, as is often the case when it is a question of convincing others about the need for reform, the innovators alleged that religion and religious practices had been in some way "obscured". The theory that Ricci proposed at Pistoia did not enthrone private interpretation and individual inspiration, but rather the inspired character of every particular church, whether diocesan or national. It still retained the principle of obeying the Bishop of Rome in catechetical and liturgical matters—provided that his proposals and his teaching could be examined freely by the subordinate churches.[4]

Pistoia teaches us that it is always detrimental to the faith of baptized Catholics for official documents from Rome concerning divine worship to be examined systematically by subordinate groups that, by dint of trying to adapt the liturgical celebrations to the conditions in the local churches, end up distorting the Church's liturgy and thus falsifying the relations between God and men.[5]

---

[4] *Dictionnaire de théologie Catholique*, vol. 12 (Paris: Letouzey et Ané,); Romano Amerio, *Iota Unum* (Paris: Nouvelles Éditions Latines, 1987).

[5] John Paul II, *Letter to all the Bishops of the Church on the Mystery and Worship of the Holy Eucharist*, February 24, 1980 (see in particular no. 12).

14

THE ROMAN LITURGY DURING THE FIRST
EMPIRE AND UNDER NAPOLEON III

At the beginning of the nineteenth century, the intellectual climate following the Revolutionary period was not just Gallican or Jansenist: it had also become antireligious and, more particularly, anti-Catholic. Within this context, parish churches were being sold and turned into stables, granaries, and storage sheds. In the sanctuaries that were still used for worship, what had survived of the Roman liturgy was gradually replaced by the worship of the Supreme Being, then by the cult of the goddess of Reason.

During the religious ceremonies people would sometimes sing revolutionary tunes; it was thought that this might establish firm ties between Christianity and the spirit of 1789.[1]

As for the liturgy, it appears to have collapsed: out of a total of 130 dioceses in France, only about a dozen preserved the Roman rite as codified following the Council of Trent. The priests were the first "victims" of this situation: arrested, imprisoned, and tortured, they proved to be incapable of reciting a Divine Office together[2] or of celebrating a Mass according to a common rite.

In 1797, however, Abbot Gregory (a constitutional bishop) tried to reconcile the nonjuring priests with the priests who had taken the oath by proposing the creation of a common liturgy that would be "adapted" and celebrated in French. His plan remained a dead letter.

---

[1] The day arrived when they did not hesitate to play "*La Marseillaise*" on the organs in certain parishes, which made it possible, granted, to mollify the most zealous revolutionaries and thus to save from planned destruction a good number of instruments dating from the *Ancien Régime*.

[2] In 1798, nine hundred priests who had been rounded up on the convict ships of Rochefort to be martyred could not recite the Office in common, so great were the differences in their breviaries.

The Concordat of Napoleon I

Despite the vicissitudes that the liturgy went through, and notwithstanding the persecutions suffered by the clergy, French society remained attached to Catholicism, even though religious practice was at an extreme low.

Napoleon would make use of what seemed in his view to be a "social Catholicism", which he considered practical, above all: religious customs, kept up by a clergy that was generally ill formed and completely controlled by a centralized, powerful political authority—could they not become a serviceable instrument for the cause of reunifying the country?[3] Having understood that the people were still attached to the traditional values of religion (or at least to some of its external practices), the Emperor signed in 1801 a Concordat aimed at bringing about a religious peace that would complement and assist the establishment of a lasting political peace.[4]

And so, with a view to pacifying minds and hearts, the organic articles of 1802 (which completed the 1801 Concordat) state that "there will be only one liturgy and one catechism for all the Catholic churches of France." No doubt the liturgical and catechetical unification that the Emperor dreamed of was dictated more by the will to power than by a sincere intention to restore the rights of the Church. Although a certain religious appeasement was obtained, the price to be paid was the manipulation of the Church by the political authorities. The members of the clergy, having become civil servants, would henceforth be appointed by the State; the bishops were selected by Napoleon and, after swearing the oath, received a spiritual investiture from the Pope. Thus was established "a servile, often mediocre Church, at the mercy of pragmatic unbelievers".[5]

Religious and liturgical practice during the First Empire

At the beginning of the nineteenth century, the anticlericalism inherited from the French Revolution was still latent, even though it

---

[3] Cf. Lionel de Thorey, *Histoire de la messe de Grégoire-le-Grand à nos jours* (Paris: Édition Perrin, 1994), pp. 288 ff.

[4] The Concordat of 1801 was still in force in the *Départements* of Alsace (Diocese of Strasbourg) and Moselle (Diocese of Metz).

[5] Thorey, *Histoire de la messe*.

had lost a bit of its vehemence in everyday life. In 1832 Pope Gregory XVI observed, "The See of Peter is shaken; the bonds of unity slacken day by day. The Church is exposed to the hatred of the peoples."

In this situation, the liturgy could still be on occasion the subject of more or less lively controversies. If anyone still attended church at all, it was often out of purely human considerations rather than for truly spiritual reasons. The imperial court wished to reintroduce a pomp and magnificence recalling that of the *Ancien Régime*, and so the bishops subservient to the political authorities fell in step by organizing in turn more pompous ceremonies (contemporaries remarked that they savored more of opera than of authentic Christian liturgy). A Commission held meetings to try to bring about the unification of the "national" liturgy demanded by the organic articles of the Concordat, and it envisaged the compilation of new books (the missal, breviary, catechism); it was hoped that they would quickly become common in all the dioceses in France. But the work was not completed, which meant a return to the multiple liturgies of pre-Revolutionary days.

Given the fact that, during the same period, the diocesan boundaries were redrawn,[6] the problems became, so to speak, ubiquitous. The Bishop of Langres, in traveling about his diocese, had to be capable of celebrating according to five different rites—likewise the Bishop of Orléans in his ecclesiastical territory.

In spite of the problems posed by the disparity of diocesan liturgical practices, no new missal capable of restoring liturgical unity was compiled under the Empire. Worse still: the process of fragmentation in worship got its second wind in 1815, the year in which several dioceses that hitherto had managed to keep the Roman rite adopted neo-Gallican liturgies of their own, modeled on the one in Paris.[7] And so we can say that in 1835 (the year in which a neo-Gallican rite was adopted in the Diocese of Quimper) the liturgy

---

[6] The 1801 Concordat reduced the number of dioceses from eighty-three to sixty. New ecclesiastical territories would be carved out in 1817.

[7] Thus the dioceses of Brittany, one by one, abandoned the Roman rite; new ways of celebrating the Eucharist then appeared in Nantes, Rennes, Vannes, Saint-Brieuc, and finally in Quimper.

in France was in a worse state than in 1801, that is, at the moment when the Concordat was signed.[8]

Attempts to restore the Roman liturgy

The collapse of the Roman liturgy in the nineteenth century did not take place in a climate of complete indifference; despite everything, some reactions appeared here and there. The year 1811 saw the publication of a work that discussed the hypothetical advantages of restoring the "Roman chant" in all the churches in France.

Three years later, Louis XVIII commanded that the Roman rite be adopted again in his royal chapel. The decision was well received by the publication *Ami de la religion*,[9] which noted:

> His Majesty has just ordered that the Roman practices be substituted for those of Paris and used exclusively in the services of the royal chapel. In making this decision, His Majesty gives an example that one would do well to hope to see imitated perpetually by all the churches in the kingdom.

A work begun by Dom Prosper Guéranger

It is chiefly with Abbot Prosper Guéranger that the liturgical question would acquire a new dimension.

Born in April 1805 in Sablé-sur-Sarthe, Prosper Guéranger entered the seminary of Le Mans in 1822. The following year he began his studies in theology, encouraged by Monsignor Bouvier, then rector, who would later become the Bishop of Le Mans.

Since he was too young to be ordained a priest when he completed his studies, Prosper Guéranger was named personal secretary to his ordinary, Bishop de la Myre-Mory. It was not until October 1827 that he was finally ordained a priest by the Archbishop of Tours. A pungent note was not lacking in the ceremony. Abbot Guéranger himself relates the incident:

---

[8] This information was kindly forwarded to the author by the Reverend Father Guy-Marie Oury, a monk of Solesmes.

[9] *Ami de la religion* is a periodical dealing with church history that appeared for the first time in 1814.

The ordination ceremony had started. I was following with recollection all the formulas of it, which were very familiar to me. After the litanies, I noticed that the bishop was not laying his hands upon my head, nor the priests who were present, but that he had proceeded instead immediately to the exhortation, *Oremus, fratres carissimi, Deum Patrem omnipotentem* [Let us ask, dearest brothers, God the Father almighty], and that neither he nor the priests were holding their right hands over me. Disturbed to the utmost by this omission, which was about to render my ordination dubious, I believed that I ought to object: "*Monseigneur,*" I said to the Archbishop, "you are omitting the imposition of hands." Surprised by this interruption on the part of an ordinand, the prelate replied, "*Monsieur l'Abbé,* everything is taken care of; mind your own business." Then he continued to read the formula, as though nothing were the matter, still without imposing his hands. I insisted once more, and finally the two priests, who read more carefully the rubric preceding the exhortation, warned the Archbishop, who said to me quite simply, "You are right; I beg your pardon." Immediately he came up to me, imposed his hands, and the priests did so after him.[10]

From 1840 to 1841 Abbot Guéranger published the *Institutions liturgiques*; that was the start of a controversy but also, in a certain way, the beginning of the movement that would lead to the restoration and the unification of the Roman liturgy.

The arguments set forth by Prosper Guéranger in favor of the rite inherited from Rome did not always please the French bishops, the chief reason being that they viewed the steps recommended by the young priest from Le Mans as an infringement upon their authority. Nevertheless, his new ideas eventually bore fruit, thanks mainly to two favorable circumstances: the gradual decline of the Gallican spirit on the one hand, and on the other hand, the support given by Monseigneur Parisis, the Bishop of Langres.

The decline of Gallicanism

Abbot Guéranger was thoroughly convinced that the Gallican spirit, which had been a root cause of the fragmentation of the Roman

---

[10] Dom Cuthbert Johnson, *Prosper Guéranger (1805–1875), a Liturgical Theologian: An Introduction to His Liturgical Writings and Work* (Rome: Pontificio Ateneo S. Anselmo, 1984).

liturgy into particular diocesan rites, was coming to an end. Now this heralded end was soon hastened by the policies of Napoleon III[11] as well as by the flight of Pius IX from Rome in 1848. The flight of the Pope would quickly give rise to a veritable ultramontane movement,[12] not only in France but also throughout Christian Europe.

The support of Monseigneur Parisis

Like most bishops of that period, Monseigneur Parisis did not object in principle to diocesan liturgies. However, the five different rites in use in his diocese presented certain administrative difficulties for him. That is why, in 1836, he opted for a return to the Roman breviary, thus preparing his priests to adopt the Roman Missal later on.

In October of 1839 Bishop Parisis made the use of the Roman rite the general rule for his entire diocese, giving five reasons for his choice: the antiquity of this liturgy, its universality, its unchangeable character, its fullness, and its authority.[13]

With that, the movement in favor of returning to the Roman liturgy started; the provincial councils that would be held in France during the second half of the nineteenth century give us the best proof of that.[14]

The provincial councils

The decline of Gallicanism, together with the work of Abbot Prosper Guéranger, facilitated the gradual return of the Roman liturgy in the parish churches.

---

[11] See André Castelot, *Napoléon III* (Paris: Édition Perrin, 1999).

[12] Ultramontanism (beyond the mountains) is a collection of doctrines and attitudes in favor of the Roman primacy and opposed to the Gallican positions that defended the autonomy of the national churches and the intervention of the State in religious affairs. Ultramontanism developed in France particularly in the nineteenth century; influential figures in this movement were Joseph de Maistre, Lamennais, Cardinal Pie, Louis Veuillot, and others. Cf. *Dictionnaire des mots de la foi Chrétienne* (Paris: Édition du Cerf, 1968).

[13] See Johnson, *Prosper Guéranger*, pp. 200–202.

[14] See Dom Prosper Guéranger, *Institutions liturgiques*.

In France

The council that was held in Paris in 1849 acknowledged the primacy of the Supreme Pontiff and admitted his authority in all departments of ecclesiastical discipline. From then on it was forbidden for priests to introduce new changes into the liturgy. That same year, the council of Soissons recalled the authority of the Holy See and condemned the Gallican claim that decisions by Rome have no validity until they are recognized by the civil authority.

Thus a series of local councils pursued a common objective: to remember the role of Peter in the Church.

The council of Rennes emphasized that unity of faith must be manifested through unity of liturgical worship. It favored the return to the Roman liturgy.

The council of Albi, in turn, decided to resume the use of the Roman liturgy as soon as possible. Identical decisions were reached, starting in 1850 in Lyons, Bordeaux. In Clermont the return to the Roman liturgy was presented as a sign of devotion and filial obedience toward the person of the Roman Pontiff.

The council of Aix forbade unauthorized changes to the liturgy and favored the adoption of the Roman rite. In 1851 the council of Auch stressed that the level of liturgical practices should be raised and their forms restored. That same year, the council of Amiens resolutely condemned Gallicanism and in a way sounded the final victory of the ultramontane movement.

During that period, a new Benedictine community, founded by Dom Prosper Guéranger and based in Solesmes, set out on a new path, as far as the liturgy is concerned. According to Dom Guéranger (who had become the first Abbot of Solesmes), the celebration of the liturgy ought to have the highest priority for a monk. It is the center of monastic life, because it witnesses to the fundamental values of the Gospel; the liturgy is the means by which one is incorporated, as it were, into the salvific mysteries of Christ and becomes directly involved in the living experience of the Church.

Subsequently the movement to restore the Roman liturgy would be spearheaded and informed by Solesmes; from the second half of the nineteenth century on, the Benedictines of this community would play a dominant role that continues today.

In German-speaking lands

Beginning in the second half of the eighteenth century, because of the influence of Josephism, German-language missals spread rapidly. Furthermore, in order to promote the participation of the people during liturgical celebrations, the sung prayers in the Ordinary of the Mass were gradually replaced by acclamations or hymns directly inspired by Lutheran chorales, which were themselves derived from late Gregorian melodies that were distorted to fit a measured rhythm.[15] The *Kyrie eleison* became *Herr, erbarm dich unser*,[16] the *Gloria* was replaced by *Allein Gott in der Höh sei Ehr*,[17] and the *Sanctus* gave way to *Heilig, heilig ist der Herr*.

Eventually, liturgical chant was forced to give way to a so-called "sacred" music, modeled on the polyphony that was in use in the princely courts of the eighteenth century (i.e., Haydn and Mozart). Against the backdrop of the grand Baroque churches, then, the faithful witnessed the triumph of the chorale and the *"Deutsche Singmesse"* [Mass sung in German], even though a few dioceses—such as the Diocese of Mayence—remained attached to Gregorian chant.

In 1894, however, a decree prohibited the *Singmesse*; the German-speaking churches were invited then to return to the Latin and Gregorian liturgy as it was codified in the missal published after the Council of Trent.

The return to this more "official" liturgy would come about through the agency of the larger monasteries, some of which maintained close ties with Solesmes.[18]

In England

The liturgical question here should be studied in light of the conflicts between the Anglicans and the Catholics.

[15] The *Orgelbüchlein* [Little Organ Book] of Johann-Sebastian Bach offers many examples of harmonized chorales based on Gregorian themes.

[16] The melody indicated by Herrnut in 1784, which very closely resembles a Gregorian acclamation, can be used with either German or Latin words.

[17] The well-known melody dates back to before the Reformation (Niklaus Decius, d. 1529).

[18] The Abbey of Beuron, for example, would follow closely the liturgical studies of Solesmes.

The ostracism that victimized English Catholics came to an end with the 1829 Act of Emancipation. Until then the official policy of the British government had forbidden Catholics to celebrate the Eucharist according to the ritual of the Catholic Church. The only places where one could find a genuine liturgy were in London, in the chapels of the ambassadors of certain Catholic countries. These sanctuaries—veritable refuges—were the only places remaining where English Catholics could have contact with the "Baroque" Roman liturgy as it was celebrated on the Continent.

Fortunately, just as in France, nineteenth-century England saw the gradual development of a movement in favor of Catholicism. On the one hand, Romanticism contributed to an interest in studying the Middle Ages,[19] and this led many assuredly influential Anglican intellectuals[20] to turn to Catholicism; on the other hand, an infatuation with theological studies hit the major universities. This was the beginning of what would be called the "Oxford Movement".

In this favorable set of circumstances appeared the figure of John Henry Newman.

Raised in the Anglican faith, Newman converted to Catholicism, was ordained a priest, and then became a cardinal; Newman introduced the Oratorians[21] to London as well as to Birmingham. Now one characteristic feature of the Oratorians is the great emphasis that they place on liturgy and chant. But to chant the Mass and Solemn Vespers every day requires trained singers.

Although Newman demanded quality, he was rather reserved with respect to Gregorian chant and polyphony. In his opinion, the nineteenth-century musical principles were unsuitable for the perfect performance of ancient works. That is why he preferred to hear choirs perform the works of Haydn, Beethoven, or Cherubini. His musical choices were a perfect reflection of the ideas and tastes of the period; this was the heyday of the "concert Masses" accompanied either by an orchestra or else by a solo organ having

---

[19] We recall in this regard Sir Walter Scott.

[20] An example is Auguste Pugin, who went on to develop the neo-Gothic style, even in rural churches.

[21] The Oratorians is a priestly association founded by Saint Philip Neri.

many stops, ranked in a way designed to replace a symphony orchestra.

The Oratory would have to await the coming of Henry Bird Collin to enter a new stage in its rediscovery of the Roman rite. After becoming a Catholic in 1898, this musician was employed by the Oratorians in Birmingham. There he faithfully worked for the revival of Gregorian chant along the same lines as Dom Guéranger.

Harmoniously complementing the liturgical movement that was already well established in his time, Henry Bird Collin initiated a musical movement that is still active today in Great Britain.[22]

---

[22] This is according to a conference given by Fr. Guy Nicholls (of the Birminham Oratory) during a Colloquium at Solesmes. See *Actes du Colloque* (Rosheim, France: Association *Pro Liturgia*).

VATICAN I AND THE CONTEMPORARY "LITURGICAL MOVEMENT"

The Church's confrontation with modernity

During the nineteenth century the Church was confronted with new ideas that circulated mainly in Europe, urged on by the action of certain governments:[1]

> The materialistic mindset and progress of the sciences gave birth to doctrines that posed dangers for religious life, such as liberalism, positivism, and materialism. The social problems created by industrial development were at the origins of socialism and communism, which were both hostile to the Church.

Endowed with a lively sense of the authority of the papacy in doctrinal matters, Pope Pius IX (1846–1878) perceived the dangers to which all these new ideas exposed the Catholic Church. That is why he drew up a veritable catalogue of erroneous doctrines. Appearing on the list—and condemned—were rationalism, pantheism, indifferentism, naturalism, communism, false notions about Church-State relations, as well as certain statements concerning morality.

Then, on June 29, 1868, after consulting with several cardinals, Pius IX published a Bull in which he announced his intention to convene a Council on December 8, 1869.

On the date that he had arranged, the First Vatican Council began in Saint Peter's Basilica with a Solemn High Mass. At the conclusion

---

[1] It is appropriate to note that in France the Church would have to make compromises, first with the imperial authorities, and then with the conservative Republic of Thiers and Mac-Mahon. Citation is from Lionel de Thorey, *Histoire de la messe de Grégoire-le-Grand à nos jours* (Paris: Édition Perrin, 1994), p. 293.

of the liturgy, the Secretary of the Council placed the open Gospel book upon the altar and, after the official sermon given by one of the bishops in attendance (there were more than 770), the prelates paid homage to the Supreme Pontiff. After that, they invoked the Holy Spirit before singing the Litany of the Saints.

Then there was a Gospel reading about the sending of the disciples on a mission (Lk 10:1–16), and the Pope intoned the *Veni Creator*.[2]

Vatican I and the Roman liturgy

The liturgical question was not the main subject of discussion at Vatican I: the real purpose of this Council was to affirm the primacy of the papacy[3] and to "remove the dust" that had settled on canon law, so that it could better meet the challenges of the modern world.

The liturgy was not mentioned until the seventeenth session (January 3, 1870). The Fathers limited themselves to confirming the decrees of the Council of Trent, with the intention of maintaining the dignity of divine worship. Their caution is explained by a fear of having to witness a new and uncontrollable fragmentation of the Roman rite.

Several exceptions to ritual unity appeared nevertheless: on January 19, 1870, a Mass was celebrated in the Ambrosian rite in Milan.

In other respects, from an ecumenical point of view, Vatican I, while holding firm on questions pertaining to the unity of the liturgy in the West, proved to be very broadminded with regard to the diversity of Eastern rites. Thus the Christians of the East who wished to remain in communion with Rome would benefit from a genuine freedom of expression in their respective cultic practices.

But Vatican I had to suspend its work: the [Franco-Prussian] War of 1870 broke out. The attachment to the Roman liturgy as codified following the Council of Trent, added to the discovery of the

---

[2] Francis Dvornik, *Histoire des Conciles, de Nicée à Vatican II*, in the Collection "Livre de vie" (Paris: Édition du Seuil, 1962).

[3] Vatican I would lead to the proclamation of the dogma of papal infallibility. A minority of baptized Catholics opposed this definition, which resulted in the schism of the Old Catholics (presently found mainly in Germany and Switzerland).

diversity of rites in the Eastern churches, already induced certain scholars to intensify a "liturgical movement" that had been initiated by Dom Guéranger and his close collaborators.

The contemporary liturgical movement

What is generally referred to as the "contemporary liturgical movement" is a group of initiatives and concrete programs whereby some scholars and pastors sought to comply with the wishes of the Church and to restore to the Roman liturgy its true form, its true stature, its true meaning.

This movement had been started by Dom Guéranger and the Benedictines of Solesmes, among others. However, in Solesmes, the research being done on the liturgy and Gregorian chant was not primarily intended to affect the liturgical practice of the faithful.

Belgium and Germany, rather, were the starting points for pastoral action aimed at associating the Christian people more directly with the liturgical spirituality that was being rediscovered. A broader movement would be launched by Dom Lambert Beauduin (1873–1960) and would be carried on very effectively by several large Benedictine monasteries.

Indeed, ever since the seventeenth and eighteenth centuries, the result of the pompous and complex form assumed by the liturgical ceremonies was that many of the faithful, even diligent, practicing Catholics, did not always manage to take part in the genuine devotion of which the Roman rite is the bearer—hence the development of a personal devotion that was seconded by popular religious manifestations, which meant that often, during the celebration of the Eucharist, many of the faithful focused more on "secondary mediations"[4] than on the mystery of Christ, who was active upon the altar.

In 1923 the Eucharistic Congress in Paris echoed this situation in which the Catholic lay faithful had been plunged:

> Experience proves that three-quarters of all Christians, even practicing Catholics, do not know exactly what the Holy Sacrifice of the Mass consists of; they do not even know how they should take part in it.

---

[4] This expression is Jungmann's. (Cf. *Lexikon für Theologie und Kirche*, XII, p. 10.)

What astonishment there would be among the great majority of the faithful, if they were to learn that every true Christian must not only attend the Holy Sacrifice, but also offer this sacrifice with the priest.[5]

Once launched, the liturgical movement would soon be able to find support in two major documents: the Motu Proprio *Tra le sollecitudini* of Pius X (1903) and the Encyclical *Mediator Dei* of Pius XII (1947).

As a result of the teaching of the Supreme Pontiffs, the celebration of the Eucharist could no longer be mistaken for a purely ritual ceremony carried out by a clergyman trained in a sort of erudite choreography, while the faithful focused their attention on a choir that performed its splendid program from the choir loft.

The Mass would once again have to be understood and experienced as the center of Christian life in the Church, simultaneously as a sacrifice and as a banquet.[6] The liturgy in its entirety would have to be built upon the *Credo*, because it is, for every believer, his faith: professed, experienced, prayed, sung, and brought into contact with the faith of the whole Church.[7]

The work of Saint Pius X and [Venerable] Pius XII

The contemporary liturgical movement was encouraged principally by the two Roman Pontiffs who initiated the studies that would lead to a complete revision of the Roman rite: Saint Pius X and [Venerable] Pius XII.

With Saint Pius X the work of restoring the Roman liturgy more completely would begin. The Supreme Pontiff declared it himself: his work would be only "the first toward revising the Roman breviary and the Roman missal".[8]

Bishop Piacenza, an active member of the Commission appointed by the Pope, specified the aims that this "restoration" would pur-

---

[5] *Congrès eucharistique national* (Paris, 1923), p. 94.

[6] This is a paraphrase of Dom Guy-Marie Oury, "*De Mediator Dei a Sacrosanctum Concilium*", in *Actes du Colloque de Solesmes* (Rosheim, France: Association *Pro Liturgia*).

[7] This is a paraphrase of Dom Lambert Beauduin, *La piété de l'Église* [The Church's piety], cited by Dom Oury, op. cit.

[8] Latin: "*primum gradum ad Romani breviarii et missalis emendationem*".

sue: revising the rites and then proceeding to a general alteration of the rubrics concerning the liturgy.

A letter written by Pius X to the Cardinal-Vicar of Rome suggests the state that the liturgy had reached at that time:

> The desire to see the splendor, the dignity, and the holiness of the liturgical offices flourish again everywhere has convinced us to make known by a special act what our will is with regard to sacred music, which contributes so abundantly to the service of worship.
>
> ... Good example must be given to the whole world. Indeed, bishops and lay faithful come from all parts to Rome to see the Vicar of Christ and to fortify their souls by visiting our venerable basilicas and the tombs of the Martyrs, by attending with redoubled fervor the solemnities that are celebrated there with great pomp and splendor in every season of the year.... We ardently desire that they should not return to their homeland scandalized by our customs.... Supposing that someone has come from a country where musical instruments are not used, what judgment would he pass upon us when he hears them in our churches, just like in the theaters or in other profane places?
>
> ... Then, too, Your Eminence, ... there will be much to suppress or to correct in the singing at Mass.... The liturgical regulations ... are no longer applied.... They have substituted interminable musical settings of the words of the psalms, compositions resembling old theatrical works and, for the most part, of the same paltry artistic value.... The fastidiousness of some is satisfied by this, but most of the listeners ... are surprised that such an abuse could still continue. We therefore want it to disappear entirely.[9]

"Old theatrical works", says Saint Pius X in speaking about the music being made in the churches. But is it not the liturgy as a whole that has become theatrical, according to the tastes of the

---

[9] In December 1903 Pius X published a Motu Proprio determining the manner in which the restoration of sacred singing should be carried out. The text provides for the creation of a Commission charged with bringing the work to its conclusion. The revision of the Gregorian chant books would be entrusted to the Benedictines of Solesmes, who, at that time, already had at their disposal a considerable amount of material allowing them to study Gregorian chant and the Roman liturgy simultaneously. On this question, see Dom Pierre Combe, *Histoire de la restauration du chant Grégorien d'après des documents inédits: Solesmes et l'édition Vaticane* [History of the restoration of Gregorian chant, based on unpublished documents: Solesmes and the Vatican edition] (Solesmes: Édition de l'Abbaye, 1969).

time? In 1909 Father Garreaud de Mainvilliers, recalling a situation that he knew quite well, spoke of

> the theatrical pomp displayed in our cathedrals on feast days; that motley of dalmatics and copes that are stiff as tin-plate, ascending and descending in the chancel; the battalions of thurifers swinging their censers like slings toward the vaulted ceilings and catching them in flight, like jugglers; the criss-crossing lines of choirboys, which evolve into a quadrille at the signal from the clapper of the master of ceremonies.[10]

Thus Saint Pius X intended to recall what people still seemed to forget at the start of the twentieth century: the fact that liturgy never meant organizing "theatrical" ceremonies that permitted the participant to cajole his own feelings by making a fuss over complex rituals; instead, true liturgy consists of performing the rites freely and easily so as to allow oneself in a docile way to be formed by the spiritual message, for which the rites have become the privileged vehicle by the very fact that the Church has chosen them.[11]

On November 20, 1947, Pope Pius XII issued the Encyclical *Mediator Dei*.[12] This is a major document in which the liturgy is defined as being the "integral worship of the Mystical Body". The word "integral" has an important signification here: it teaches that the liturgy must no longer be only a "cult", that is, a ceremony in praise of God, but must be "integral worship", that is, a cultic action involving at the same time—and in an inseparable manner—Christ and his Church.

The liturgy must be "integral" worship in the sense that the celebration of the sacraments provides a setting for both the prayer

---

[10] See Dom Guy-Marie Oury's article "*La liturgie*", in the periodical *France-Catholique*, October 1999.

[11] "The solemnity of worship is an integral part of the Catholic liturgy and must be cultivated as one element of its own message, provided always that this solemnization does not become bogged down in what is pompous and mannered. Embellishment is most successful when it is so fitting that it causes one to forget that it is there." This is a reminder from a contemporary monk from the Abbey of Sainte-Madeleine in Le Barroux; quoted in *Quatre bienfaits de la liturgie* [Four benefits of the liturgy] (Le Barroux: Édition Sainte-Madeleine, 1995).

[12] The document is summarized by Dom Bernard Capelle, in *Revue Grégorienne*, no. 1–2, January 1957, Solesmes.

of the people of God and for the sacrifice of the Lord, for both the annual cycle of the mysteries of Christ and for the sanctoral cycle.

Pius XII shows that in every liturgical action the Church is actually present, and at the same time, her Divine Founder. Christ is present in the Holy Sacrifice of the altar in the person of his minister and above all in the Eucharistic species. He is present in the praises and the prayers addressed to God, since he has said: "Where two or three are gathered in my name, there am I in the midst of them."

An understanding of this unceasing union of Christ with his Church is of capital importance: it reveals to us the most essential reason for always joining the interior homage of the soul to the visible rite, and it places us on our guard against a piety that would lead us to think that grace depended solely upon the efficacy of the rituals, which consequently would mean neglecting the moral gift of oneself.

Liturgical rituals, indeed, need to be enlivened by morality; this point, recalled again and again in the Encyclical of Pius XII, runs counter to the habits that were developed from the seventeenth century on and strongly affirmed in the nineteenth century, when many thought that carrying out the rubrics scrupulously could be enough to nourish the piety of the faithful effectively.

As a result of the teaching of Pius XII, greater care would be taken so that the performance of every sacred ritual would reflect the double character of the liturgy, which is at the same time spiritual and visible.

Provided that the liturgy is spiritual and visible, it is living. Pius XII concludes from this, accordingly, that the liturgy must be capable of adapting to the laws of evolution: the divine elements established by the Lord remain unchangeable, whereas other elements can be modified, like any human production.

> Hence, the Supreme Pontiff says, the marvelous variety of Western and Eastern rites; hence the progressive development of cultic elements ... as well as the rebirth of practices that had fallen into disuse. These changes are due to a more precise doctrinal formulation, or else to new pastoral needs. They testify magnificently to the ongoing growth and vitality of the Church.[13]

[13] *La liturgie*, no. 540 (reprinted by Dom Bernard Capelle, ibid.).

The Encyclical cautions the faithful about another pitfall: in the liturgical realm, changes cannot be fruitful unless they are disciplined. Otherwise it leads to anarchy and to chaos. Pius XII declares:

> It follows from this that the Sovereign Pontiff alone enjoys the right to recognize and establish any practice touching the worship of God, to introduce and approve new rites, as also to modify those he judges to require modification. Bishops, for their part, have the right and duty carefully to watch over the exact observance of the prescriptions of the sacred canons respecting divine worship.
>
> Private individuals, therefore, even though they be clerics, may not be left to decide for themselves in these holy and venerable matters, involving as they do the religious life of Christian society.... For the same reason no private person has any authority to regulate external practices of this kind. [*Mediator Dei* 58.]

Thus the general direction of the liturgy is recalled and the laws for its celebration are set. Is it not obvious that *Mediator Dei* contains the seed of all the work of restoring the Roman rite that would be carried out later by the Second Vatican Council?

Some architects of the contemporary "liturgical movement"

Several noteworthy figures are connected with the "contemporary liturgical movement"; they worked so that the Church's liturgy might be celebrated more fittingly and experienced more fruitfully by the entire Christian people. We might mention several names:

Pius Parsch (1884–1954)

A canon regular of Klosterneuburg, Pius Parsch sought to communicate a sense of the liturgy among the Christian people in the parishes. In 1930 he published more than twenty-five million copies of his *Texts of the Sunday Mass*, in which liturgical instruction is combined with biblical teaching. He also inaugurated the "choral Masses" and the "popular choral offices", during which more emphasis was given to the participation of the faithful.

Dom Lambert Beauduin (1873–1960)

Dom Lambert Beauduin was a parish priest before entering the Benedictine Monastery of Mont-César in Belgium. As a monk he gained a deeper appreciation for the Roman liturgy, according to the principles disseminated by Dom Guéranger. His primary concern, then, was to make sure that such a liturgy would no longer be the sole province of contemplative religious, but might become an action in which all the faithful could take part.

In order to allow greater access to the official prayer of the Church, Dom Beauduin promoted the publication of "Mass books" to be used by the faithful; the [French-language] missals of Dom Cabrol and Dom Lefebvre would be widely diffused and, later on, the missal of Fr. Feder, which was compiled in the same spirit.

Romano Guardini (1885–1968)

Romano Guardini is known above all for his work *The Spirit of the Liturgy* [1918], which has served to the present day to explain the perspective from which one should approach Eucharistic worship.

Unfortunately, as it often happens, disciples sometimes make their master say more than he intended, and often the young "pupils" of Guardini, gathered together as the "Quickborn" Association, have gone beyond certain principles that are defined in *The Spirit of the Liturgy*.

That is why Romano Guardini is suspected by certain bishops of wishing to short-circuit the hierarchy of the Church. Following some misunderstandings, Guardini tried to dispel possible points of contention in a letter that he wrote in 1940 to Archbishop Stohr of Mainz: several German and Austrian bishops had reacted, fearing that the movement launched by Guardini would eventually undermine their authority.

On December 24, 1943, the Vatican Secretary of State himself wrote to the wary bishops, asking them to renounce the exercise of their proper authority in purely liturgical questions. At the same time, he authorized the celebration of the "Great German Mass", a liturgy during which the celebrant recited everything in Latin while the people sang appropriate hymns.[14] This practice enjoyed great success, since it tied in with what had already been done during the eighteenth and nineteenth centuries; as a result the transition from Latin to the vernacular language after Vatican II would be facilitated in German-speaking lands. Conversely, there would be less tension in those same countries than in France when the faithful would express their desire to participate in the current Roman liturgy, celebrated in its Latin and Gregorian form.

What clarifications did Guardini make in his letter to the Archbishop of Mainz? He denounced four erroneous approaches.

1. "liturgism", which occurs when something important is underestimated, until someone rediscovers it again and assigns an exaggerated place to it. Guardini specified that this error in appreciation occurs when one's thinking and sensibility is no longer governed by reason but only by estheticism.

2. "pragmatism" [*"practicisme"*], which consists of replacing true pastoral theology in liturgical matters with practical activities derived from pedagogy. "Pragmatism" is based on an unawareness of the essence and the dignity of religious life, which is in the first place interior and should not be subordinated to solely material and practical objectives. Overlooking the fact that the liturgy is not something useful per se, "pragmatism" places divine worship "at the service of moral conduct and inspiring initiatives",[15] while forgetting the primary and most important aspect of the liturgy: the fact that it is utterly gratuitous.

3. "dilettantism", which occurs when a current popular trend ends up thrusting itself upon the awareness of the faithful through the modification of liturgical practices. And Guardini gives us examples drawn from his experience:

> Starting from the idea that man can only pray in the language in which he lives, great importance has been assigned to German. Convinced of the importance of liturgical symbols, some have tried to bring them out more clearly and to give to sacred actions a more popular look.... [It quickly became apparent, however,] that not only was the Latin not known, but the German wasn't either. Particularly serious, further-

---

[14] See A. Adam, *La liturgie aujourd'hui* [Liturgy today] (Paris: Édition Brépols, 1989).

[15] See Alfons Kirchgässner, *Unser Gottesdienst* [Our Mass] (Freiburg im Breisgau, 1961).

more, was the fact that the liturgical theme became associated with other themes, such as confused notions as to the place of the laity in the Church or concerning the relation between ethics and religion.[16]

These examples remain urgently relevant today;[17]

4. "conservatism", which consists of rejecting from the liturgy anything to which one is not accustomed. Speaking of adherents to liturgical "conservatism", Guardini says that they do not understand that "the elements [to which they cling] ... come from the most sterile religious period—the nineteenth century, and that these very elements supplanted many riches of the Church's piety".

According to Guardini, the adherents of liturgical "conservatism" make the same mistake, century after century: they assimilate the liturgy of the Mass to popular and private devotions, which are often of dubious value. The reception of the sacraments, then, is "detached from its important context, so as to become a purely external ritual".[18] Some conservative forces often do not have "a true concept of what the liturgy really is"; many see in it nothing but "the external aspect, without really understanding the meaning of it".[19]

Guardini is reacting here against a liturgical formalism inherited from the eighteenth and nineteenth centuries and still very much alive in his day.

Dom Odo Casel (1886–1948)

A monk at Maria Laach, Odo Casel used his study of the Fathers of the Church as a basis for demonstrating that the liturgy is a

---

[16] Ibid.

[17] It can be noted today that, the more the liturgy deteriorates, the more "socializing" or "moralizing" homilies become, but rarely are they spiritual. To verify this, one need only listen to the religious programs televised on Sunday mornings [in France] and compare the subjects treated by the Orthodox Christians with those treated by the Catholics: spirituality in the first case, predominantly social themes in the second. Is it any wonder, then, that the West is going through a serious crisis in spirituality? Is it any wonder that, every year, hundreds of individuals abandon the Christian faith and go off looking in other religions or philosophies for a spirituality that they no longer find in our Western churches?

[18] Quoted in Kirchgässner, *unser.*

[19] This is based on the discussion of Wolfgang Graf, "L'encyclique *Mediator Dei* et la doctrine eucharistique", in *Actes du second colloque d'études historiques, théologiques et canoniques sur le rite catholique romain*, C.I.E.L., Montrouge, Oct. 1996.

"celebration of mystery" in which Jesus Christ, considered as the "original mystery", makes his work of redemption fully effective.

He shows, moreover, that the liturgy is, in the first place, the reflection of the essential realities of the Christian faith.[20]

The works and essays of Dom Casel were published from 1921 to 1941 in the *Jahrbuch für Liturgiewissenschaft* [Yearbook for liturgical studies].

---

[20] See Dom Odo Casel, *Das christliche Kultmysterium*; published in English as *The Mystery of Christian Worship*, ed. Burkhard Neunheuser (New York: Crossroad Publishing, 1999).

16

ON THE EVE OF VATICAN II

The period in which Vatican II took place was also the one in which a number of ancient texts and documents discovered in the previous century were being studied. We mention here in particular *The Travels of Egeria to Jerusalem*, which dates from the fourth century; the *Didache* (late first century); and the *Apostolic Tradition* by Hippolytus of Rome, which goes back to the beginning of the third century.

In *The Travels of Egeria to Jerusalem*, Egeria [in Latin, "Aetheria"], a nun from Gaul or Spain, has left an important historical record on the subject of the liturgies celebrated in the Holy Places. As for the *Didache*, it shows us what the instruction of the catechumens consisted of: it is still one of the most ancient documents we have of the early Church. Finally, the *Apostolic Tradition* presents itself as a collection of texts providing precious information about the Roman liturgy (ordinations, the Eucharist, Baptism, etc.).

Many scholars launched into an in-depth study of these ancient texts and published the results of their research. *La Faculté de Théologie de Strasbourg*[1] played an important role; situated at the joining of Latin Europe and Germanic Europe, this academic center facilitated the exchange of ideas and fostered dialogue among researchers with complementary perspectives.

A fragmented liturgical movement?

In the decades leading up to Vatican II, however, the liturgical movement did not have the homogeneity that many would like to ascribe to it. Some were more in favor of a theological liturgy designed to

---

[1] The Theology Faculty of Strasbourg enjoys a unique status in France: it offers state certification that is also canonically approved.

give glory to God, while others wanted a liturgy that would be more missionary and pastoral. There was also evidence, in certain individuals, of a desire to go beyond the guideposts set by the Holy See. As early as 1948, when Fr. Doncoeur, a Jesuit, and Fr. Duployé, a Dominican, met in Trier [Trèves], Germany, with professors von Balthasar Fischer and Johannes Wagner the day after a liturgical meeting at the Abbey of Maria Laach, Fr. Duployé taunted Professor Fischer, saying, "You know, we could accomplish many things together, and if they knew in Rome that Paris and Trier were marching together, that would be the end of the hegemony of the Congregation of Rites."[2] This was to say that, in such an intellectual climate, the directives in *Mediator Dei* ran the risk of remaining a dead letter—just like the subsequent decisions of Vatican II, which constantly refer to *Mediator Dei*.

Le Centre de Pastorale Liturgique

On May 20, 1943, in the midst of the German occupation, *Le Centre de Pastorale Liturgique* [Center for liturgical-pastoral theology, abbreviated C.P.L.] was founded. At first it was an unofficial organization, created at the initiative of Dominican Fathers Roguet and Duployé and supported by the publishing house Éditions du Cerf; its mission was to promote the "liturgical movement" by organizing conferences and by publishing liturgical studies.

In 1949 Fr. Aimé-Georges Martimort, a professor at the Catholic Institute of Toulouse, replaced Fr. Duployé as co-director of the C.P.L.

In 1965 the C.P.L.—which had become the focal point of research conducted by theologians, exegetes, liturgists, archeologists, musicians, pastors, patristics, and scholars—[3] merged with the *Commission Épiscopale de Liturgie* [Bishops' commission on the liturgy, C.E.L.][4] to become *Le Centre National de Pastorale Liturgique* [National cen-

---

[2] This is recounted by Dom Guy-Marie Oury, "*De Mediator Dei à Sacrosanctum Concilium*" in *Actes du Colloque de Solesmes* (Rosheim: Association *Pro Liturgia*).

[3] According to Oury, op cit.

[4] C.E.L. was founded in 1951.

ter for liturgical-pastoral theology, C.N.P.L.], an official structure of the French bishops.

Preparing for the Second Vatican Council

There is no doubt that these were the studies conducted by scholars that would assist in the renewal of the liturgy. However, considering the present state of the Roman liturgy, there is no denying that certain mistakes were made.

Too often, in the general enthusiasm aroused by the preparations for Vatican II, intellectuals who were caught up in their studies and their research did not always notice the discrepancy between the ideal of liturgy that they were proposing and the realities in the parishes.

Furthermore, when the Council was about to be convened, the liturgy did not seem to be an essential issue for the Fathers who were gathered in Rome. Did not Cardinal Montini, Archbishop of Milan and the future Pope by the name of Paul VI—the "Pope of the Council"—declare himself that the renewal of the liturgy was not a priority?

Indeed, at that point in time when the Council was being planned, the pastors and the faithful were so accustomed to seeing the Roman Mass celebrated according to the rituals contained in the missal inherited from the Tridentine codification, that they did not imagine that the manner of celebrating the Eucharist could be changed some day. The majority of the pastors themselves had still been formed in such a way that they had a scrupulous respect for the rubrics of a liturgy that, they supposed, had always been just as they knew it: a priori, then, there was no reason to change anything at all. At the most, they would agree to make some adjustments, thinking that the priests who were docile in following the Tridentine Roman Missal would follow just as scrupulously a Roman Missal that had been somewhat modified. Now, history would later show that disobedience was latent, even before Vatican II.

If discussions arose on the subject of the form that the Roman liturgy should have, they were generally "debates" among specialists, which were of no interest to Catholics in the parishes, or even to the diocesan bishops.

Now the conciliar work on the liturgy would begin and would be carried out. The form that the restored liturgy would assume was imposed, then, rather than proposed: imposed on the diocesan bishops, who perhaps felt that they were outclassed by the "specialists" and the "experts", and imposed on the faithful who, over the course of a few weeks, discovered in their parishes a manner of celebrating the Roman rite that they did not expect and that, in certain cases, went so far as to be spiritually "destabilizing".

Some years later, Cardinal Ratzinger summed up this situation—which was painful for many—in these words: the Roman liturgy as revised following Vatican II seemed more like the product of the work of bureaucrats and commissions than like the result of a process of organic development and maturation.[5]

The Roman liturgy on the eve of Vatican II

What did the celebration of Mass according to the Roman rite look like on the eve of the Council that opened in October 1962?

Beneath the unity of the rituals, it was possible to distinguish several differences, depending on whether the Mass was celebrated in an urban or a rural area, in a "practicing" region or in one that had been "dechristianized", in a middle-class or working-class neighborhood. But these differences had to do with the practical setting for the *Missale Romanum*, and not with the way in which the liturgy was adapted. Besides, the Roman Missal in Latin did not allow that many adaptations: all the parts of the Mass were so interconnected that it was scarcely possible for a celebrant to interrupt the course of a celebration to introduce his own subjectivity into the liturgical rite.

Mass in the city

It used to be in the major city parishes that the liturgy could best be carried out following the directions given by the Roman Missal.

---

[5] See Cardinal Joseph Ratzinger, *The Ratzinger Report* [1985], *Feast of Faith* [1986], and *Milestones: Memoirs 1927–1977* [1998] (all published by Ignatius Press, San Francisco).

Numerous clergy were on hand (when a bishop celebrated High Mass, his assistants assumed the roles of deacon and subdeacon), the altar servers were readily available and well trained, a choir sang polyphonic works, while a schola took care of the Gregorian chant. And so, thanks to the general availability of the "personnel"— especially in an era when no one dreamed of deserting the cities to go somewhere for the weekend—it was possible to celebrate magnificent liturgies.

However, despite several attempts to simplify the rituals and make them less burdensome, the Roman liturgy (before Vatican II) did not manage to rid itself of a *decorum* that was often ponderous, inherited in part from the eighteenth, but especially from the nineteenth century. To be convinced of this, it is enough to look at the clothing that prelates had to wear:[6] the bishop wore a train, put on embroidered gloves (until the offertory), and had to have silk stockings and sandals in the liturgical colors.

Alongside these so-called "beautiful" Masses, the suburban parishes generally offered liturgies that were more simple. It should be noted, however, that almost everywhere, even in places with limited means, every effort was made to embellish the liturgy. Although there was as yet no talk of "liturgical planning" [*animation liturgique*], in medium-sized parishes Catholics of good will could be found who were willing to help the priests to the best of their ability, without encroaching upon the role of the priest, properly understood.

Mass in the country

In rural parishes, the form of the liturgy often varied, according to whether or not one was in a region where the faith was practiced.

The tourist traveling in Alsace [in northeastern France], for instance, would be surprised to see the churches filled with parishioners,

---

[6] During the singing of the Office of Terce, which precedes the celebration of High Mass, the bishop, at his throne, was clothed publicly in the vestments of a prelate, somewhat in the way that the Sun King [Louis XIV of France] was dressed in the presence of his courtesans.

even on ordinary Sundays; the smallest church in this province had an organ[7] and a choir, often in robes, that provided Gregorian chant for the Proper and the Common and sang polyphonic works on feast days. Due to the influence of German-speaking countries and Protestantism, the congregation had no difficulty in singing an extensive repertoire, ranging from Latin chant to French hymns, sometimes via German.

In Brittany, Normandy, the Vendée, and other traditionally Catholic regions, it was generally a cantor at the lectern who led the chant in the smallest rural churches. The congregations knew certain parts of the Proper, as well as the sung parts of the Ordinary, which they sang antiphonally with the clergy. In Brittany, the lay people learned traditional hymns in the Breton language, which were collected in the volume *Kantigou Brezhoneg*, edited in 1934 in Saint-Brieuc. In the days when there was no clergy shortage, the parish harmonium [small organ] was generally manned by an assistant priest who had learned the basic principles of accompaniment during his formation at the diocesan major seminary.

In contrast, such liturgies were virtually unknown in other provinces: whole regions had remained dechristianized [since the French Revolution].

Now the difficulty in those days was that there was no question of the celebrant curtailing the liturgy on the pretext that attendance in church was low; for better or for worse, it was necessary to do everything prescribed by the rubrics of the Roman Missal.

As one can imagine, the burden quickly became overwhelming for a village curate who was obliged to carry out, for example, the long and complex rituals of the Easter Triduum in front of a congregation of as few as a dozen people, who were scarcely capable of understanding the full significance of a liturgy celebrated entirely in Latin.

---

[7] The local law of Alsace requires schoolmasters to provide the services of a chant *schola* to the parish church. The *École Normale* [teacher-training institute] of Strasbourg, accordingly, has an organ, which allows future teachers to learn how to accompany the Mass and [Sunday] Vespers. Primary school students, especially in rural communities, are "recruited" by the teacher either as altar servers or as choristers.

The Roman liturgy before Vatican II:
Its strengths and weaknesses

It is easy to understand that, before the Council, the Roman liturgy was judged, first of all, with respect to the place where it was celebrated; depending on the parish, one could find that it had great qualities or, on the contrary, a certain number of inadequacies, if not flaws.

The same Mass was found everywhere . . .

One of the advantages of the Roman Missal in use before the Council was to leave little room for the private initiatives of the celebrants. Thus the Catholic who was traveling and who went into a church to attend Mass was assured of finding almost everywhere the liturgy that he knew: he could participate in it easily by finding in his own "Sunday missal" all the prayers prescribed by the Church.

In those days the liturgy truly appeared as a unifying factor: it allowed the faithful to have the sense that the Church transcended national boundaries and that her official prayer was not limited to a given linguistic area.[8]

. . . but it was not always adapted to the variety of situations that the Church encountered.

Considering the great diversity of parish situations that one encountered, it is clear that the Roman Missal drawn up following the Council of Trent was an ill-adapted work: designed for the celebration of "Low Masses", the liturgy that it requires became a burden for a priest serving in a dechristianized locality. No provisions are made, indeed, for adapting the liturgy to conditions that may be particularly difficult: thus a missionary celebrating in the middle of the jungle, with limited resources, as one might imagine, is obliged to follow exactly the same liturgy as the Archbishop of Paris celebrating in his cathedral.

---

[8] We see today how troublesome this loss of unity can be whenever there is a royal wedding in Belgium, a country where the variety of languages gives rise to political and diplomatic problems that can sometimes be thorny.

Such a situation cannot help but raise questions of a pastoral nature. Now these questions emerged precisely at the point in time when there were more and more experiments aimed at making the Roman liturgy something less fixed, more adapted to the diversity of contemporary mindsets.

To these multiple questions the Second Vatican Council would have to apply the correct answers: at the same time it would have to take into account the specificity of the Roman rite, respect the datum of the history of the liturgy, manifest its fidelity to tradition while putting to good use the discoveries of contemporary theology, channel and direct the (more or less anarchical) experiments being conducted in the name of "pastoral liturgics", and prepare the faithful for changes—something to which they were not accustomed or which they were not ready to receive.

For the Council Fathers, this was a gigantic task, the extent and danger of which, at the time, was not always appreciated, it seems.

In October 1962, at the point in time when the Second Vatican Council was convened by John XXIII, the Catholic Church had to brave the eddies and currents of the modern world. She was confronted by the Modernist crisis, by the spread of Marxist thought in intellectual circles, by the so-called "death-of-God" philosophies, by rationalistic thinking, historical criticism, positivism, the emergence of the social sciences, the questioning of traditional values, changes affecting culture and morality, liberation theology, the claims of the feminist movements, etc.[9] She would yet have to withstand the crisis[10] of May 1968 and find a way for herself through societies governed by new technologies and dominated by moneyed interests.

John XXIII marks out the path of the Council

To understand better the situation of the Church at that point in time when the Second Vatican Council was about to launch into its work on a plan for revising the liturgy, it is helpful to recall several statements by John XXIII. Addressing the Congregation of

---

[9] This is a paraphrase of Elie Maréchal in *Le Figaro*.

[10] André Frossard later said that the student demonstrations in 1968 were a great Pentecost to which they had forgotten to invite the Holy Spirit.

Catholic Seminaries and Universities on June 17, 1961, the Pope declared:

> In order that the law of belief might be determined by the law of prayer, the Apostolic See, from the very beginning of the Christian religion, was accustomed to inculcate the following: "Besides these hallowed ordinances of the most blessed and Apostolic See, in accordance with which the most pious Fathers, after casting aside the pride of pernicious novelty, have taught us to refer to Christ's grace both the beginnings of good will, and the advances in commendable devotions and the perseverance in these unto the end, let us be mindful also of the sacraments of priestly public prayer, which, handed down by the Apostles, are uniformly celebrated in the whole world and in every Catholic Church." [11] In order that clergymen and properly instructed faithful might apply themselves to this duty with an active zeal, the Roman Pontiffs have constantly exhorted them to consider in greater depth and to procure by every possible means "the connection between dogma and the sacred liturgy, as well as between Christian worship and the sanctification of the people": they have done so in our era by the Apostolic Constitution *Divini cultus* of Pius XI of blessed memory, and especially by the Encyclical *Mediator Dei*, published on November 20, 1947, by his successor Pius XII of blessed memory.

The teaching of the Supreme Pontiff is clear: the connection between the liturgy and dogma is so close that a modification of the liturgy could be beneficial only to the extent in which it corresponded to a deepening of dogma and resulted in a greater sanctification of the Christian people. John XXIII is recalling, then, that change for the sake of change, in liturgical matters, would inevitably lead to failure— just like adaptations that, being too dependent upon pastoral considerations or trends, no longer took dogma sufficiently into account.

On April 15, 1962, John XXIII spoke to bishops, the guardians of the liturgy:

> However matters and the times may develop, the episcopal office will be absolutely incapable of bringing forth abundant fruits, unless those

---

[11] Council of Ephesus, *Indiculus* ["The Catalog, or the Authoritative Statements of the Past Bishops of the Holy See Concerning the Grace of God"], Denzinger, 139.

who are rightly called *"Sacrorum antistites"* [presiders of the saints] take care to permeate their labors with abundant prayer, as if with a gentle dew.

And they must first draw this abundance of divine graces from the Most Holy Sacrifice of the Altar. It is especially by this means that the price of the blood shed by Christ is applied to men. From this same sacrifice, in which every priest enters as if into a mystical embrace with Christ, it is impossible that the bishop should not find a pious alleviation of his labors, particularly if he celebrates very religiously, if he prepares himself holily, if he performs afterwards the acts of thanksgiving due to God, who is immortal and all-good. Indeed, if the most pious and most experienced of Christ's faithful are distinguished by their devotion to the most august Sacrament of the Eucharist—and that is correct and certain—how could the bishops not venerate this Sacrament with a very lively devotion, so as to draw therefrom, as from their principal source, grace, consolation, strength and serenity? How could they not ardently wish to betake themselves to the sanctuary of the Blessed Sacrament and to abide there, inflamed with the desire for rest in the midst of the increasing labors and cares of their office?

Finally, speaking to priests on May 26, 1962, the Supreme Pontiff declared:

Let the priests, too, take care that they do not abandon themselves completely to the restlessness and the external works of the holy ministry. For an uncontrolled thirst for action impoverishes the soul little by little; and neither the good of the parish nor the manifold interests of the diocese can justify it. Moreover it cannot help but cause grave harm to candidates for the Priesthood. Indeed, how will young men be able to appreciate as they ought the seriousness of the priestly office if, when they look at the priest, they cannot find in him an example of perfection to be imitated?

But in order to be capable of setting an example to be followed, let the priests remember the principal duties of their office: to offer worthily the Sacrifice of the altar, to proclaim the Word of God, to administer the Sacraments, to visit the sick (especially those who are near death), to instruct those who do not know the faith. The rest, which does not pertain to these obligations, must be left aside or else tolerated in the last place.

17

THE SECOND VATICAN COUNCIL

When he decided to convoke a Council to complete the work of Vatican I, John XXIII was not planning to "reform" the Roman liturgy, but to "restore" it.

It was clear that the Council Fathers would not have the task of "making" a new missal; they would simply be asked to enunciate general principles, on the basis of which it would be possible to impart more vitality and more truth to the official prayer of the Church, which at that time had still not succeeded in extricating herself completely from the constraints and the rigid practices that were among the less beneficial aspects of the nineteenth-century heritage in the religious sphere.[1]

The Commission responsible for preparing the work of the Council

Organizations to prepare for the Council were appointed and were ordered to gather the propositions, the wishes and the questions issuing from the bishops, the universities, and the various dicasteries of the Roman Curia. On the basis of the sum total of responses received, a Commission was subsequently put in charge of elaborating a schema to be used in composing the conciliar Constitution on the Sacred Liturgy.

This Commission was presided over at first by Cardinal Cicognani, who almost immediately obtained the assistance of a Secretary: Fr. Annibal Bugnini, a professor of liturgy at the Lateran University.

---

[1] Perhaps one could hazard a comparison between the stiffness of the flat chasubles inherited from the nineteenth century (and not from the sixteenth, as is generally believed) and the rigidity of the attitudes—if not of the mindsets—that sometimes used to promote a certain manner of viewing and experiencing the liturgy before the Council.

On August 26, 1960, an initial list of nineteen members and thirty-two consultors was established. Curiously, not one name of a French or German bishop appeared on the list, nor the name of anyone in charge of a French or German liturgical institute. It seems that the Holy See wished to indicate its mistrust of those who, intoxicated by the unauthorized liturgical experiments that they had launched, ended up going beyond their competence and not always showing respect for ecclesiastical discipline.

Nevertheless, a complementary list of consultors was drawn up the following October 24, in which the "deliberate omissions" of that summer were remedied.[2]

The preparatory schema for the Constitution
Sacrosanctum Concilium

The preparatory schema for the Constitution on the Liturgy was on the desk of Cardinal Cicognani on January 22, 1962. The next day it was approved in a plenary session of the Commission.

On October 11 of that same year, John XXIII opened the first session of the Council in the presence of 2,540 Council Fathers. In his inaugural speech, the Pope invited them to promote a "dialogue" between the Church and the world. In no uncertain terms he stated that the Church can no longer be content to live enclosed like a hothouse plant [*vivre en vase clos*]; in keeping with the parable of the sower, she must take into consideration the quality of the soil in which she must sow the Good News of Christ.

Yet the "dialogue" between the Church and the world, as the Pope envisaged it, does not mean the "subordination" of the Church to the world; it was still clear that the world must be renewed in Christ according to the Gospel, without rendering the Church insipid by hitching it to the wagon of the present age.

The first conciliar schema to be discussed was the one concerning the renewal of the liturgy. It recommended seeing to it that the faithful would be able to participate more fully in the liturgical

---

[2] Dom Guy-Marie Oury, *"De Mediator Dei à Sacrosanctum Concilium"*, in *Actes du Colloque de Solesmes* (Rosheim: Association *Pro Liturgia*).

actions.[3] Since the debates were drawing on at some length, the Council Fathers were invited to put aside discussions pertaining to the details and to speak only on more general questions having some relation to the pastoral aspect of the liturgy.

Therefore it was not a question of changing the Mass, or of inventing new rites or of modifying those that are part of tradition, or of bringing about continual reforms or fine-tuned adaptations, but rather of making the liturgy better suited to signifying the mystery that it celebrates. It was quite true, nevertheless, that in order to carry out this program, it would sometimes be necessary to resolve to do away with certain practices introduced at a late date into the liturgy,[4] or to reinstate some gestures and prayers that had been lost over the course of the centuries.

Certainly, the appearance of the Roman rite would be modified somewhat: some new features would appear in the manner of conducting the liturgy, and some gestures that had been considered venerable, simply because the most recent generations had seen them performed, would have to be dispensed with. However, if they were understood correctly and put into effect properly, these adjustments would be for the benefit of a greater clarity as to what the essential rites of the liturgy symbolize and effect.

Approval of *Sacrosanctum Concilium*

On November 14, 1962, the text of the Constitution on the Sacred Liturgy was approved by a vote of 1,922 to 11. Its preamble opens with these Latin words, which serve as the name by which we refer to the document: *"Sacrosanctum Concilium"*.

> The sacred Council has set out to impart an ever-increasing vigor to the Christian life of the faithful; to adapt more closely to the needs of our age those institutions which are subject to change; to foster whatever

---

[3] It is in any case regrettable that this schema was still too dependent upon the pastoral preoccupations of the postwar period and consequently did not sufficiently take into account the contemplative dimension of the liturgy. On this question, see Dom Cipriano Vagaggini, "Contemplation et Liturgie", in *Revue Grégorienne*, nn. 5 and 6 (Abbaye de Solesmes, 1962): pp. 179–91; 219–28.

[4] This was often for reasons that were more sentimental than theological.

can promote union among all who believe in Christ; to strengthen whatever can help to call all mankind into the Church's fold. Accordingly it sees particularly cogent reasons for undertaking the reform and promotion of the liturgy.

Sacrosanctum Concilium: A Constitution to read with the eyes of the Catholic faith

"Renewal" [or "restoration"] and "progress": these are, to be sure, the two key words to keep in mind when we read the Constitution *Sacrosanctum Concilium* with a view to understanding its spirit and applying its principles intelligently.

Contrary to what has sometimes been supposed, said, or taught, the Second Vatican Council was not a beginning or an ending: it was only a stage in the life of the Church. It can be understood, therefore, only in light of the councils that preceded it and with our eyes set on the Church of the future—as limited as our perspective on that might be.

In order to grasp the genuine magnitude and extent of the liturgical renewal desired by the Church, it is therefore fitting to consider it through the eyes of an authentic faith.

The place of the Constitution *Sacrosanctum Concilium* in the history of the liturgy

In a few remarkable lines, Pope John Paul II explains to us the place that the Constitution on the Sacred Liturgy occupies in the life of the Church:

> In response to the requests of the Fathers of the Council of Trent, concerned with the reform of the Church in their time, Pope Saint Pius V saw to the reform of the liturgical books, above all the Breviary and the Missal. It was towards this same goal that succeeding Roman Pontiffs directed their energies during the subsequent centuries in order to ensure that the rites and liturgical books were brought up to date and when necessary clarified. From the beginning of this century they undertook a more general reform.
>
> Pope Saint Pius X established a special Commission for this reform, and he thought that it would take a number of years for it to complete

its work; however he laid the foundation stone of this edifice by renewing the Roman Breviary.[5] "In fact this all demands", he affirmed, "according to the views of the experts, a work both detailed and extensive; and therefore it is necessary that many years should pass, before this liturgical edifice, so to speak, ... reappears in new splendour in its dignity and harmony, once the marks of old age have been cleared away."[6]

Pope Pius XII took up again the great project of liturgical reform by issuing the Encyclical *Mediator Dei*[7] and by establishing a new Commission.[8] He likewise decided important matters, for example: authorizing a new version of the Psalter to facilitate the understanding of the Psalms;[9] the modification of the Eucharistic fast in order to facilitate access to Holy Communion; the use of contemporary language in the Ritual; and, above all, the reform of the Easter Vigil[10] and Holy Week.[11]

The introduction to the *Roman Missal* of 1963 was preceded by the declaration of Pope John XXIII, according to which "the fundamental principles, related to the general reform of the Liturgy, were to be entrusted to the Fathers in the forthcoming Ecumenical Council."[12]

Such an overall reform of the Liturgy was in harmony with the general hope of the whole Church. In fact, the liturgical spirit had become more and more widespread together with the desire for an "active participation in the most holy mysteries and in the public and solemn prayer of the Church",[13] and a wish to hear the word of God in more abundant measure. Together with the biblical renewal, the ecumenical movement, the missionary impetus, and ecclesiological research, the reform of the Liturgy was to contribute to the overall renewal of the Church. I draw attention to this in the Letter *Dominicae Cenae*: "A very close

---

[5] See Apostolic Constitution *Divino afflatu*, November 1, 1911, in *AAS* 3 (1911): 633–38.

[6] See Motu Proprio *Abhinc duos annos*, October 23, 1913, in *AAS* 5 (1913): 449–50.

[7] See Encyclical *Mediator Dei*, November 20, 1947, in *AAS* 39 (1947): 521–600.

[8] See Sacred Congregation of Rites, Historical Section, no. 71, *Memoria sulla riforma liturgica* (1946).

[9] See Pius XII, Motu Proprio *In cotidianis precibus*, March 24, 1945, in *AAS* 37 (1945): 65–67.

[10] See S. Congregation of Rites, Decree *Dominicae Resurrectionis*, February 9, 1951, in *AAS* 43 (1951): 128–29.

[11] See S. Congregation of Rites, Decree *Maxima redemptionis*, November 16, 1955, in *AAS* 47 (1955): 838–41.

[12] See John XXIII, Motu Proprio *Rubricarum Instructum*, July 25, 1960, in *AAS* 52 (1960): 594.

[13] See Saint Pius X, Motu Proprio *Tra le sollecitudini dell'officio pastorale*, November 22, 1903, in *Pii X Pontificis Maximi Acta*, 1:77.

and organic *bond* exists *between the renewal of the Liturgy and the renewal of the whole life of the Church.* The Church not only acts but also expresses herself in the Liturgy and draws from the Liturgy the strength for her life." [14]

The reform of the rites and the liturgical books was undertaken immediately after the promulgation of the Constitution *Sacrosanctum Concilium* and was brought to an effective conclusion in a few years thanks to the considerable and selfless work of a large number of experts and bishops from all parts of the world. [15]

This work was undertaken in accordance with the conciliar principles of fidelity to tradition and openness to legitimate development; [16] and so it is possible to say that the reform of the Liturgy is strictly traditional and in accordance with "the ancient usage of the holy Fathers". [17] (*Vicesimus quintus annus,* nos. 3–4). [18]

The Constitution recalls the great principles of the liturgy

The introduction to *Sacrosanctum Concilium,* as well as chapters 1 and 2, contain teaching that is valid for the liturgy in general, regardless of the legitimate rite in which it is celebrated. Thus, for the first time in the history of the Church—and even though the liturgical revision foreseen by Vatican II applies only to the Roman rite—the liturgy is approached from the angle of its universality and considered in terms of its solemnity.

The liturgy is then presented within the framework of the economy of salvation: the Constitution shows the role that it plays in the Church and in the life of each individual Christian. Repeating almost verbatim a formulation from *Mediator Dei* [par. 20], the Council teaches [SC 7] that every liturgical celebration is "full public worship ... performed by the Mystical Body of Jesus Christ, that is, by the Head and his members".

[14] See Letter *Dominicae Cenae,* February 24, 1980, no. 13, in *AAS* 72 (1980): 146.

[15] Cf. SC 25.

[16] Cf. SC 23.

[17] Cf. SC 50 and see *Missale Romanum,* Preamble, 6.

[18] John Paul II, apostolic Letter *Vicesimus quintus annus* [English translation at the Vatican website], nos. 3–4.

Such worship can be rendered only through a double movement: a descending movement, in which God has the initiative in bestowing his divine gifts upon man, and an ascending movement, in which man, as a response to what he has received from his Creator, sends up to God his praise and gives expression to his adoration.

Finally, the conciliar document insists upon the different modes of God's presence in the liturgy: God is present in the proclamation of his Word, in the priest who celebrates, and, in a very special way, in the consecrated species of Bread and Wine.

The "pastoral" aspect of the Roman rite restored after Vatican II

To be sure, as it had been called to do, the Council placed the emphasis on the "pastoral" aspect that every liturgy ought to have. It may be necessary to explain here the meaning of the word "pastoral", a term often used in the years following Vatican II.

Genuine "pastoral concern", as Paul VI himself describes it, ought to consist, in the first place, of making the liturgical ceremonies clear and accessible to the faithful. It must not be confused with an impoverishment or a reduction of the liturgy that aims to adapt the celebrations to what one imagines to be the capacity of the faithful.

Authentic "pastoral concern" consists of providing the means by which the liturgy can be celebrated in all its dignity and without undergoing any distortion: for a liturgy that someone deforms, thinking that this will make it more lively or more meaningful, is a liturgy that leads astray instead of safeguarding, a liturgy that often irritates instead of calming those who take part in it. Thus, any "pastoral program" that tended to promote continual creativity would be dubious, not to mention dangerous. Based on the erroneous assumption that the rite should express the feelings of the faithful and be their work, it would end up proliferating ceremonies of a psychologizing and subjective sort. Now experience shows that, although such ceremonies express the feelings and ideas that the faithful have about the divine, they are, on the contrary, incapable of presenting what is authentically divine to man.

The implementation of the liturgical renewal would quickly be confronted with this issue of "pastoral concerns". It must be admitted today: a false concept of "pastoral concerns" has sometimes led to a distortion of the Roman liturgy, to varying degrees.

Consequently, those who wanted to adapt liturgical celebrations so as to be "pastoral" have too often ended up transforming the liturgy in an "odd, shabby show that it is not worth going to every Sunday".[19] This was surely not what Vatican II intended.

[19] This is an expression by Cardinal Danneels, Archbishop of Malines, Belgium, quoted in *Documentation catholique*, no. 2132.

18

THE CONSTITUTION
SACROSANCTUM CONCILIUM

The conciliar Constitution on the Sacred Liturgy is divided into several chapters, preceded by a brief introduction. Let us quickly go through the different parts of this magisterial document, which, in the first sections, insists on the idea of "active participation" in the liturgy.

The Introduction

It consists of three major sections. The first describes the orientation that the liturgical renewal is supposed to have. The second recalls the importance of the liturgy and its place in the work of redemption wrought by Christ. The third section, finally, indicates that, even though all of the lawful rites recognized in the Church are equal in right and in dignity,[1] the Council intends to address only the question of restoring the "Roman rite".[2]

It is indeed, then, a matter of revising the Roman liturgy, and particularly the Roman Missal as it was handed down by the living tradition of the Church and in the state that it was in at the time of Vatican II. At no point did the Council consider making a brand-new liturgy that could coexist alongside the old one.

The Introduction insists furthermore on a point that too often goes without comment: it shows that the life of faith presents a twofold aspect, at once human and divine, visible and invisible, tending to action and tending to contemplation. However, the

[1] See pages "22" [in chapter 2 of this book] and following (on the different lawful liturgical families in the Church).
[2] See SC 3.

Council also says, "*The human is directed toward and subordinated to the divine, the visible to the invisible, action to contemplation.*" [3]

So, too, must the liturgy of the Church be: essentially subordinate to the divine, to what is invisible, and to contemplation, even though in practice it appeals to the human faculties, with all the dullness and clumsiness that that sometimes involves.

Chapter 1

This chapter describes the nature of the liturgy and its importance in the life of the Church. Citing the most ancient liturgical texts (such as those of the Leonine Sacramentary [*Sacramentarium Veronese*], for example), or the teachings of earlier councils (such as the Council of Trent), the conciliar document shows that the whole sacramental life of the Church was born from the side of Christ as he slept the sleep of death upon the Cross.[4]

The chapter then points out the modes of Christ's presence in the liturgical actions: during Mass, our Lord is present in the person of the priest, who is acting *in persona Christi*, and, preeminently, in the Eucharistic species. In the celebration of the sacraments other than the Eucharist, the Lord is present in the Word and in the singing or recitation of the psalms:

> The liturgy, then, is rightly seen as an exercise of the priestly office of Jesus Christ. It involves the presentation of man's sanctification under the guise of signs perceptible by the senses and its accomplishment in ways appropriate to each of these signs. In it full public worship is performed by the Mystical Body of Jesus Christ, that is, by the Head and his members.[5]

Lastly, this first chapter underscores that, although the liturgy does not constitute the sole activity of the Church, it is nonetheless "the source and the summit" of the Church's life.[6] Thus it can be said that to warp or betray the liturgy is to pollute or dry up the foun-

[3] SC 2.
[4] SC 5.
[5] SC 7.
[6] SC 10.

tain that waters the entire Church. Consequently, a crisis in the liturgy inevitably leads to a crisis in the Church, and vice versa.

Finally, even though this first section ends by restating the full importance that "pious exercises" and popular devotions should have, when the latter, under the vigilance of the pastors, become engrafted onto the liturgy,[7] it recalls especially that the perfect execution of a rite is not sufficient to guarantee the effectiveness of a liturgical celebration.

The first condition to be fulfilled is to have the "proper dispositions". Only the interior disposition can assure that the graces procured by the liturgy are not received in vain. And so, the conciliar document adds:

> Pastors of souls must, therefore, realize that, when the liturgy is celebrated, something more is required than the laws governing valid and lawful celebration. It is their duty also to ensure that the faithful take part fully aware of what they are doing, actively engaged in the rite and enriched by it.[8]

This last reminder sounds a bit like a warning against a certain "rubricism" inherited from the eighteenth and nineteenth centuries, when so much attention was paid to the perfect execution of the ceremonies that the clergy often ended up forgetting the faithful,[9] when the ceremonies fanned the flames of an entirely personal piety to such an extent that sometimes the true "spirit of the liturgy" became utterly impenetrable.

Many remember nothing about this passage of the Constitution except the expression "active participation"; they have made it, so to speak, the point of departure for an entire "liturgical-pastoral theology".

---

[7] SC 12–13.

[8] SC 11.

[9] Paul Claudel evokes the atmosphere of a Sunday Mass in Paris In 1917: "One [Massgoer] pretends to read from a book, while the other fusses with her hat. It is not that the proceedings are uninteresting, and it is certainly not a matter of being bored. Everyone knows that he is there to wait until it is over, and vaguely watches the priest at the altar, who is busy with who knows what", in *Oeuvre poétique complète*, Pléiade edition; quoted by Fr. A. Bandelier, *Simples questions sur la Messe et la liturgie* (Tours: Édition CLD, 1999).

It is interesting to note here that the English expression "active participation" is not a correct translation of the original Latin expression *"participatio actuosa"* [actual participation]. In fact, the *"participatio actuosa"* so much hoped for by Vatican II must not be confused with a *"participatio activa"*.[10] Too often people make the mistake of trying to promote "active participation" in the liturgy by means of an "activist participation": this has produced agitating—not to mention stress-producing—liturgies, which do not always observe "the laws governing valid and lawful celebration". Too often the result has been a "deformation of the liturgical reform" and a cheapening of the celebrations that people thought they were making more accessible and more attractive.[11]

Pope John Paul II has clearly reminded us what true "active participation" ought to consist of:

> Nothing of what we do in the Liturgy can appear more important than what in an unseen but real manner Christ accomplishes by the power of his Spirit. A faith alive in charity, adoration, praise of the Father, and silent contemplation will always be the prime objective of liturgical and pastoral care.[12]

True *"participatio actuosa"* in the liturgy, as intended by Vatican II and to which we are called by the Church, has as a prerequisite, therefore, a sort of self-effacement, a submission to something that does not come from ourselves but is given to us from on high.

The idea of "the reform of the liturgy" in the Constitution *Sacrosanctum Concilium*

Chapter 1 of *Sacrosanctum Concilium* deals with the way in which the entire Church views the renewal of the Roman rite. In order to do this, the conciliar document begins by reiterating what the "restoration" work ought to consist of: "Both texts and rites should

[10] This confusion seems to be perpetuated today by numerous publications on "liturgical planning", which seem to be more important to some Catholics than the Roman Missal itself.

[11] On this subject see the study by Bernard McElligott in *A Voice for All Time* (Association for Latin Liturgy, 16 Brean Down Avenue, Bristol, Great Britain, BS9 4JF).

[12] John Paul II, Apostolic Letter *Vicesimus quintus annus*, no. 10.

be drawn up so as to express more clearly the holy things which they signify", so that the faithful can understand them and participate in them more readily.[13]

The general norms that should guide the "restoration" of the rite

The Constitution begins by specifying who has the authority to revise the liturgy: the Apostolic See, inasmuch as the power exercised by the Church has been entrusted to it. Since the liturgy is something sacred for the benefit of the whole Church, no one else may, on his own authority, remove or change any part of it at all.[14]

The passage deals next with the prudence required to "revise" those parts of the liturgy that need revision:

> [T]here must be no innovations unless the good of the Church genuinely and certainly requires them, and care must be taken that any new forms adopted should in some way grow organically from forms already existing.[15]

Therefore it is not a matter of making the rites more pleasing, as might have been believed on certain occasions, but rather of giving them greater communicative force.

The renewal envisaged [by the Constitution] was to take place along two lines: first, by way of rediscovering the place that Sacred Scripture should have in every liturgical action, and, second, by way of revising the liturgical books based on consultations with the bishops throughout the world.[16]

The Council demonstrates here the full importance of Scripture: we sing under its inspiration; from it we receive instruction; it prompts us to action; it imparts the true significance to the symbols used in the liturgical celebrations.

---

[13] See SC 21.
[14] SC 22.
[15] SC 23.
[16] SC 24–25.

The Church's liturgy: An action that is both hierarchic and communal

Because the liturgy is an action that is simultaneously hierarchic and communal, it is not possible to celebrate it in an arbitrary form. This point is one of the fundamental reminders of Vatican II.[17]

"Hierarchic" by nature, the liturgy requires that it be executed in a certain order, with a certain logic that does not depend, strictly speaking, upon the one who is responsible for implementing it in the name of the Church. Being "communal", the liturgical actions should not appear to the faithful as a sequence of private actions, nor as a means of promoting devotions that, though admirable in themselves, would be merely personal.

These two points will have two important consequences: the first is that every liturgical celebration will always have to manifest the public and social nature of the liturgy;[18] the second is that "in liturgical celebrations each person, minister, or layman who has an office to perform, should carry out all and only those parts which pertain to his office by the nature of the rite and the norms of the liturgy."[19]

That is why those who are called to exercise a "ministry" (celebrants, servers, lectors, commentators, choir members, and so forth) must do so with the piety and the orderliness that the people of God have a right to demand of them: "Consequently they must all be deeply imbued with the spirit of the liturgy, each in his own measure, and they must be trained to perform their functions in a correct and orderly manner."[20]

The didactic and pastoral character of the liturgy implies the application of certain principles

At the basis of the liturgical renewal there is, as we have seen, a "pastoral" concern. Consequently the Second Vatican Council would emphasize the importance of the "active participation" of the peo-

[17] SC 26.
[18] SC 27.
[19] SC 28.
[20] SC 29.

ple of God: a manner of participating that involves a willingness to be open, to be well disposed to receive the teaching that the liturgy conveys and transmits.[21]

True "participation" occurs, first of all, when we make our own the actions, prayers, and songs that form part of the worship of the Church, and not by "adapting" liturgical celebrations to make them more "meaningful" or pleasant.[22]

In order to promote a real participation that allows the faithful to receive the grace of God abundantly, the liturgy must either make innovations or else recover certain fundamental features that it has lost over the course of the last centuries. Among these features, the Council emphasizes

- the transparency, brevity, and noble simplicity of the rites.[23] This means taking as a model the Roman rite as it was before it had been influenced by a subjective and sentimental piety and decked out with external pomps that imitated the pageantry that was fashionable in the high society of the *Ancien Régime*;[24]
- the intimate union between the ritual and the Word: the latter must be clearly manifested, more particularly through the selection of biblical readings that are varied and better suited to the feasts being celebrated;[25]

---

[21] SC 33.

[22] One should always beware of liturgical celebrations that have been "adapted"; generally they are nothing more than ceremonies that have been modified so as to accommodate error.

[23] SC 34.

[24] Article 32 of the Constitution on the Liturgy specifies, moreover: "In the liturgy, apart from the distinctions arising from liturgical function or sacred orders and apart from the honors due to civil authorities in accordance with liturgical law, no special exception is to be made for any private persons or classes of persons whether in the ceremonies or by external display."

[25] One often forgets that the biblical passages are found not only in the Liturgy of the Word itself, but also in the Gregorian chants (entrance, offertory, and Communion antiphons, the Gradual, and Alleluia), the order of which has been modified so that they can be more readily adapted to the different celebrations of the liturgical year.

- the possibility of celebrating the liturgy using the vernacular languages:[26] the Latin language remains the language of the Roman liturgy, but it is no longer the only language that has to be used; alongside it will appear the languages commonly spoken, allowing the faithful to have direct access to the liturgical texts;
- the possibility of introducing diverse cultural riches into the heart of the liturgy—while observing certain principles—so that the liturgical celebrations can speak more effectively to the sensibilities of the various peoples of the world;[27]
- the development of a true liturgical life at the diocesan and parish level, centered around the bishop, the guardian and promoter of the authentic liturgy, or around his representative;
- the implementation of a true "liturgical pastoral program" at the diocesan level, for which the bishop will be primarily responsible, the purpose of which will be to promote the harmonious application of the principles of the liturgical renewal called for by the Council.

Why have these principles, which are indisputably excellent, not been followed obediently everywhere? Why have they been warped to the point of being the source of errors and blunders that have seriously wounded the people of God?

One answer seems to be the most accurate: at the time of the Council there was a lack of formation that dated back to the time before the Council.[28] To be sure, the majority of the faithful in the

---

[26] SC 36.

[27] SC 37–40.

[28] Before Vatican II it was not necessary to insist on liturgical formation, since it was enough to copy what one had always seen others do. Abbot Maurice Gruau tells of his priestly ordination on June 29, 1995, in the Cathedral of Laval: at the end of the ceremony, which had begun at 8:00 in the morning and concluded at noon, the Bishop said to the new priests, "Before you celebrate Mass, ask experienced priests to teach you how to say it." And the author continues, "We had not expected the bishop to make this recommendation. First of all, because before being able to celebrate Mass, each of the new priests had often attended Mass. Secondly, because before their ordination, there had been an examination on the Mass; a priest who had been our regular spiritual director brought to our attention the mistakes that we were making, or the things that he just didn't like, even though they are not written down anywhere.... Celebrating Mass presupposes a know-

Church were animated by a sincere piety, but often there was no firm theological foundation for this piety to rest on. Now the parish priests often came from the ranks of these faithful. Consequently there were very few who were capable, immediately after the Council, of thoroughly understanding what was really at stake in the liturgical renewal. The only "formation" that most of them had was that which was provided by periodicals that were either not entirely objective or else insisted unilaterally on one aspect of the Council or another.

Many found in the new Roman Missal promulgated by Paul VI little more than an occasion to liberate themselves from the constraining rubrics found in the old Tridentine Missal that they had used thus far.

Suddenly, as many celebrants saw it, the liturgy appeared to be no longer a homogeneous unit constructed according to a definite plan [*une véritable logique*], but a sequence of words and rituals that one could "pick and choose", depending on the circumstances. From there it was a short step to more daring and imaginative things.[29]

Not knowing the meaning of the realities that make up the liturgy, a great number of them thought that the rituals could be manipulated and that they even should be manipulated so as to conform better to the needs of the new pastoral approach. "And when persons who have had a bad formation form others...."[30]

---

how that is not learned from books but is handed on by tradition. It is the same with singing the various parts of the Mass, in particular the prefaces; it was useless trying to learn with the help of a musician. We had heard them so often that we duplicated the same mistakes as our predecessors"; quoted in *L'homme rituel; anthropologie du rituel Catholique Français* (Paris: Édition Métaillé, 1999).

[29] This is paraphrasing Cardinal Danneels, in *Documentation Catholique*, no. 2145, pp. 840 ff.; quoted by Fr. Bandelier in *Simples questions*.

[30] Fr. Bandelier, *Simples questions*, pp. 50–51.

19

THE MYSTERY OF THE EUCHARIST
ACCORDING TO VATICAN II

The participation of the faithful in the Eucharist

Chapter 2 of the Constitution *Sacrosanctum Concilium* addresses more directly and concretely the topic of the celebration of the mystery of the Eucharist.

After recalling briefly the origin of the Mass and the profound and essential meaning with which the Eucharistic liturgy ought to be endowed (sacrament of love, bond of charity, paschal feast in which Christ gives himself, channel of grace and pledge of future glory), the conciliar document points out the fundamental principles for renewing the Roman liturgy.

First, however, the Constitution recalls what true participation in the liturgy should consist of: offering oneself with Christ in union with God.[1]

Then, in a single sentence, the conciliar document introduces the essential point: the revision and renewal of the rite of the Roman liturgy.

This revision is supposed to be carried out in such a way that the liturgical rites themselves, by their own pastoral effectiveness, might invite the faithful to participate completely in the Eucharist by involving their minds, hearts, and bodies [*literally*: their consciousness, piety, and deportment] in the sacred action.[2]

---

[1] SC 47–48.
[2] SC 48.

The revision of the Eucharistic liturgy

In articles 52 through 58, the Constitution *Sacrosanctum Concilium* enumerates the points that will be affected by the renewal of the Roman liturgy.

It will be necessary to make more evident the [underlying] unity of the rituals of the Mass. They should not appear to be an arrangement of prayers that have been added over the centuries, nor an accumulation of gestures and symbols, but rather should constitute a whole, the parts of which follow one another with a clear plan and a genuine harmony.

In this "whole", the Word of God is essential. This is why an important place will again be given to the proclamation of the biblical readings and meditation on them.

For pastoral reasons already mentioned above, local languages can be used—without imposing them as an obligation.[3] In that case, care should be taken, however, that the faithful always know the Latin chants of the Ordinary of the Mass (the *Kyrie, Gloria, Credo, Sanctus, Pater noster*, and *Agnus Dei*).

Holy Communion remains the sign of total participation in the Eucharist; it should be encouraged and can take place under both species in certain instances.[4]

The Liturgy of the Word and the Liturgy of the Eucharist, properly so-called, constitute one single act of worship; it is required to

---

[3] Many theologians and historians remind us that introducing the local languages for the purpose of promoting participation of the faithful was not a novelty at the time of Vatican II. But very few of them inquire as to whether, from the eighth to the thirteenth centuries, for example, the introduction of the vernacular really allowed the faithful to "understand" what was sung in the sanctuaries of the churches. Indeed, considering the lack of a sound system (which meant that the pulpits were placed in the middle of the congregation), the noise that people made coming and going in the nave and the side aisles, and possibly the noise made by the manual bellows of the organ, etc., one is entitled to ask whether the sense of participating in the Eucharist necessarily depended upon understanding the words of the celebrant. (We should mention also the darkness that prevailed in church buildings; the spotlights that we are accustomed to use falsify the picture that we have of the liturgy in the past.)

[4] "The dogmatic principles ... laid down by the Council of Trent remain intact" (SC 55). Cf. Council of Trent, sess. 21, July 16, 1562, "The Doctrine on Communion under both Species and that of Little Children", chaps. 1–3.

participate in the totality of this act on Sundays and holy days of obligation; these two parts of the Mass, therefore, should be closely united.

Finally, the possibility for priests to concelebrate the Eucharist is expanded. Whereas the Roman rite inherited from Trent had preserved concelebration only for the ordination ceremony of priests,[5] the Second Vatican Council, faithful to a practice that has been maintained throughout the Church, extends the possibility to several circumstances: the Mass on Holy Thursday; Masses celebrated on the occasion of a synod, a council, or an assembly of bishops; Mass celebrated for the consecration of an Abbot in a monastery; conventual Masses; and, with the permission of the diocesan bishop, the principal Masses celebrated in parish churches.

Plainly, the conciliar document does not foresee that concelebration would become a convenient solution or an habitual practice: in no case may concelebration deprive the faithful of Masses that could be celebrated in sanctuaries other than the ones in which several priests gather.[6]

The goal of the Council

When one reads the text of the Constitution *Sacrosanctum Concilium*, the objective being pursued by the Council in restoring the Roman rite appears quite clearly. It is twofold:

- to make the rites clearer by disentangling them from elements that were added during periods when religious sentiments had sometimes gained the upper hand, to the detriment of a real sacramental theology, and
- to bring the liturgy out of the private domain of individualism[7] and to reaffirm the fact that every liturgical celebration

---

[5] The Roman Missal revised in Trent notes that, during the ceremony in which new priests are ordained, they are supposed to celebrate the Mass after the offertory rite: they kneel around the altar and recite all the words of the Eucharistic Prayer (Roman Canon) with their bishop.

[6] Article 58 of the Constitution states that a new rite of concelebration should be composed and incorporated into the Pontifical and the Roman Missal.

[7] "It must be admitted that the old liturgy had strayed too far into the realm of individualism and private devotions, and that there was insufficient communion between the

of the Church is by its very essence a communal act, just as Pius XII had already affirmed in the Encyclical *Mediator Dei*.

Likewise we see that, contrary to what is sometimes said or believed, the Council did not invent a new rite and was not "fabricating" a "new liturgy". It simply laid the foundations for a *restoration* of the Roman rite, so as to make possible and accomplish the work of revising the liturgy that had been begun in the nineteenth century and was often called for by the Popes in modern times.

That is why, on the twenty-fifth anniversary of the Constitution *Sacrosanctum Concilium*, John Paul II would recall that "the reform of the liturgy is strictly traditional." [8]

The revision of the rites associated with the other sacraments

Chapter 3 of the Constitution *Sacrosanctum Concilium* is devoted entirely to the sacraments other than the Eucharist.

The document begins by making a distinction between "sacraments" and "sacramentals"; the former confer grace, while the latter have effects that are essentially spiritual. Both of them, nevertheless, flow from the mystery of the Passion and Resurrection of our Lord and are directed toward the sanctification of man and at the same time toward the praise of God.[9]

The conciliar document then outlines in broad strokes the plan for revising sacraments: the rites used must clearly signify the nature and the purpose of each sacrament, and local languages can figure more prominently in celebrating them.

Besides the Roman ritual that will be composed in this way, there can also be particular rituals that take into account to a greater

---

priest and the faithful", Cardinal Joseph Ratzinger, "Conference on the tenth anniversary of the Motu Proprio *Ecclesia Dei adflicta*", in *Documentation Catholique*, no. 2197, p. 144.

[8] John Paul II, Apostolic Letter *Vicesimus quintus annus*, no. 4 (December 1988).

[9] SC 59, 60, 61.

degree—subject to the approval of the Holy See—the needs and requirements of particular regions.[10]

Baptism[11]

The rite would be revised so as to adapt the baptismal ceremony to concrete situations that children encounter today (Baptisms that are celebrated late, children born within the context of unbelief, children raised in one-parent families, Baptisms performed by catechists in mission lands where the infant mortality rate suggests urgency, etc.).

Furthermore, Baptism itself can be preceded by an adult catechumenate, that is, by a gradual process of formation that occurs in several stages.

Confirmation[12]

The rite of Confirmation would be revised with a view to demonstrating more clearly the connection between this sacrament and the entire process of Christian initiation.

Penance (Sacrament of Reconciliation)[13]

Here the conciliar document is particularly laconic: with regard to "Confession", it is content to emphasize that the rite must "more clearly express both the nature and effect of the sacrament".

Anointing of the Sick[14]

The old "Extreme Unction" becomes the "Anointing of the Sick". A simple change of title? No, indeed. It is a matter of making the faithful understand and admit that this sacrament is not reserved for those who are actually dying, but that it also concerns those who

[10] SC 62–63.
[11] SC 64–70.
[12] SC 71.
[13] SC 72.
[14] SC 73–75.

are simply approaching death, whether by reason of sickness or of old age.

The Sacrament of Holy Orders[15]

The rites and the prayers of priestly or diaconal ordination must be revised; the use of the vernacular is permitted for the addresses given by the bishop.

The Sacrament of Matrimony[16]

The rites and the prayers of the marriage celebration must signify more clearly the grace of the sacrament and emphasize the duties of the spouses.

Furthermore, since marriage often assumes popular trappings, it will be possible to introduce certain local customs into the religious ceremony, provided that they are in harmony with the Christian meaning of the sacrament.

Sacramentals

The conciliar document mentions only two sacramentals here, although the number of them is not being fixed once and for all:[17]

Religious profession[18]

The rites of religious profession should take place preferably during the course of a Eucharistic celebration. Three aspects of the ceremony should be highlighted: its unity, its sobriety, and its dignity.

[15] SC 76.
[16] SC 77–78.
[17] SC 79.
[18] SC 80.

Funerals[19]

The late Middle Ages had often given a dramatic character to the funeral liturgy. Today it is the Paschal character of the rites that should be highlighted above all: from the practical point of view, this modification will lead to a greater variety of readings for Masses of Christian Burial, to the introduction of the Alleluia, and omission of the sequence *Dies irae* during the Eucharistic liturgy.

The rite of burial for infants will be revised and provided with a proper Mass, the purpose of which could be to refine the theology concerning the eternal destiny reserved for very young children who die before they can be baptized.

The Council sets guidelines to be followed

As one can verify by reading the Constitution *Sacrosanctum Concilium*, the Council does not specify the modifications that must be made to the liturgy; it limits itself to indicating the main lines of a liturgical renewal aimed at giving clearer expression to the coherence between the Catholic faith and the manner in which that same faith must be celebrated in the Church.

Furthermore, the correct application of the principles spelled out in the Constitution *Sacrosanctum Concilium* is closely bound up with ecclesiological doctrine, that is, with the knowledge about the Church that every believer who belongs to that same Church by Baptism has a right to have. In order to understand better the importance of the liturgical renewal intended by Vatican II, we must remember that

> a very close and organic bond exists between the renewal of the liturgy and the renewal of the whole life of the Church.
>
> The Church not only acts but also expresses herself in the liturgy, lives by the liturgy, and draws from the liturgy the strength for her life.[20]

Are we not obliged to admit, then, that to misunderstand the liturgy, as it is intended by the Church, is to misunderstand the Church herself?

---

[19] SC 81–82.

[20] John Paul II, Letter *Dominicae Cenae*, no. 13, February 24, 1980, in *AAS* 72 (1980): 146; Apostolic Letter *Vicesimus quintus annus*, no. 4 (December 1988).

20

THE DIVINE OFFICE AND
THE LITURGICAL YEAR

In chapter 4, the conciliar Constitution on the Liturgy arrives at the subject of the Divine Office, by which the Church addresses her praise to God, day and night, especially through the voices of her priests, monks, and nuns.

The value of the Divine Office

The Council begins by recalling the singular value of the Divine Office, the praise of those who stand before the throne of God, in the name of the Church, to sanctify the Christian day.[1]

This praise should be based principally on the psalms (their distribution will be modified), readings from the Fathers of the Church, and accounts from the lives of the saints that have been rendered more historically accurate, that is, expurgated of fanciful legends that had been added in later centuries.[2]

The arrangement of the Office

In certain periods of Church history, the Divine Office might have seemed like a burdensome "chore" that had to be done as quickly as possible to get it over with. It is not so long ago that there were canons in some churches who would "string together" several Hours of the Divine Office, one after the other, so that they managed to say Compline (the final night Hour) even before celebrating the capitular Mass in the morning!

[1] SC 83–86.
[2] SC 90–92.

It was to avoid this "bargain-basement" approach to prayer that the conciliar document foresees a revision of the way in which the various Offices are distributed over the course of the day: "[T]he traditional sequence of the Hours is to be restored so that, as far as possible, they may again also become in fact what they have been in name." [3]

Henceforth the prayer of the Church would turn upon the two hinges of the daily Office: Lauds, or Morning Prayer, and Vespers, or Evening Prayer.

Furthermore, the Office of Compline must indeed mark the close of the day.

Besides these Hours, Matins—[traditionally] a nocturnal prayer of praise—was to be adapted so that it could be celebrated at any hour of the day, as a concession to the time constraints of modern life.

The three "Minor Hours" of Terce, Sext, and None would be maintained by those who celebrate the Divine Office in choir. Outside of a monastic community, it would be permissible to say only one of these Hours, at the time that is most appropriate.

Who must recite or chant the Divine Office?

The Office must be said in its entirety or in part—according to the categories enumerated by the Council—by canons regular, monks, and nuns, by cathedral or collegial chapters, by clerics in Major Orders—that is, deacons and priests—and by the members of certain institutes of religious life. [4]

Whether this Office is recited alone or chanted by a monastic community, it is always prayed in the name of the whole Church: it is the voice of the Church rendering public praise to God.

Furthermore, the lay faithful are strongly encouraged to join in this official form of prayer, particularly by chanting Vespers [Evening Prayer] on Sunday and on solemn feast days. [5]

[3] SC 88.
[4] SC 95–98.
[5] SC 99–100.

In order to remain within the great tradition of the Western Church, clerics are required to preserve the Latin language when they chant the Divine Office in community;[6] the option of saying the Hours in the local language can, however, be granted in individual or particular instances. In the latter case, the translations used must be approved.[7]

The liturgical year

In chapter 5, the document deals with the topic of the liturgical year, that is, the cycle of time during the course of which the liturgy unfolds, allowing the faithful to commemorate on predetermined dates the great mysteries of Redemption associated with the life of Christ.

Included also in this liturgical cycle are the feasts of the Virgin Mary, who was united to her Son in a singular manner, as well as commemorations of the saints and martyrs, whose lives were exemplary and who therefore already possess eternal salvation.[8]

The Council recalls, furthermore, that throughout the year Sunday holds a place of the highest rank: it is the day on which Christians join together to celebrate the Paschal Mystery. Consequently it is "the foundation and kernel of the whole liturgical year".[9]

In order to help the faithful to rediscover the profound meaning of the Christian year, Vatican II proposed a revision of the liturgical cycle: the feasts of the Lord should again have priority and no longer be eclipsed by the feasts of the saints, which had become preponderant, especially since the seventeenth century. As for Lent, it would once again serve as a time of preparation for Baptism; while still being first and foremost a penitential season, it would also take on a social and external dimension.

As for the feast days of the saints, they would be reduced [both in number and in solemnity], while leaving to each particular Church

---

[6] SC 101.

[7] The Council plainly speaks of "translations" and not of "adaptations", which raises several questions, for example, as to the legitimacy of the book *Prières du temps présent* [Prayers of the present time], which is used as a "breviary" by many priests and religious.

[8] SC 102–5.

[9] SC 106.

the possibility of celebrating local saints, always provided that the feasts of the Lord take precedence.[10]

The renewal of the liturgical year intended by Vatican II was devised, then, to manifest more clearly the fact that time, punctuated by the cycles of the day and the seasons, is something other than a blind march toward a destiny that eludes us.

For the believer, time is a path that has been well marked out by Christ, who leads man onward to God. Along this path, every feast day celebrated by the Church is an important phase, during which we find refreshment and regain our strength by saying together with the whole Church: "today"—*hodie*. And so these are not past actions that the liturgy asks us to celebrate, but rather deeds that are "realized" unceasingly, through which God sanctifies us.

So it is that by accepting the rhythm of the liturgy, we agree to advance toward God through the mystery of passing time. In this "time" that we seek to measure with ever-greater precision, in order to satisfy our desire to calculate everything and have an equation for everything, each minute that passes must become a moment of grace. Participation in the liturgy of the Church is designed to remind us of this, also.

[10] SC 107–111.

21

SACRED MUSIC: THE PLACE AND ROLE OF GREGORIAN CHANT

When it is celebrated according to the Roman rite, the liturgy ought to be sung in its entirety: this is the "normal" form. All parts of the Mass or of the Divine Office, from the simplest prayer to the most complicated readings, including of course the recitation of the psalms, are in fact meant to be declaimed according to principles that obey the laws of music.

That is why the Second Vatican Council devotes considerable space to the question of chant, recalling that the initiatives of Saint Gregory the Great led to the creation of a repertoire of liturgical chants that constitutes the musical tradition of the Church as well as an invaluable treasure.[1]

Sacred chant combined with the words of the liturgy, then, is a necessary or integral part of the solemn form that the liturgy should assume whenever possible.[2]

The function of chant and the role of musicians in the liturgy

The conciliar document [the section on "Sacred Music"] begins by referring to Scripture and the Church Fathers, as well as to the studies conducted at the request of Saint Pius X in the modern period,[3] to recall the fact that sacred song in and of itself exercises a ministerial function in the liturgy.[4]

---

[1] John Paul II, "*Allocution aux Pueri Cantores*" [Address to the choirboys], le 31 décembre 1999 (*Osservatore Romano* [édition française], no. 3, janvier 2000).

[2] SC 112.

[3] See page 51.

[4] SC 112.

But what is sacred music? Does every song that is performed during a liturgical celebration deserve to be designated as "sacred"?

The Council replies to this twofold question by specifying that sacred music must be closely connected with the liturgical action that is being carried out, and that it must enhance the solemnity of the rites by making prayer more "pleasing".[5]

In order for chant to fulfill its purpose, it must be cultivated, taught at a very young age, and handed down by carefully trained choirmasters. The treasure of sacred chant should be preserved principally in the seminaries and in religious houses, by musicians who have had serious liturgical formation.[6]

Gregorian chant: Sacred song par excellence[7]

If there is one kind of singing that possesses all the qualities of liturgical song, if there is one sort of music that has developed in close contact with the liturgy itself, it is certainly Gregorian chant.

The Council states again forcefully: the Gregorian repertoire constitutes the chant proper to the Roman liturgy. Consequently it deserves to have pride of place in the sacred actions that are carried out in the name of the Church.[8]

Other sorts of music, certainly, can be introduced into the Roman rite, provided, on the one hand, that it is not to the detriment of Gregorian chant, and provided, on the other hand, that these other types of music have qualities suited to the liturgy. This is tantamount to saying that not all kinds of music are suited to liturgical actions, however pleasant they may be to our contemporary ears or however insistently they may appeal to our emotions.

Without saying so explicitly, the Council recalls here that the encounter with God which takes place during a liturgy is not limited to the simple psychological feelings that could be aroused by a sort of music that aimed to please the faithful.[9]

---

[5] Ibid.

[6] SC 114–15.

[7] See Appendix III.

[8] SC 116.

[9] Giacomo Biffi, *Musica sacra e liturgia* (Casale Monferrato: Edizioni Piemme, 1992).

The qualities of Gregorian chant

With respect to the liturgy, Gregorian chant must not be considered as one musical form that is more interesting than another, or, more simply, as singing that is added to the liturgy "to make it beautiful". It is more than that; it is more than a type of "religious" music: it is sung prayer, the most perfect rendition of the Roman liturgy on the musical plane. It is itself, in a way, this liturgy, but as though expanded, as though raised to its highest degree of expression. It follows that Gregorian chant is capable of spreading among the faithful a message that is more universal, more complete, more capable of being "interiorized" than would be the message of a liturgy that had simply been embellished with ordinary hymns.[10]

The Church recognizes the didactic value of Gregorian chant; this is because she sees that, when it is added to the rites of a celebration, it fosters that openness of heart and soul which enables the faithful to receive the means of living the doctrine that is conveyed by the liturgy. Gregorian chant sets into motion a process of knowing divine realities that passes more through the channel of the senses and experience than along the single path of conceptual thought. The richness of this chant is derived, then, from the fact that it does not open the way solely to a theological (and biblical) content that is accessible to reason alone, but carries the listeners toward a perfect expression of the faith that is to be lived and transmitted.

As Cardinal Daneels has emphasized, "the liturgy cannot become the expression of ourselves." Thus, if there is always a danger of celebrating only so as to "master the rituals" and, in that way, to make the liturgy a means to an end, there is also another danger: that of singing solely for one's own enjoyment. To be sure, the liturgy and chant appeal to our senses, but in that capacity they are not supposed to cajole them. There can be a great sensible joy in singing a beautiful polyphonic work or a simple popular hymn; but

---

[10] The common hymn, inasmuch as it is an adaptation of a popular devotion, must be purified, as it were, by the liturgy (cf. John Paul II, *Vicesimus quintus annus*). Gregorian chant is already purified because it is the expression of the liturgy: it emanates from the liturgy and owes its development to it.

this joy, legitimate in itself, must in the first place be—within the specific framework of the liturgy—at the service of our interior dispositions, which make use of the sensible elements of the sacred rites to lead us toward the contemplation of the Invisible. Now Gregorian chant has understood this perfectly: it does not caress our feelings but channels them, purifies them, so as to put them at the disposal of our capacity to apprehend the mystery being celebrated.

Just like all true liturgy, all liturgical music must be first and foremost a gift, a gratuitous praise that the Church directs to God through Christ's sacrifice of thanksgiving; it should not be merely an intellectual construct aimed at expressing or intensifying personal feelings that are more or less orderly, more or less appropriate. And for this reason, because it is at the same time a gift and praise, liturgical music, like the liturgy, must be "fitting and just".

A type of music that was only beautiful but not "fitting" or "just" would run the risk of being perceived as nothing more than entertainment, as a means of satisfying a desire for estheticism, as an object of amusement and enjoyment—as is the case with musical numbers performed in concert. Now the liturgy and liturgical song absolutely must watch out and steer clear of this dangerous reef, so as to remain "icons", that is to say, sense-images inhabited by a presence, and not by emanations of some human feeling that is part and parcel of a superficial religiosity guided by the subjectivism that characterizes our post-Christian societies.[11]

Now Gregorian chant avoids the dangers that we have just enumerated: prior to being a cause of esthetic pleasure, it is a language that brings about that which it enunciates,[12] a language that allows

---

[11] Cf. Luigi Giussani, *La conscience religieuse de l'homme moderne* [The religious awareness of modern man] (Paris: Éditions du Cerf, 1999).

[12] "The British linguist Austin deserves the credit for having pointed out the fact that certain linguistic acts are not only *constative* but actually bring about, themselves, the action that they enunciate; he calls this type of language *performative* or *illocutionary*, terms that were immediately adopted by liturgists and applied to the sacraments. In them, the language act is an *operative expression*. Austin's terminology allows us to distinguish in liturgical language between the simply *locutionary* dimension (the information or the meaning), the *perlocutionary* dimension (that is, the effect produced upon the hearers), and lastly the *illocutionary* dimension that is present in the sacrament but also in the profession of faith and,

the listeners to grasp more fully the liturgy as a whole instead of under-standing individual rituals in a fragmented way.[13] It is also the sort of singing that best promotes "active participation" in the liturgy.[14]

By revealing to us the God who, through the liturgy, acts at the very heart of the created world, Gregorian chant leads us to discover and to revere the mystery of the Divine Presence. It teaches us about what is sacred, places us in a sort of "preserve" where the most del-icate and most endangered dimensions of human life are protected.[15]

Gregorian chant is a sensitive master who takes his time in teach-ing us: although he loves to cover the words that we sing with a veil, with a shadow, it is not in order to disguise the meaning of what we are proclaiming, but rather to make sure that this meaning is only gradually revealed to us, so that we might never be tempted to celebrate ourselves, but rather might remain turned toward him who acts at the heart of the liturgy.[16]

---

finally, in a general way, in the liturgical action as a whole inasmuch as it is an expression of the Christian identity" (Marie-Laure Bourgueuil; quoted by Denis Crouan et al., *Le chant grégorien redécouvert* [Gregorian chant rediscovered] [Tours: Éditions C.L.D., 1997]).

[13] The verb *saisir* in French ["to grasp", "to seize"] has the advantage of being a syn-onym of "understand", while being capable of expressing also, in the passive form, the fact that one is "seized" or "caught up" by the action that is being carried out. Now, strictly speaking, the liturgy is not primarily something that must be understood; it is presented to us as a source of understanding and hence is meant to make us enter into the Mystery of the Covenant. Therefore we are not the ones who in the first place must understand the liturgy; rather, the liturgy must make us comprehend, that is to say, must enable us to establish a relationship with the divine. This is the same perspective in which we should reframe the question about Gregorian chant after the liturgical renewal of Vatican II.

[14] The "active participation" in the liturgy called for by the Church is not an "activist" participation whereby everyone seeks to busy himself or to put himself forward. Quite on the contrary: true "participation in the liturgy" is a participation of the heart, consisting of the intention to carry out as well as possible—with genuine sincerity—what the Church asks us to accomplish in her liturgy.

[15] Cardinal Godfried Danneels.

[16] Cf. the contributions of various authors to Crouan's *Le chant grégorien redécouvert* and cf. Appendix IV. See Cardinal Joseph Ratzinger, *A New Song for the Lord: Faith in Christ and Liturgy Today*, trans. Martha M. Matesich (New York: Crossroad Publishing, 1996). Berna-dette Lecureux, *Le latin, langue de l'Église* [Latin, the language of the Church] (Paris: Éditions Spes, 1964); there is a new edition of this work, with a preface by Dom Philippe Dupont, Abbot of Solesmes. Dom Jacques Hourlier, *Entretiens sur la spiritualité du chant grégorien* [Talks on the spirituality of Gregorian chant] (Solesmes: Éditions de l'Abbaye, 1985).

22

THE FORM OF THE ROMAN LITURGY, AS RESTORED AFTER VATICAN II

On April 3, 1969, with the apostolic Constitution *Missale Romanum*, Pope Paul VI promulgated the Roman Missal that had been restored by the decree of the Second Vatican Council.

This Constitution is made up of three parts:

- a short historical retrospect,
- a presentation of the new Roman Missal,
- a review of the objectives of the renewal of the Roman liturgy.

Historical retrospect

The Roman Missal promulgated in 1570 by Pius V, pursuant to a decree of the Council of Trent, provided priests of the Latin rite for four centuries with the norm for celebrating Mass. The arrangement of the Mass, as it had been specified in this work, dated back in its essential features to Saint Gregory the Great.

Now, the new conditions in which the Church must carry out her work have clearly shown that the formulas of this "Tridentine" Roman Missal had to be revised or enriched.

That is why

the ... Second Vatican Ecumenical Council, by its Constitution *Sacro-sanctum Concilium*, laid the foundations for the general revision of the Roman Missal. The Council has decreed that "both texts and rites should be drawn up so that they express more clearly the holy things which they signify";[1] that "the rite of the Mass is to be revised in such a way that the intrinsic nature and purpose of its several parts, as also the connection between them, may be more clearly manifested and that

[1] SC 21.

devout and active participation by the people may be more easily achieved";[2] further, that "the treasures of the Bible are to be opened up more fully, so that richer fare may be provided for the faithful at the table of God's word";[3] and finally that "a new rite for concelebration is to be drawn up and inserted into the Pontifical and into the Roman Missal."[4] ...

Quite soon after the Council of Trent, as is apparent from the Apostolic Constitution *Quo Primum* of our predecessor St. Pius V, the study and comparison of ancient manuscripts available in the Vatican Library and elsewhere contributed not a little to the revision of the Missal. Since that time many other very ancient liturgical texts have been discovered and published, and texts from the Oriental Churches have also been studied. Many have expressed the desire that the riches of faith and doctrine contained in these texts should no longer remain hidden in the darkness of library cupboards and shelves, but should be brought out into the light to warm the hearts and enlighten the minds of the Christian peoples.[5]

Presentation of the new Roman Missal

After this brief historical retrospect, the Constitution *Missale Romanum* of Paul VI presents the new version of the missal. The volume consists first of a "General Instruction", which sets forth the rules for celebrating Mass: rites, the functions and duties of each participant in the liturgy, material things required for the celebration, and the arrangement of the sanctuary.

The Constitution then presents the elements that had been introduced or reintroduced into the Roman liturgy; some of them, although traditional, had been discarded so long ago that they could be mistaken for "novelties". These elements are

- the penitential rite at the beginning of Mass,
- the Prayer of the Faithful (after the Creed),
- the reading of a passage from the Old Testament (or, during the Paschal season, from the Acts of the Apostles),

[2] SC 50.
[3] SC 51.
[4] SC 58.
[5] *Missale Romanum*, Decree of Promulgation, third and fourth paragraphs.

- several Prefaces that are newly composed or drawn from the Roman tradition,
- three Eucharistic Prayers, and
- a Consecration formula that permits the faithful to sing the *Anamnesis.*

Furthermore, the Sunday readings are distributed over a three-year cycle, and certain rites that were needlessly duplicated—especially in the Mass that was sung according to the "Tridentine" Roman Missal—are suppressed.

Finally, the Constitution of Paul VI retains the use of the *Graduale Romanum* as far as liturgical chant is concerned.[6]

The objectives of the renewal of the Roman liturgy

The revised Roman liturgy, as defined in the Missal promulgated by the authority of Paul VI, explicitly aims to be a sign and an instrument of unity among Christians, in imitation of what the Roman rite managed to accomplish, as codified in the missal that resulted from the Council of Trent.

The renovated Roman Missal, which has the force of law for the Eucharistic liturgy, replaced the old missal, said to be "of Saint Pius V", starting on November 30, 1969, the First Sunday of Advent.

The new missal recalls that the celebration of Mass, which is the center of all Christian life, must be regulated in such a way that all the faithful can participate in it according to their circumstances and receive the fruits that the Lord intended to bestow in instituting the Eucharist and in entrusting it to his one Church.

It is likewise reiterated that, since all of the liturgy is carried out with the help of sensible signs that nourish, strengthen, and express

[6] The Benedictine monks of Solesmes were invited to revise the distribution of the entrance antiphons (*Introit*) and Communion verses, so that they would be better suited to what is being celebrated by the liturgy; to restore ancient musical pieces of unquestionable value and to omit pieces of a more dubious musical quality. (Cf. Dom Jean Prou, *Le chant grégorien et la spiritualité des fidèles*; Dom Eugène Cardine, *La sémiologie grégorienne: Graduel neumé; Graduale Triplex*; Dom Saulnier, *Le chant grégorien par un moine de Solesmes; Requirentes modos musicos* [Latin: Seeking musical modes]; and numerous articles by Dom Jean Claire on Gregorian modes. See also the *Études grégoriennes* published by the Abbey of Solesmes.)

the faith, it is necessary for liturgical celebrations to be organized as the Church requires, that is, following the rules given by the Roman Missal.[7]

The order of the Mass according to the Roman rite as restored after Vatican II

In a subsection [of chapter 2] of the "General Instruction", entitled "The Structure of the Mass as a Whole", the revised missal presents very clearly the way in which the Mass should now unfold when celebrated according to the Roman rite.

This is the typical form that must be followed and carried out when there is no obstacle; according to Canon Law, exceptions to this form are licit only when one has first sincerely attempted to carry out what the Church requires, but external circumstances prevent one from following faithfully the rules for celebrating that are given in the missal.[8]

The typical form of the current Roman liturgy[9]

The introductory rites

Once the faithful have gathered, the priest and the ministers, wearing liturgical vestments,[10] process toward the altar in the following order:

[7] "General Instruction on the Roman Missal" [1970, abbreviated "GIRM"], chapter 1, "Importance and Dignity of the Eucharistic Celebration".

[8] See also Dom Cuthbert Johnson, *Progetto liturgico* [Italian: Liturgical plan] (Rome: Edizioni liturgiche, 1992). *Enchiridion Documentorum Instaurationis Liturgicae* [Latin: Compendium of documents of the liturgical renewal], Vols. 1–3 (Rome: Edizioni liturgiche).

[9] See also Dom Robert Le Gall, *La messe au fil de ses rites* [The rites of the Mass, step by step] (Tours: Éditions C.L.D., 1992).

[10] For the priest-celebrant, the liturgical vestments are the alb (and possibly the amice to cover the collar of his street clothes), the cincture or girdle (which prevents the alb from flowing like an "evening gown"), the stole, and the chasuble. The liturgical vestment common to all the ministers who perform a duty at the altar is the alb, tied at the waist by a cincture (cf. GIRM 297–310). See Appendix VI.

- the server who carries the burning censer;[11]
- the servers who carry the candles and, between them, the server who carries the cross;
- the acolytes and the other ministers;
- the lector, carrying the Book of the Gospels; and
- the priest who will celebrate the Mass.[12]

During the procession, the entrance antiphon or hymn is sung. "Its purpose is to open up the celebration, to foster union among the people, to direct their minds to the sacred mystery being celebrated, and to accompany the incoming procession."[13]

Upon arriving at the altar, the priest and the ministers venerate it in the requisite manner: they either make a profound bow, or, if there is a tabernacle with the Blessed Sacrament, they genuflect.

The processional cross is placed near the altar so as to be readily visible, the candles are set in their proper places on or around the altar, and the Book of the Gospels is placed upon the altar.[14]

---

[11] This is done if incense is used. The revised missal returns to the ancient liturgical tradition, since it specifies that incense is placed in the censer before the procession begins, that is to say, at the sanctuary, and no longer right before the altar is incensed.

[12] If a deacon is present, he walks directly in front of the priest and carries the Gospel book, since his function makes him a minister of the Word of God.

[13] GIRM 25. It must be acknowledged here that the hymns and songs that are sung today in most parishes (with words that generally have nothing to do with the official texts of the Mass) do not accomplish the objectives set by the liturgy.

[14] Note that the new missal always gives general instructions, in contrast to the pre-Vatican II missal, which belabored every detail. For example, with regard to the candles, a genuine freedom is given to those who plan the liturgy to place them around the altar. On the other hand, it is necessary for these liturgical planners to have good taste and common sense in order to do things correctly and harmoniously. One might say, then, that the current missal grants more "responsibility" to the participants in the celebration than the old missal did; with the latter it was at most a matter of following the rubrics obediently without necessarily asking any questions. This docility might have suited certain scrupulous minds that were worried about always having reassuring norms, but did it produce a genuine flourishing? We are obliged, nonetheless, to add that this docility had one great advantage: it guaranteed for all a liturgy that was celebrated with precision, which is no longer the case today when the current Roman Missal falls into the hands of a celebrant who imagines that, as a matter of principle, the virtues of a "pastoral approach to liturgy" are incompatible with the rules for celebrating that have been formulated by the Church.

The priest ascends to the altar, venerates it with a kiss, then incenses it while walking around it.[15] After that, he goes to his chair.

Then the people finish singing the entrance antiphon.

Turned toward the faithful and extending his hands, the priest greets the congregation with one of the formulas offered by the missal.[16]

The penitential rite

The preparatory penitential rite, which is always obligatory, can be performed by means of various formulas given in the missal, one of which is the *Confiteor*.[17]

It is worth explaining here that the singing of the *Kyrie eleison* cannot serve as the penitential rite unless it is preceded by prayer intentions.

The opening prayer

After the penitential rite, the *Kyrie* and then the *Gloria* are recited or chanted.[18] After that, the celebrant invites the faithful to pray: he says, "Let us pray" (or *"Oremus"*), allows a few moments of

---

[15] Returning here, as well, to the ancient tradition, Vatican II asked that—to the extent possible—the altar should be separate from the wall of the apse so that one can walk around it (see chapter 7 of *Sacrosanctum Concilium*).

[16] The celebrant or another minister can introduce the liturgy of the day "briefly" (*sic*) in a few words.

[17] The text of this prayer has been modified so as to avoid the repetition of certain formulas.

[18] "How should this *Glory to God* be sung? It's quite simple, it would seem. Straight through. And yet nowadays in France, we have not managed to find melodies that catch on readily in the various congregations. . . . And so, to avoid a dull recitation of the *Gloria*, alternating between the celebrant and the congregation, they interrupt the text with a refrain. This is a mistake! Why? Because in doing that, they respect neither the style nor the nature of this hymn and transform it into a song with a refrain. A comparison makes this very clear. Take a great aria from an opera. Imagine that instead of being sung, it is recited and, what's more, it is interrupted at intervals by a short sung phrase, by a refrain" (Cardinal Jean-Marie Lustiger, *La messe* [The Mass] [Paris: Éditions Bayard, 1988]).

silence for personal prayer, and then, extending his hands, says the Opening Prayer (Collect), to which the faithful respond, "Amen".

The Liturgy of the Word

After the Collect, the celebrant and all the others in attendance sit down. The lector goes to the ambo to read the First Reading.

After that, the Responsorial Psalm or the "Gradual" is sung.

Then comes the Second Reading, after which the *Alleluia* of the day is sung (or, during Lent, the Gospel verse or "Tract").[19] While this music is being sung, the priest puts incense into the censer that the acolytes present to him. Then he goes in front of the altar, makes a profound bow to recite the prayer *"Munda cor"* with his hands joined, goes to take the Book of the Gospels, which was placed upon the altar at the beginning of Mass, and goes to the ambo to proclaim there the Gospel of the day.

As the celebrant walks from his chair to the ambo, he may be accompanied by acolytes, forming a procession and carrying the censer and the candles.

At the ambo, the priest opens the Book of the Gospels and says, "The Lord be with you" (*Dominus vobiscum*). After the congregation's response, he announces, "A reading from the holy Gospel according to N." (*Lectio sancti Evangelii secundum N.*), while making the Sign of the Cross with his thumb on the book, then on his forehead, lips, and heart. He then incenses the Book of the Gospels.

After the Gospel has been read, the celebrant proclaims, "The Gospel of the Lord" (*Verbum Domini*), kisses the book while the congregation responds, and says in a low voice, "Through the words of the Gospel may our offenses be blotted out."

The celebrant then gives a homily to explain to the faithful some aspect of the Scripture passages that have just been read, or he may speak about texts from the Ordinary or the Proper of the Mass.[20]

---

[19] The present liturgy has restored the custom of having three readings. Charlemagne was the one who had omitted one of the readings formerly presented in the course of Mass in the Roman rite.

[20] GIRM 41.

After the homily, the entire congregation recites or sings the "Profession of Faith", that is, the Creed (*Credo*).[21]

Following the *Credo*, the "Prayer of the Faithful" is recited, in keeping with an ancient custom that, before the Council, had been observed only during the Good Friday liturgy. The faithful are invited to pray for the Church, for world leaders, for those who suffer from various afflictions, for all mankind, and for the salvation of the whole world.[22] It is the celebrant's duty to invite the faithful to pray and to conclude the intercessions.[23]

After each prayer intention, the faithful can either sing a short response or observe a moment of silence.

The Liturgy of the Eucharist

While the schola begins the offertory hymn, the acolytes prepare the altar by placing upon it the corporal, the purificator, the chalice, and the missal. When everything is ready, the celebrant goes to the altar to receive the gifts there: the paten containing the hosts, the cruets of wine and water.

If a deacon is present, he is the one who receives the gifts brought up by the acolytes and presents them to the celebrant.

These actions and rites are accompanied by formulas given by the liturgical tradition and specified in the missal.[24]

The offertory hymn continues at least until the gifts are placed upon the altar by the deacon or the priest.

After offering the bread and the wine, the celebrant incenses the gifts that are on the altar, then the altar itself.[25]

---

[21] The *Credo* is a dogmatic text elaborated at the time of the Councils of Nicea and Constantinople (325–381) so as to safeguard the unity of Christians. To respect and learn well the words of the *Credo* is a pledge of unity in the faith and in ecumenical hope. That is why the liturgy has the duty of permitting the faithful to memorize the text of the *Credo*. In order to do this, it is essential not to replace the official words of this hymn with any other words whatsoever. Cf. Cardinal Jean-Marie Lustiger, *La messe*.

[22] Cf. SC 53.

[23] See Appendix VII.

[24] Cf. GIRM 102–3.

[25] Cf. GIRM 163.

After completing the incensation and returning to his place at the middle of the altar, the celebrant bows to say the prayer "Lord, we ask you to receive us . . ." (*In spiritu humilitatis*), then he goes to one side of the altar to wash his hands while saying the designated prayer in a low voice.

After returning to the middle of the altar, the priest turns toward the people, extends his hands and says, "Pray, brethren, that my sacrifice and yours . . ." (*Orate fratres: ut meum ac vestrum sacrificium* . . .). After the response of the congregation, he begins the Preface dialogue, then the Preface itself. Upon the completion of the latter, the entire assembly sings together the *Sanctus-Benedictus.*

What follows is the Eucharistic Prayer. It can simply be recited, but it can also be sung in its entirety, which is more in keeping with tradition and with the spirit of the liturgy.[26]

Shortly before the Consecration and the elevation, an acolyte may call the attention of the faithful with a bell; he will also ring it at the elevation of the Host and the chalice.[27]

The celebrant can choose among several Eucharistic Prayers:

- Eucharistic Prayer I, or the "Roman Canon", is the one that was already found in the missal before Vatican II; it is, in a certain way, the most "traditional".
- Eucharistic Prayers II, III, and IV were introduced into the current missal following Vatican II. They were composed using elements from very ancient texts.[28]
- Other Eucharistic Prayers have been approved. They are in many cases the fruit of the immediate postconciliar period, during which the idea probably was to arouse the interest of the

---

[26] The liturgy, after all, is not a private affair of the celebrant.

[27] GIRM 109.

[28] Eucharistic Prayer II is the shortest; it is inspired by the *anaphora* of Hippolytus of Rome (third century), the earliest Eucharistic Prayer of the West that has come down to us. Eucharistic Prayer III was composed on the basis of Roman, Gallican, and Mozarabic elements; it also uses texts originating in the tradition of Antioch. Eucharistic Prayer III is inspired directly by the New Testament and is modeled upon the arrangement of Eastern anaphoras. A very thorough and clear study of these three Eucharistic Prayers has been made by Dom Guy-Marie Oury, *L'Ami du Clergé* (a publication now entitled *Esprit et Vie* [Spirit and life]), published in Langres, no. 29, 18 juillet 1968.

faithful in the liturgy by incessantly creating prayers "for every occasion". We emphasize that not all of these Eucharistic Prayers are successful compositions and that they often are no more than incidental experiments that therefore have never deserved to be an official part of the missal, even though one has the right to use them in certain circumstances.

All of the Eucharistic Prayers conclude with a doxology ("Through him, with him, and in him ..."; *Per ipsum et cum ipso et in ipso ...*), to which the congregation responds, "Amen".

Then the "Our Father" (*Pater noster*) is recited, which continues with the prayer and the Sign of Peace.

After that, all sing the "Lamb of God" (*Agnus Dei*); meanwhile the celebrant breaks the Host and lets a particle from it fall into the chalice while saying the designated liturgical prayers.

Then comes the Communion rite: the celebrant receives the Body and Blood of Christ, then gives Communion to the ministers who wish to receive, and finally goes to give Communion to the faithful who approach the altar in procession.

During this time, the schola sings the Communion antiphon and some psalm verses. The text of this antiphon corresponds to the theme of the Gospel of the day and often takes up again, in a more concise form, some aspect of the thought developed in the entrance antiphon (*Introit*) of the Mass.

The concluding rite[s]

When Communion has been distributed, the celebrant returns to the altar and proceeds to purify the sacred vessels; these are then placed by an acolyte on the credence table, so that the altar once more appears as bare as it was at the beginning of the Mass, a sign that the liturgical action is coming to an end, that the Lord's banquet is completed.

After a moment of silence to foster meditation and acts of thanksgiving by all, the celebrant rises to say the concluding prayer (Postcommunion); the congregation responds, "Amen".

After this prayer, if necessary, the celebrant or another minister may make several brief announcements for the parish.

Then the priest extends his hands to greet the faithful one last time while saying, "The Lord be with you" (*Dominus vobiscum*); he immediately adds: "May Almighty God bless you ..." (*Benedicat vos omnipotens Deus ...*).

The priest venerates the altar by kissing it, as at the beginning of the Mass; then, together with all the ministers, he salutes it (by bowing or genuflecting). They all then form a procession so as to return to the sacristy. The celebrant, aware of the action that he has just performed, is invited to meditate in silence and to give thanks to the Lord; to assist him in doing this, the missal proposes a series of prayers.

Conclusion

As you see, this "typical form" of the revised Roman liturgy has several advantages:[29]

- The connection between the congregation and the celebrant is affirmed more clearly.
- The essential rites have been trimmed of later additions that had grown cumbersome—and esoteric—over time.

[29] "The rite of Paul VI remains a rite in Latin; it does not oblige but only allows the priest to celebrate facing the people; celebrations in the vernacular—however legitimate they may be—are likewise merely authorized, whereas the majority of French priests have made them a general rule. Hymns and religious songs have also become the general rule, as opposed to Gregorian chant, which remains the traditional chant of the Latin Church.... One can note several errors in the French translation of the Our Father (*'ne nous soumets pas à la tentation'* = 'do not put us to the test'), and in the Creed, with the phrase *'de même nature que le Père'* (= 'one in nature with the Father'), which the Pope refused to say during the World Youth Days, saying 'one in being with the Father' instead and, to emphasize the error, repeating the same term in Latin (*consubstantialem Patri*). [The French version] also translates *una cum papa nostro* [= with our Pope] as: 'with *the* Pope, John Paul". A vestige of Gallicanism? Yet in no instance can these abuses be blamed on the rite of Paul VI." François Biju-Duval, *Les traditionalistes face à la tradition* [Traditionalists confronting tradition] (Paris: Édition Téqui, 1999).

- The roles of the individual participants in the liturgy are better defined and do not encroach upon one another.
- Duplicated prayers have been eliminated.
- The form of the liturgy that has been determined in this way—when it is properly observed—is astonishingly close to that of the first known form of the Roman rite.[30]

[30] See chapter 4 ("The 'Roman' Liturgy") and chapter 10 ("A Particular Case: The Dominican Liturgy"); Dom Guy-Marie Oury, *La messe: spiritualité, histoire, pratique* [The Mass: spirituality, history, practice] (Tours: Éditions C.L.D., 1985).

23

HOW THE REVISED ROMAN
LITURGY WAS RECEIVED

The principles articulated at Vatican II were demanding. In order to be applied in an exact and deliberate manner, they should have been entrusted to pastors who had a solid formation in all areas of theology. Well, we know now that they were handed over to priests who certainly had plenty of good will and self-denial but were often hardly capable of appreciating what was truly at stake, theologically and pastorally, in the changes brought about by the conciliar directives.

Indeed, when the first decrees for implementing the liturgical renewal were published,[1] the priests who had the difficult responsibility of putting them into effect in the parish communities were generally clergymen who, in the major seminaries of their day, had been the beneficiaries of a formation provided by professors who themselves had been formed according to the principles of the nineteenth century.[2]

Suddenly, now, parish priests were expected to "modify" the liturgy that they had celebrated themselves and had always seen celebrated. And so as to carry out this "modification" properly, each diocese organized "formation sessions" and "workshops" to retrain them. Today we see that such educational efforts could have borne fruit if they had not been aimed solely at transmitting the ideas of a few pastoral "experts" who were in charge, who as a matter of

---

[1] The most important liturgical documents of the postconciliar years are collected by Austin P. Flannery, ed., in *Documents of Vatican II* (Grand Rapids, Mich.: Wm. B. Eerdmans Publishing, first printing 1975), pp. 1–282.

[2] Paul Vigneron, *Histoire des crises du clergé Français contemporain* [History of the contemporary French clergy crises] (Paris: Éditions Téqui, 1976).

principle favored any and all innovations and new liturgical experiments. Consequently, from the very onset of the liturgical renewal, they tried to do something radically new with the liturgy instead of improving the manner in which it was celebrated by reinstating the Roman rite in its integral form and by fostering a new development that was organically connected to its history and its origin.[3]

Was that not courting failure from the start?

The liturgical renewal from the layman's perspective

In order to study the actual impact of the liturgical renewal, it is necessary to consider three points:

- what the Catholic layman knows about the liturgy,
- what he sees and hears when he participates in the celebration of the Eucharist, and
- what he experiences when he attends Mass.

What the Catholic layman knows about the liturgy

More than forty years after the start of the implementation of the liturgical renewal called for by Vatican II, it is evident that the majority of Catholic lay people no longer know anything about their liturgy: it is enough to ask them a few questions to determine that they have become "orphans" with respect to the sacred, and that they are unaware of their liturgical patrimony. Very few of them are acquainted with the order of the Mass, and still fewer could explain the meaning of the current rituals of the Eucharistic celebration.

Numerous priests themselves (and, among them, bishops) admit that they do not really know the liturgy that they are called, nevertheless, to celebrate daily: the older ones have introduced into the current liturgy some rites, customs, and gestures that belonged to the preconciliar Mass and have not been retained in the current Roman Missal. Even if this is not a serious matter per se, it is

---

[3] Fr. Louis Bouyer, *Le métier de théologien* [The theologian's profession] (Paris: Éditions France-Empire, 1979). See especially pp. 67–79.

nonetheless proof that the meaning of the Council's liturgical renewal has not really been understood and assimilated.

As for the younger clergy, who have had no in-depth liturgical formation at all during the years that they spent in a diocesan or interdiocesan seminary, at best they try to copy, more or less felicitously, what they have seen and liked in this religious community or that monastery.

In either case, the liturgy is neither taken for what it is nor is it lived from within: a subjective slant has been introduced, and once the liturgy has been set adrift, it runs every risk imaginable, veering from the trite to the tasteless, while never achieving an authentically "Catholic" and worthy celebration.

What the Catholic layman sees and hears when he participates in the celebration of the Eucharist

Generally speaking, the Catholic layman who still has a certain degree of confidence in the clergy, but whose judgment in liturgical matters has been largely spoiled by several decades of neglect of the Roman rite, thinks that what he sees the priest do and hears him say around the altar is the result of the proper implementation of the conciliar directives. However, if he compares what is done with what is prescribed in an official missal, he can easily determine that, in general, the liturgical celebrations available for him to participate in are practically never in conformity with the Roman rite as it stands today.

What does this layman find in most parishes?[4]

- that the liturgy is devised by "teams" or committees that rely more on "liturgical planners' magazines" than on the directives in the missal;
- that the texts of the "Proper" and the "Ordinary" of the Mass are often replaced by completely unauthorized texts;
- that many celebrants [in France] use photocopied sheets disguised as a missal;

---

[4] I am leaving aside here, for purposes of discussion, the few "privileged" parishes and monasteries where today's liturgy is celebrated respectfully, in a form that can be described as "classical".

- that the gestures and movements of those officiating are lacking in dignity;[5]
- that the penitential rite at the beginning of Mass no longer exists;
- that the offertory rites are truncated (the washing of the hands disappears);
- that the embolism that follows the Our Father is more and more often omitted;
- that Gregorian chant is only parsimoniously tolerated—when it is not forbidden, pure and simple, by the local authority;
- that the use of incense seems to have been abolished;
- that liturgical vestments (most often the chasuble) are no longer worn;
- that when saying the prayers, the celebrants give the impression of addressing the congregation rather than God;
- that altar rails have been removed (except when they have been declared part of a historical monument);
- that [the old ornate] altars [set against the back wall] have been abandoned in favor of tables (or makeshift and often rickety arrangements in small parishes with limited financial means);
- that the space left around these tables does not allow at all for the performance of the rites;
- that the altar servers, when they are present, no longer have anything to do (and are reduced to the decorative status of flowerpots).

What the layman experiences when attending Mass

The result of all this is that nowadays, in liturgies that get farther and farther away from the Roman rite, the more faulty, fragmented, and reassembled they are, boredom prevails for the most part. The obvious absence of culture and of a sense of the authentic tradition leads to the planning of random ceremonies that all too often have no other common element than their mediocrity. Thus, for the Catholic layman, an Easter Mass has no more solemnity

[5] The gestures often vary widely between the "melodramatic" and the "cramped". On this subject, see Michel Guérin, *Philosophie du geste* (Paris: Éditions Actes sud, 1995).

than a Sunday Mass in Ordinary Time, and a wedding Mass ends up resembling a funeral Mass, aside from a circumstantial decorum that must not be mistaken for the liturgy itself.[6]

It must be acknowledged that the refusal to implement the Council—even among those who invoke its spirit—has led to the contrivance of liturgies loosely based on the pattern of the Roman rite that have no other purpose than to cater to the sensibilities of this or that group of Catholics. But these "do-it-yourself" ceremonies, modeled on arbitrary initiatives that are devoid of any biblical, theological, or historical foundations, leave the faithful with a deep sense of uneasiness: not enough of the sacred, not enough silence, a lack of dignity, too much chit-chat and commentary.

Thus everyone agrees that, in the turbulence of the postconciliar period, pastors allowed an approach to worship to develop that has resulted in the prevalence of a liturgy that has become "dull and boring because of its fondness for banality and mediocrity, to such a degree that it makes one shudder".[7]

Liturgical crisis or crisis of modern man?

History shows us that no one can tamper with the liturgy; you can't do anything else with the liturgy than that which it is made for, and no one can pass himself off for something other than what he really is.

The liturgy, therefore, tends to reveal our deepest personality, and the way that we treat and carry out the liturgy (as well as the way in which we comport ourselves during the liturgy) are indicators of our genuine human make-up, with its strengths and weaknesses.

And so, even though he may not be much of a psychologist, anyone who watches the ministers officiating at the altar can discern, through their behavior, their gestures and their bearing, the true personality of each one of them.[8]

---

[6] See Maurice Gruau, *L'homme rituel; anthropologie du rituel Catholique Français* (Paris: Éditions Métailié, 1999).

[7] Cardinal Joseph Ratzinger, quoted by Dom Gérard Calvet, *Les Amis du Monastère*, bulletin of the monastery of Sainte-Madeleine du Barroux, no. 95 (août 2000).

[8] Tony Anatrella, *Non à la société dépressive* [Say no to the society of depression] (Paris: Éditions Flammarion, 1993). Jean-François Catalan, *Dépression et vie spirituelle* [Depression

Thus any Catholic who is the least bit attentive can discover, through the manner in which the liturgy is carried out, the way in which the celebrant understands and inwardly experiences the realities of the faith that he celebrates and, furthermore, the quality of the relationship that he has, both with God and with himself.

Well, nowadays, the way in which the liturgy is treated in many parishes tends to show that certain pastors have not harmoniously integrated the different components of their humanity. Hence there is an interior conflict, which they think that they can resolve by the intervention of "liturgical planning", but they continue to be preoccupied even more by the conflict until it leads them, sooner or later, into a false relationship with God and with the Church. The reason why these pastors who are prey to a lack of well-being set out to "tinker" with the liturgy, with the support of liturgical committees,[9] is that they are convinced that a "modified" celebration will better soothe their existential anguish.[10]

This is why, in our [Western] societies, which are undergoing a serious spiritual crisis, you find so many Catholics who are capable of tampering with the liturgy by subverting its rites. So many celebrants today set out to rewrite the rituals in order to adapt them to their own preferences;[11] they devise new prayers and new gestures. Is this not, in the first place (even if done under the pretext of being "pastoral"), in order to conform the celebration to their real character and to the role that they would like to be able to play in public? Is it not so as to create for themselves a persona through which they hope to disguise their real character, which perhaps is no longer truly in harmony with their priestly state?[12]

---

and the spiritual life] (Paris: Éditions Desclée, 1996); Catalan, *L'Homme et sa religion; approche psychologique* [Man and his religion, a psychological approach] (Paris: Éd. Desclée, 1993).

[9] Sometimes certain members of these committees seem to have the same problems that they do.

[10] Of course, we should not pass any judgment on their emotional state.

[11] Or what they imagine to be the mentality of the faithful.

[12] "Those who celebrate a feast need some external motive empowering them to do so. They cannot do it of themselves. There needs to be a reason for the feast, an objective reason prior to the individual's will. In other words, I can only celebrate freedom if I *am* free; otherwise it is tragic illusion. I can only celebrate joy if the world and human existence really give me reason to rejoice. *Am* I free? *Is* there cause for joy? Where these

Those who tamper with the liturgy always run the risk of throwing into even greater relief their real character and their true identity: a character and an identity that they may fear or even reject.

Other clergymen unceasingly adapt the liturgy to what they imagine to be the mentality and the tastes of the faithful who are in front of them; are they not actually revealing their unconscious desire to be "of the world"? Now, this desire can be tragic if it becomes apparent, with the passage of time, that it is turning into regret for having once chosen the consecrated life (a choice that the cleric can no longer affirm gladly and peacefully). Is it not tragic, really, when you see that the vocations of some men were built solely upon their ideal image of themselves, but that this ideal crumbled as they lost certain supports that, for them, were primarily of an emotional sort?[13]

And so, one can say that it is the desire to be "of the world", compounded by inadequate human formation, that drives numerous celebrants today to disregard the liturgical rites and to tamper

---

questions are excluded, the "party"—the post-religious world's attempt to rediscover the feast—is soon revealed as a tragic masquerade. It is no coincidence that, wherever people go to parties looking for 'redemption', i.e. the experience of liberation from self-alienation, from the constraints of everyday life, from a society which represses the self, such parties burst the bounds of middle-class entertainment and become bacchanalia. The taking of drugs is 'celebrated' together, a way of journeying into a realm which is completely 'other', a liberating excursion from the daily round into a world of freedom and beauty. But in the background there is the number one question concerning the power of suffering and death which no freedom can resist. To avoid these questions is to inhabit a dream world, artificial and insubstantial. It takes more than emotional declamations about the suffering of oppressed peoples—which have become the stock in trade of so many of these homemade 'liturgies' to conceal their fundamental lack of grip [on reality]. In other words, when 'celebration' is equated with the congregation's group dynamics, when 'creativity' and 'ideas' are mistaken for freedom, the fact is that human nature is being soft-pedaled; its authentic reality is being bypassed. It does not take a prophet to predict that experiments of this kind will not last long; but they can result in a widespread destruction of liturgy" (Cardinal Joseph Ratzinger, *Feast of Faith*, trans. Graham Harrison [San Francisco: Ignatius Press, 1986], pp. 63–64).

[13] For example, the cassock, Latin chants, the "beautiful" ceremonies of yesteryear, the warm, congenial atmosphere of the major seminary, etc.

with the liturgy.[14] Hence it is obvious that, for many of them, a lack of respect for the liturgy is accompanied by a painful and increasing inability to accept fully the priestly state, which is a state of life consisting of voluntary acts of self-denial, of choices clearly established with a view to their own salvation and the salvation of the faithful who are entrusted to them by the Church. Many are the victims of this state of affairs; they then embark upon a tragic process of desacralization, which inevitably leads to their becoming completely secularized, actors in a real personal tragedy.

There you have the whole problem with the liturgy today: a problem with human origins that ends up having serious repercussions on the spiritual life, that is, on the deepest, most comprehensive existential plane.

A very serious aspect of the crisis is that today no one has yet calculated the extent of the psychological and moral suffering of many priests who are confronted by these deep existential problems; the diocesan authorities, who are unfortunately weak and unreliable, content themselves with persuading their priests that they will find consolation in throwing themselves headlong into activism:[15] regional meetings, faith discussion groups, continuing education courses, etc.

Let us stop hiding from reality. The crisis ravaging the Church today—which manifests itself as much in the collapse of the liturgy as it does in the popularization of false liturgies resulting from the immature behavior of certain celebrants who are ill at ease—is a crisis of an anthropological sort, first and foremost. It is a basic anthropological imbalance[16] that, in man, no longer allows the development of a proper Eucharistic spirituality.

---

[14] This is made easier for them nowadays by the general ignorance of Catholics, who are ready to accept any sort of ceremony when Sunday comes around, and also by the popularity of liturgical planning manuals that can be described as "dubious".

[15] Whereas the real solution would be to organize gatherings for priests, during which they could chant the Office in a traditional form that would need little preparation and thus regain a taste for praise and adoration and then, based on that, an honest sense of priestly fellowship.

[16] This is manifested also by the fact that many clerics are now foundering in a state of depression.

As long as those in authority in the dioceses are unwilling to acknowledge that the origin of a great number of difficulties met with nowadays lies there, and not somewhere else,[17] all the analyses of the present situation and all the elaborate attempts to remedy it, by means of diocesan synods and pastoral or liturgical experiments, can be multiplied endlessly: they will still circle around the problem without daring courageously to root out the evil that has attacked the Church by infiltrating and dismembering the liturgy.[18]

[17] But will they be able to see this, when often they are dealing with the same problems to some extent?

[18] This is paraphrasing Bruno Hetsch, *Ne dissimulons plus les vraies raisons de la crise* [Let us stop hiding the real reasons for the crisis] (Bulletin Pro Liturgia, juin 1999). These observations were reiterated, in part, by Fr. Alain Bandelier, *Simples questions sur la Messe et la liturgie* (Tours: Éditions C.L.D., 1999).

24

THE CONTEMPORARY LITURGICAL CRISIS

It is clear that it was not the liturgical renewal of Vatican II that was the problem: the great majority of Catholics accepted it confidently, without the least hesitation, because it brought with it a genuine enrichment in many respects.[1]

What was the problem and what continues to be the problem is the manner in which the magisterial documents have been hijacked and used to take the Roman liturgy where the Church never wanted it to go. As a consequence of the abuses and mistreatment of the Roman rite that have become so widespread—to the point that they have become customs that are found with few variations in almost all the parishes—the Catholic faithful have had the sense that the liturgy was no longer something sacred, a living organism, but rather the result of the deliberations of some self-declared "specialists".

For the first time ever in its long history, the Roman liturgy at present appears no longer as a precious, unified heritage that one can make one's own, but rather as a more or less felicitous assembly of disparate elements, a sort of permanent "work-in-progress" ["bricolage"] subject to the decisions and preferences of someone or other, to which each individual is free to give or withhold his assent.[2]

Because the official form of the Roman liturgy, in the aftermath of Vatican II, has been denied to the Catholic faithful, who would have accepted it without raising objections, the Church has seen her people divided summarily into four camps:

[1] Joseph Ratzinger, *Milestones: Memoirs 1927–1977* (San Francisco: Ignatius Press, 1998), p. 148.

[2] See Claude Barthe, *Reconstruire la liturgie* [Reconstructing the liturgy] (Paris: Éditions F. X. de Guibert, 1997).

- the camp of those who have stopped practicing their faith and who go to church only at Christmas, Easter, and on important family occasions;
- the camp of those who have never known anything but the *Ersatz* forms of the Roman liturgy and have become accustomed to and content with what is offered to them in the parishes;
- the camp of those who hope for a correct implementation of Vatican II directives; and
- the camp of those who reject the conciliar liturgical renewal because, in their opinion, it is the source of the present crisis.[3]

Those who are content with what is offered in the parishes

There is quite a lot of variation in the way that the present liturgy is celebrated. Perhaps the most striking aspect, which has sparked the most debates, has been the liquidation of a whole patrimony of chants, of formulas, of customs, which neither the Council nor the reforms that came after the Council had asked for in the first place, but which was considered as part of the liturgical reform.[4]

This comment made by a French bishop demonstrates that today the Roman Missal is no longer considered as the point of reference to be followed in matters concerning worship celebrations, but rather as an open-air quarry[5] where anyone responsible for the liturgy and lacking in inspiration can come to find building blocks that he can use to reconstruct a ceremony suited to his taste.[6]

---

[3] See other works by Denis Crouan: *The Liturgy Betrayed* (San Francisco: Ignatius Press, 2000); *The Liturgy after Vatican II* (Ignatius Press, 2001).

[4] Bishop Georges Lagrange, quoted in Claude Barthe, *Reconstruire*.

[5] Charles Wackenheim, *Entre la routine et la magie, la messe* [Between routine and magic, the Mass] (Paris: Éditions du Centurion, 1982). Jean and Colette Guichard, *Liturgie et lutte des classes* [Liturgy and class conflict] (Paris: Éditions de L'Harmattan, 1976). Michel Deneken, *Le salut par la croix* [Salvation through the cross] (Paris: Éditions du Cerf, 1988). Alain Woodrow, *L'Église déchirée* [The Church, torn] (Paris: Éditions Ramsay, 1978).

[6] Cardinal Lustiger recalls that "the Mass is an act *codified* with reference to Jesus, not only in its [general] intention, but also in the details of its gestures, postures, and words.... [T]he prayer that concludes the introductory rite of the Mass, therefore, is not just a casual comment in which the personality or the originality of the celebrant should be apparent; he does not have to 'express himself' to us." See Dom Guy-Marie Oury, *La messe: Spir-*

However, the same bishop reminds us: "Some respect is due to the Christian people. The Code of Canon Law is quite insistent on this point: Christians have the right to a liturgy that is the liturgy of the local Church and not the fanciful invention of the celebrant or the local pastor." [7] The reason for this is simple: it is the Church that celebrates the Eucharist and, when she does,

> she acts with the gestures and the words of Jesus' prayer, handed down by apostolic Tradition. And when he was celebrating the Last Supper with the Twelve, Jesus followed the Jewish Passover ritual, which itself was exactly and minutely codified. That is why, in the Eucharistic Prayer, there is no room for improvisation.[8]

The ritual is a minutely codified Jewish Passover ritual, he says. Indeed, this is the ritual that is the source of our Eucharistic liturgy, as we have seen in the early chapters of this survey.

One important question remains, nevertheless: Where did this codification of the Jewish Passover ritual come from? In order to answer this question, we must plunge into the Old Testament; there we find the roots of the Christian faith that we celebrate in the course of every liturgical ceremony.

> In the accounts of the events leading up to Israel's flight from Egypt, as well as in those that describe the flight itself, the Exodus appears to have two distinct goals. The first, which is familiar to us all, is the reaching of the Promised Land, in which Israel will at last live on its own soil and territory, with secure borders, as a people with the freedom

---

itualité, histoire, pratique [The Mass: Spirituality, history, practice] (Tours: Éditions C.L.D., 1985), pp. 17 and 61. "The Church rejects this specious argument that the liturgy is for the people and not the people for the liturgy. The Church does not intend for the liturgy to be adapted to the people, but rather for the people to adapt to the liturgy. There is no way to make anyone accept this apparent paradox unless he recognizes that the Church has a transcendent personality; ... it is as a transcendent person that she celebrates her own worship, with her own language, with her own chant, with her own art.... The Church is well aware that those of her members who want to adjust the liturgy to the people misunderstand her own Mystery and do not sufficiently revere the transcendence of her own Person" (V. A. Berto, *Le Cénacle et le Jardin* [The upper room and the garden] [Bouère: Éditions D.M.M., 2000]).

[7] Bishop Georges Lagrange, quoted in Claude Barthe, *Reconstruire*.

[8] Cardinal Jean-Marie Lustiger, *La messe* [The Mass] (Paris: Éditions Bayard, 1988), p. 117.

and independence proper to it. But we also hear repeatedly of another goal. God's original command to Pharaoh runs as follows: "Let my people go, that they may serve me in the wilderness" (Ex 7:16). These words—"Let my people go, that they may serve me"—are repeated four times, with slight variations, in all the meetings of Pharaoh with Moses and Aaron (cf. Ex 8:1; 9:1; 9:13; 10:3). In the course of the negotiations with Pharaoh, the goal becomes more concrete. Pharaoh shows he is willing to compromise. For him the issue is the Israelites' freedom of worship, which he first of all concedes in the following form: "Go, sacrifice to your God within the land" (Ex 8:25). But Moses insists—in obedience to God's command—that they must go out in order to worship. The proper place of worship is the wilderness: "We must go three days' journey into the wilderness and sacrifice to the LORD our God as he will command us" (Ex 8:27). After the plagues that follow, Pharaoh extends his compromise. He now concedes that worship according to the will of the Deity should take place in the wilderness, but he wants only the men to leave: the women and children, together with the cattle, must stay in Egypt. He is assuming the current religious practice, according to which only men are active participants in worship. But Moses cannot negotiate about the liturgy with a foreign potentate, nor can he subject worship to any form of political compromise. The manner in which God is to be worshipped is not a question of political feasibility. It contains its measure within itself, that is, it can only be ordered by the measure of revelation, in dependency upon God. That is why the third and most far-reaching compromise suggested by the earthly ruler is also rejected. Pharaoh now offers women and children the permission to leave with the men: "Only let your flocks and your herds remain" (Ex 10:24). Moses objects: All the livestock must go too, for "we do not know with what we must serve the LORD until we arrive there" (Ex 10:26). In all this, the issue is not the Promised Land: the only goal of the Exodus is shown to be worship, which can only take place according to God's measure and therefore eludes the rules of the game of political compromise.

Israel departs, not in order to be a people like all the others; it departs in order to serve God. The goal of the departure is the still unknown mountain of God, the service of God. Now the objection could be made that focusing on worship in the negotiations with Pharaoh was purely tactical. The real goal of the Exodus, ultimately its only goal, was not worship but land—this, after all, was the real content of the promise to Abraham. I do not think that this does justice to the seriousness that pervades the texts. To oppose land and worship makes no sense. The land is given to the people to be a place for the worship of the true God. Mere possession of the land, mere national autonomy, would reduce Israel to the level of all the other nations. The pursuit of such a goal would be a misunderstanding of what is distinctive about Israel's election. The whole history recounted in the books of the Judges and Kings, which is taken up afresh and given a new interpretation in the Chronicles, is intended to show precisely this, that the land, considered just in itself, is an indeterminate good. It only becomes a true good, a real gift, a promise fulfilled, when it is the place where God reigns. Then it will be not just some independent state or other, but the realm of obedience, where God's will is done and the right kind of human existence developed. Looking at the biblical texts enables us to define more exactly the relationship of the two goals of the Exodus. In its wanderings, Israel discovers the kind of sacrifice God wants, not after three days (as suggested in the conversation with Pharaoh), but after three months, on the day they come "into the wilderness of Sinai" (Ex 19:1). On the third day God comes down onto the top of the mountain (cf. Ex 19:16, 20). Now he speaks to the people. He makes known his will to them in the Ten Commandments (cf. Ex 20:1–17) and, through the mediation of Moses, makes a covenant with them (cf. Ex 24), a covenant concretized in a minutely regulated form of worship. In this way, the purpose of the wandering in the wilderness, as explained to Pharaoh, is fulfilled. Israel learns how to worship God in the way he himself desires. Cult, liturgy in the proper sense, is part of this worship, but so too is life according to the will of God; such a life is an indispensable part of true worship. "The glory of God is the living man, but the life of man is the vision of God," says St. Irenaeus (cf. *Adversus Haereses* 4, 20, 7), getting to the heart of what happens when man meets God on the mountain in the wilderness. Ultimately, it is the very life of man, man himself as living righteously, that is the true worship of God, but life only becomes real life when it receives its form from looking toward God. Cult exists in order to communicate this vision and to give life in such a way that glory is given to God....

What does this mean for the question we have been considering? We were looking at the two goals of the Exodus, and we saw that the issue was ultimately about the nature of the liturgy. Now it becomes clear that what took place on Sinai, in the period of rest after the wandering through the wilderness, is what gives meaning to the taking of the land. Sinai is not a halfway house, a kind of stop for refreshment on the road to what really matters. No, Sinai gives Israel, so to speak, its interior land without which the exterior one would be a cheerless prospect. Israel is constituted as a people through the covenant and the divine law it contains. It has received a common rule for righteous living. This and this alone is what makes the land a real gift. Sinai remains present in the Promised Land. When the reality of Sinai is lost, the Land, too, is inwardly lost, until finally the people are thrust into exile. Whenever Israel falls away from the right worship of God, when she turns away from God to the false gods (the powers and values of this world), her freedom, too, collapses. It is possible for her to live in her own land and yet still be as she was in Egypt. Mere possession of your own land and state does not give you freedom; in fact, it can be the grossest kind of slavery. And when the loss of law becomes total, it ends in the loss even of the land. The "service of God", the freedom to give right worship to God, appears, in the encounter with Pharaoh, to be the sole purpose of the Exodus, indeed, its very essence. This fact is evident throughout the Pentateuch. This real "canon in the canon", the very heart of Israel's Bible, is set entirely outside of the Holy Land. It ends on the edge of the wilderness, "beyond the Jordan", where Moses once more sums up and repeats the message of Sinai. Thus we can see what the foundation of existence in the Promised Land must be, the necessary condition for life in community and freedom. It is this: steadfast adherence to the law of God, which orders human affairs rightly, that is, by organizing them as realities that come from God and are meant to return to God.

But once again, what does all this mean for our [reflections upon the liturgy]? First, it becomes clear that "cult", seen in its true breadth and depth, goes beyond the action of the liturgy. Ultimately, it embraces the ordering of the whole of human life in Irenaeus' sense. Man becomes glory for God, puts God, so to speak, into the light (and that is what worship is), when he lives by looking toward God. On the other hand, it is also true that law and ethics do not hold together when they are not anchored in the liturgical center and inspired by it.[9]

Isn't it clear that the spread and acceptance of haphazard liturgies that do not observe the Roman rite, such as we see today, are only results of a long process of deceiving people into thinking that they cannot obtain the freedom promised by Christ unless they bring a new religion into being by means of a liturgy that they have devised themselves—a religion of involvement in the world,

[9] Cardinal Joseph Ratzinger, *The Spirit of the Liturgy* (San Francisco: Ignatius Press, 2000), pp. 15–20.

one that will accept the Church only insofar as she is transformed into sort of international organization whose role is limited to supporting temporal activities?[10]

Why has the Roman liturgy been the first thing to suffer from this new way of looking at things? Is it not because, having its roots in the West, it is thwarted more than any other liturgy by the "modern" ideas that shake the foundations of our societies, namely, hedonism, materialism, and pragmatism at the service of immediate profit?[11]

Those who hope for a correct implementation of Vatican II in France

Let us say it right away: they are not legion. The reason for this lack of interest in the Roman liturgy is simple, and we have already suggested it: few Catholics have had a chance to participate in a liturgy that was really celebrated according to the present Roman rite. And it is likely that, as things are going, very few Catholics will have the opportunity to see this rite in the near future. Few Catholics appreciate the importance of the liturgy in their lives and fewer are aware that the life of the Church depends upon a "correct" liturgy.

Now, since a sense of the liturgy is largely lacking in the great majority, the present situation of the liturgy due to the distortion of the conciliar directives still leaves certain questions unanswered. A letter written in 1999 by the Association *Pro Liturgia* to [the late]

[10] It is symptomatic of this confusion that Pope John Paul II is acclaimed whenever he issues a declaration on humanitarian issues, but criticized whenever he recalls the traditional principles of the Christian faith and morality.

[11] See Gérard Soulages, *Épreuves chrétiennes et espérance: lettres et documents sur la crise de l'Église* [Christian trials and hope: letters and documents on the crisis in the Church] (Paris: Éditions Téqui, 1979); *Divisions ou pacification dans l'Église* [Divisions or appeasement in the Church] (Tours: Éditions C.L.D., 1989). Valérie Hanotel, *Les cathos* [Those Catholics!] (Paris: Éditions Plon, 1995). Thierry Baffoy, Antoine Delestre, Jean-Paul Sauzet, *Les naufragés de l'esprit: des sectes dans l'Église catholique* [The spiritually shipwrecked: sects within the Catholic Church] (Paris: Éditions du Seuil, 1996). Ralph M. Wiltgen, *The Rhine Flows into the Tiber* (Rockford, Ill.: TAN Books, 1985). André Frossard, *"Be not afraid!": John Paul II Speaks Out on His Life, His Beliefs, and His Inspiring Vision for Humanity*, translated from French by J.R. Foster (New York: St. Martin's Press, 1984).

Monseigneur Billé, Archbishop of Lyons and [then] President of the French Bishops' Conference, as well as the reply that was received, testify to this malaise:[12]

Your Excellency,

The Association PRO LITURGIA ... was founded in 1988 as a voluntary association of Catholics who adhere to the Roman liturgy.

In contrast to many contemporary movements that study the liturgy or promote it in its "Tridentine" form (we mention only the most active groups: Una Voce, Oremus, the C.I.E.L., La Nef, etc.), our Association PRO LITURGIA is firmly committed to the implementation of the conciliar documents. Therefore it wishes that every Catholic could find the present Roman liturgy (said to be "of Paul VI") celebrated worthily and in its entirety, using the official books, in the vernacular languages but also, for those who prefer it, in Latin with Gregorian chant.

PRO LITURGIA works for the observance of the liturgical rites everywhere, according to the teachings of the Constitution *Sacrosanctum Concilium* and of Pope John Paul II (cf. his Letter *Vicesimus quintus annus*), so that eucharistic celebrations might free every believer from the idiosyncrasies of others and bestow on the liturgy itself a dimension that is cosmic, universal, and not exclusively geared to a particular group.

PRO LITURGIA, which presently has 400 members in France, is part of an international Federation (Confoederatio Consociationum pro Liturgia latina), which is presided over in rotation by each of the Presidents of the member associations.

Among the Associations that make up the international Federation are the movement in England and Wales (Association for Latin Liturgy) and that of the Netherlands (Vereiniging voor Latijnse Liturgie).

I think that it is worth mentioning these two Associations, inasmuch as they enjoy the support of their respective episcopates.

If I make so bold as to write to you today, Your Excellency, it is because the situation of the liturgy in France is becoming, if not alarming, then at least disconcerting for a great number of the faithful. They would like some answers to their questions with regard to the following points:

---

[12] The Association *Pro Liturgia* focuses in this letter on the present Latin and Gregorian liturgy, because its express purpose is to defend this form of the Roman rite. But besides this question it also addresses the problem of celebrations carried out without regard for the official liturgical norms.

1. The propaganda of the "traditionalist" movements

Not a day goes by without our being inundated with publications issued by traditionalist movements that are attached to the preconciliar liturgy (said to be "of Saint Pius V").

Similarly, if you check the Internet (performing a search by the word "liturgy", for example) you discover an overwhelming presence of sites dedicated to the so-called "Tridentine" liturgy, which is presented as the sole alternative to the haphazard vernacular liturgies usually found in the parishes.

In order to justify their attachment to the Tridentine liturgy, these movements—which seem to be the beneficiaries of considerable financial support, judging by the quality of their publications and their Internet websites—cite the Motu proprio *Ecclesia Dei adflicta* and at the same time point out that almost nowhere can one find the current liturgy celebrated worthily, according to the official books.

The actual situation seems to prove them right, and it is difficult to argue with them when they say, "Show us a parish where the Mass is celebrated exactly as it is described in the General Introduction to the Missal of Paul VI."

2. The rejection of the Latin Mass and Gregorian chant

More and more Catholics are sympathetic to the Latin liturgy: the older ones have memories of a liturgical patrimony that was capable of nourishing their faith, whereas the younger ones, who did not experience the disputes of the postconciliar period, are responsive to sacred surroundings that lift up their hearts to contemplate the mysteries being celebrated.

Now, even though the Council, the present Missal, and Canon Law fully acknowledge the value and the legitimacy of Masses celebrated in Latin (which can easily be found, moreover, in England, in the United States, in Italy or in the Netherlands ...), this liturgical form is always prohibited in France. For what reason?

"Pastoral reasons", we are often told. Well, those who travel through our country and see the state that the parishes are in, have reason to wonder about the effectiveness of the liturgical pastoral approach implemented since the postconciliar years. Should the "pastoral" argument still be used, then? To be honest, we no longer think so.

Furthermore, it must also be emphasized that the prohibition of Latin and Gregorian Masses adds grist for the mills of the traditionalist movements: today they are the only ones left, in France, who provide the faithful with a liturgy that is sung in its entirety and celebrated strictly according to the rubrics of "one" missal. And they are rightly proud of that fact.

3. The uneasiness of Catholics who legitimately adhere to the present Latin liturgy

This situation, indeed, places Catholics who adhere to the Latin liturgy, and who accept the Second Vatican Council without the slightest reservation, in a very difficult position.

Today, in effect, Catholics who want to participate in a Latin Mass celebrated according to the present missal are—at best—referred by the pastor whom they have consulted to a "traditionalist" community that benefits from the Indult granted by Pope John Paul II to celebrate according to the pre-conciliar rituals.

Now, they surely did not want to be "put on the Index" in this way.

Is it not obvious that this amounts to deliberately and permanently relegating them to a "ghetto"?

Isn't it obvious that this probably reflects a willingness to lump together those who reject the liturgical renewal outright (for whatever reasons) and those who in good faith want the Council—the whole Council—to be implemented?

Is this situation truly Christian? Can it continue to be justified or convincing? Our Association thinks that it is really not, inasmuch as the situation has only caused trouble and stirred up rancor, suspicion, and doubts.

4. What we would hope to see

Given the collapse of religious practice, isn't it high time to propose "also", alongside Masses in the vernacular languages, liturgies in Latin according to the present *Ordo Missae*? This could be a pastoral method of awakening in the faithful a new interest in the liturgy.

Of course, reintroducing Latin and Gregorian chant (which, it is true, was not abandoned everywhere) would have to be done prudently, so as not to offend Catholics who have too often been persuaded that to be in favor of Latin was to be "integrist" [i.e., a Tridentine "fundamentalist"] and consequently politically incorrect. . . .

The implementation of the Latin and Gregorian form of the present liturgy could be accomplished in several stages:

- During the first stage the sung prayers of the Ordinary could be introduced.
- During the second stage, the celebrant would sing the central part of the Mass, from the Consecration (*qui pridie quam patere-tur*) to the acclamation *Mysterium fidei*, and then the *Per ipsum*, followed by the *Pater noster*, and lastly, the final blessing and the *Ite missa est*.
- During the third stage, the choir would sing the entrance and communion antiphons, and the celebrant would start the preface dialogue and sing the preface itself in Latin.

And so, gradually, we could restore to the faithful a unified Latin liturgy celebrated according to the current norms.

Thus we could halt the fragmentation into parallel communities which often know nothing about each other and which lead to the creation of places of worship where everyone tries to fashion for himself a liturgy tailored to his ideas about Christianity and the Church.

Pope John Paul II has emphasized that "A faith alive in charity, adoration, praise of the Father and silent contemplation will always be the prime objective of liturgical and pastoral care" (*Vicesimus quintus annus*, 10).

Our Association is convinced that the "silent contemplation" that many individuals yearn for can be fostered to a great extent within the setting of a Latin and Gregorian liturgy.

That is why I ask you, in the name of the Association of which I am president and in the name of all Catholics devoted to Latin and Gregorian Masses, whether it would not be feasible to begin a thoroughgoing discussion (at the level of the Bishops' Conference?) on the liturgical question, and simultaneously to see to it that the places where a Latin liturgy could be celebrated according to the current *Ordo* are officially encouraged?[13]

In a letter dated May 12, 2000, *Pro Liturgia* received the following reply from Bishop Bernard Lagoutte, General Secretary of the French Bishops' Conference:

---

[13] This letter was signed by the President of the Association *Pro Liturgia*.

Monsieur President,

I have received your letter of April 19. No doubt, I would nuance somewhat several of the diagnoses that you make. Although it is true, for example, that few congregations nowadays are in a position to celebrate the Mass in Latin with Gregorian chant, there are nonetheless some churches where the *Ordo* of Paul VI is strictly followed. But I thank you for having shared with me your feelings on all the points that your letter addresses.

I am not sure that it is possible and necessary to bring back Latin Masses, at least on a regular basis. But we certainly should be checking constantly as to whether pastoral practice concerning the liturgy and the sacraments is really pursuing these objectives, namely, "praise of the Father and silent contemplation," as you quote Pope John Paul II.

This reply is interesting for at least two reasons:

- It is noted that "there are nonetheless *some churches* where the *Ordo* of Paul VI is strictly followed...."
- It is clearly stated that it is not "possible and necessary to bring back Latin Masses, at least on a regular basis".

Should we conclude, then, that the episcopal authority has determined, on the one hand, that the Roman liturgy no longer exists except in "some churches" [14] and, on the other hand, whole sections of the Constitution *Sacrosanctum Concilium* must now be considered null and void? [15]

---

[14] See for example the studies by Klaus Gamber, *The Reform of the Roman Liturgy: Its Problems and Background* (San Juan Capistrano, Calif.: Una Voce Press, 1993); *The Modern Rite: Collected Essays on the Reform of the Liturgy* (Farnborough, Hants, UK: St. Michael's Abbey Press, 2002).

[15] In that case, though, wouldn't it be fitting to revise Canon Law, which explicitly states: "Christ's faithful are at liberty to make known their needs, especially their spiritual needs, and their wishes to the Pastors of the Church" (Can. 212 §2); "Christ's faithful have the right to worship God according to the provisions of their own rite approved by the lawful Pastors of the Church" (Can. 214); "The liturgical books, approved by the competent authority, are to be faithfully followed in the celebration of the sacraments. Accordingly, no one may on a personal initiative add to or omit or alter anything in those books. The ministers are to celebrate the sacraments according to their own rite" (Can. 846 [not "841" as in French text], §1 and §2); "The eucharistic celebration is to be carried out either in the Latin language or in another language, provided the liturgical texts have been lawfully approved" (Can. 928).

Those who reject the Roman liturgy as revised after Vatican II

The present situation with the Roman liturgy, which has been the subject of numerous studies, has led the faithful—those who are searching for rituals in worship that convey the sacred—to turn to the form of the Roman rite that was in use before Vatican II, the form that is called the "Tridentine Mass" or "the Mass of Saint Pius V". These Catholics have been described as *"intégristes"*; it would be better to refer to them here as "conservatives" [*"conservateurs"*].[16]

How could these "conservatives" help being shocked, in the aftermath of the Council, by a liturgical "renewal" that had taken a truly "revolutionary" turn in many parishes?[17] It would be wrong to believe today that among the ranks of those "conservatives" there were at that time only a few bigots who were nostalgic about the Masses of their childhood; there were also—and especially—a good number of authors, artists, composers, theologians, and historians.[18]

And since they were generally not listened to by their diocesan bishops,[19] they turned to Archbishop Marcel Lefebvre,[20] a man of great prestige who had the courage to speak up forcefully to denounce certain liturgical and doctrinal deviations.[21]

In 1970 Archbishop Lefebvre founded the Fraternity of St. Pius X, the purpose of which is to form young men who, upon ordination as priests after their studies, will preserve the "Tridentine"

[16] Eric Vatre, *La droite du Père: enquête sur la tradition catholique aujourd'hui* [The right hand of the Father: an inquiry into Catholic Tradition today] (Paris: Éditions Trédaniel, 1994).

[17] Michel de Saint-Pierre and André Mignot, *Les fumées de Satan* [The smoke of Satan] (Paris: Éditions de la Table Ronde, 1976).

[18] Louis Salleron, *La nouvelle messe* [The new Mass] (Paris: Nouvelles Éditions Latines, 1970).

[19] Jacques de Ricaumont, *Visites à messieurs les curés de Paris* [Visits to the Reverend Fathers of Paris] (Paris: Éditions de la Table Ronde, 1981).

[20] Born on November 29, 1905, in Tourcoing, France, Marcel Lefebvre served as Archbishop of Dakar, Apostolic Delegate in West Africa, Superior of the missionary Congregation of the Holy Ghost Fathers, and Archbishop of Tulle before becoming, in 1970, the founder and superior of the international seminary in Écône, Switzerland.

[21] Archbishop Marcel Lefebvre, *Un évêque parle* [A bishop speaks] (Éditions Martin Morin).

liturgy. An important point is worth underscoring here: ever since its erection, the Fraternity of Archbishop Lefebvre has welcomed many young men from France who left the diocesan seminaries, which, one suspects, was not very pleasant for the diocesan bishops who during that same time were closing their seminaries one after the other for lack of candidates for the priesthood.[22]

After numerous vicissitudes, Archbishop Lefebvre was suspended *a divinis* [from sacramental ministry] by reason of illicit (albeit valid) ordinations. Despite this sanction, the former Archbishop of Dakar continued his work, convinced that it was the only way to respond to the serious crisis that was shaking the Church by undermining her liturgy and catechesis.

Given the increasing extent of the problems caused by "the Lefebvre case", in 1987 the Holy See decided to seek a solution; the following year Rome sent an apostolic visitor to Écône. An agreement was reached: the Fraternity of St. Pius X would enjoy partial autonomy and a bishop would be appointed to succeed Archbishop Lefebvre, who at that time was eighty years old.

But Archbishop Lefebvre went back on that agreement and on June 30, 1988, consecrated four bishops, even though that had been forbidden by the Pope, who alone has the right to appoint bishops in the Latin Church. The consequences of that act were serious: Archbishop Lefebvre and Bishop Castro Mayer (the co-consecrating bishop) were excommunicated, along with the four new bishops.[23]

Following that schismatic act,[24] the Vatican reacted swiftly:

---

[22] Patrick Chalmel, *Écône ou Rome? Le choix de Pierre* [Écône or Rome? Peter's choice] (Paris: Éditions Fayard, 1990). Bertrand de Margerie, *Écône, comment dénouer la tragédie?* [E., how to resolve the tragic situation?] (Paris: Éditions F. X. de Guibert, 1997). François-Georges Dreyfus, *Des évêques contre le pape* [Some bishops against the pope] (Paris: Éditions Grasset, 1985).

[23] Cf. *Osservatore Romano* [French edition] of July 3, 1988, and *Documentation Catholique*, no. 1967 (août 1988).

[24] "In reality, the Lefebvrites are part of a great crisis of obedience which has shaken the Church in the past few decades. *Ipso facto*, the Lefebvrites are hardly fighting to restore discipline in the Church; they are not even *more papist than the Pope*, given that their opposition is an attack on the authority of the pope and could constitute a precedent that would undermine the papal office. Along these lines, they busy themselves with an endless critique of the encyclicals and documents issued by Rome, attempting to minimize their authority. (It is not the Pope's duty to rally to the cause of the Fraternity of Saint Pius X.)

- Pope John Paul II published a Motu proprio beginning with the words *Ecclesia adflicta est.*
- A Pontifical Commission was created. Named the *Ecclesia Dei* Commission, its mission was to reincorporate into the Church those groups of Catholics who, while wishing to preserve the ancient Roman liturgy that was being promoted by Archbishop Lefebvre, did not concur in the act of disunity committed by the Superior of Écône in confronting the authority of Peter.

The Motu Proprio *Ecclesia Dei adflicta*

The Motu proprio of John Paul II deals with two points that shed light on our subject.

On the one hand, it explains the deep-seated reasons for the Lefebvrist split: "The *root* of this schismatic act can be discerned in an incomplete and contradictory notion of Tradition. Incomplete, because it does not take sufficiently into account the *living* character of Tradition, which, as the Second Vatican Council clearly taught, 'comes from the Apostles and progresses in the Church with the help of the Holy Spirit'."

On the other hand, the Motu proprio authorizes—under certain conditions[25]—the use of the liturgical books that predated the liturgical renewal of Vatican II.

Let us imagine for a moment that that were the case: rallying to them would be a precedent that would create anarchy, since it would subject the Pope to any number of pressure groups who would claim to be right in opposing him. It would inaugurate democracy in the Church. . . . Wouldn't that be admitting that the Modernists are right, since they demand a better hearing for the 'People of God', which is thought to be closer to God sometimes than the official hierarchy? If the Pope were to acknowledge the 'errors' committed since Vatican II, that would validate the Modernist theories, for instance, that acts of disobedience are sometimes legitimate, and that the Pope has only a relative authority.

"The Lefebvrists are therefore nothing more than schismatics. Far from being simple guardians of Tradition without any investiture whatsoever, they make a travesty of Tradition with regard to their concept of Infallibility, which is strictly reduced to a minimum, as well as on many other points" (François Biju-Duval, *Les traditionalistes face à la tradition* [The traditionalists confront Tradition] [Paris: Éditions Téqui, 1999]).

[25] The permission is an "indult", that is, a particular privilege (and not a right) granted by the Holy See for a special reason.

The Pontifical Commission *Ecclesia Dei*

Working in close collaboration with several Roman Congregations,[26] this Commission attempts to enable groups of Catholic "conservatives" to find their place in the life of the Church by allowing themselves to be incorporated as much as possible in their respective dioceses.

It must be acknowledged, nevertheless, that within the groups, associations, and fraternities that have been placed under the aegis of the *Ecclesia Dei* Commission, not all disagreements have been smoothed over: many points of contention remain, chiefly in matters concerning the liturgy. This results from the fact that in the very heart of these conservative communities there are "moderates" and "hard-liners".

The former are quite ready to accept the Roman liturgy as it was codified following Vatican II, provided always that it is truly the liturgy celebrated according to the official books and not a personal liturgy that has been "vaguely Romanized". Now, as we saw earlier, the "real Roman liturgy" in its current form is still something extremely rare.[27]

The latter—those described as "hard-liners"—reject the current Roman rite at all costs, since they continue to consider it as a "new rite" that breaks completely with the authentic liturgical tradition.[28]

The official position of the Holy See

Confronted with the near nonexistence of the postconciliar Roman liturgy, Catholic "conservatives"—joined, it is true, by other Cath-

---

[26] The Roman Congregations are the Congregation for the Doctrine of the Faith, the Congregation for Bishops, and the Congregation for Divine Worship and the Discipline of the Sacraments.

[27] This poses a real problem of conscience for priests who are devoted to the old rituals and who are required to concelebrate with the diocesan bishop according to the current rite in order to manifest their communion with the whole Church. What stance should they take when they discover that the bishop himself does not respect the present liturgy?

[28] Cf. Msgr. Camille Perl, Secretary of the *Ecclesia Dei* Commission, in a conference given on the occasion of the official presentation of the Acts of the Fifth Colloquium of the *Centre International d'Études Liturgiques* (C.I.E.L., the "International Center for Liturgical Studies") in Rome on April 5, 2000.

olics who are not satisfied with the way in which the Eucharist is celebrated nowadays in the parishes—have turned to the Holy See to demand that the use of the pre-Vatican II liturgical books be officially recognized as legitimate, for all time.

It is, of course, possible to distinguish two motives in this request. The first favors a return to the old form of the Roman rite, a step that could sooner or later call into question all of Vatican II, to the extent that the Council forms a coherent whole. Rejecting the Constitution *Sacrosanctum Concilium* would necessarily cast doubt upon the other conciliar decrees and constitutions.

The second motive consists of noting the dilapidated state of the revised Roman rite and, after realizing that it is not possible to implement it today (for whatever reasons), promoting the old form of the Roman liturgy so as to preserve at least some setting for true sacredness and liturgical dignity. This latter motive explains the position taken by a monastic community such as Le Barroux; the Father Abbot declares:

> In the turbulence of the postconciliar period, Cardinal Ratzinger denounced a certain sort of liturgy that was "dull and boring because of its fondness for banality and mediocrity, to such a degree that it makes one shudder" (*Entretien sur la foi*, chap. 9). Therefore it is not out of a spirit of contradiction but rather out of prudence that we have wished to remain faithful to the old liturgical tradition; so it is that we—and others as well—will have promoted, perhaps involuntarily, what the Cardinal calls a "reform of the reform".[29]

But can the Church accept the existence of two forms of the same rite? Must she allow groups that have refused to follow recent teachings of the Magisterium in liturgical matters to organize themselves as a Church having its own liturgy and its own calendar?

To this twofold question, the Congregation for Divine Worship has given a clear answer in an official document dated October 18, 1999:

> 1. The Roman Missal approved and promulgated on the authority of Paul VI in the Apostolic Constitution *"Missale Romanum"* of the 3rd

---

[29] Dom Gérard Calvet, *Les Amis du monastère*, Bulletin of the Abbey of Le Barroux, no. 95 (August 2000).

of April 1969 is the only form of celebrating the Holy Sacrifice which accords with the Roman Rite currently in force, in consonance with general liturgical law. The same applies, with any necessary reservations, to the other liturgical books approved after the Second Vatican Ecumenical Council.

2. The use of the form which preceded the postconciliar liturgical renewal of the Roman Rite (also known as "traditional", "ancient", "of St. Pius V", "classic", and "tridentine") is granted, under the conditions set out in the Motu Proprio *Ecclesia Dei adflicta*, to persons and communities who adhere to this form of the Roman Rite. This faculty is granted by a special indult, which in no way signifies that the two forms enjoy parity.

3. Those who enjoy the benefit of the indult granted by the Motu Proprio *Ecclesia Dei adflicta* may use this form freely both in private and in public, in the churches, and at the times expressly appointed for the faithful.

4. Since the current manner of celebrating according to the Roman Rite conforms to the common liturgical norm, there should be no talk of "two rites" or of "duality of rite". The concession given in the Motu Proprio *Ecclesia Dei adflicta* safeguards the liturgical sensibilities of those priests and those of Christ's faithful who are attached to this previous usage, but in no way establishes them as a "ritual congregation".

5. The Holy See urges bishops to be extremely tolerant to those of Christ's faithful who wish to participate in the sacred liturgy in accordance with the previous liturgical books and to keep their sensibilities constantly before their eyes.[30] These members of Christ's faithful for their part should accept the teaching of the Second Vatican Council and also acknowledge from their hearts the legitimacy and the consistency with orthodox belief of the liturgical texts promulgated after the liturgical renewal.

6. In dioceses, in accordance with varying circumstances, benevolence in dealing with those of Christ's faithful who adhere to the previous forms can be expressed either by appointing times suitable for liturgical celebration in some churches or by designating a particular church which may be convenient for these faithful under the charge of a rector or chaplain, or sometimes even by the creation of a personal parish.

---

[30] We must note that this is a particularly delicate issue; indeed, given the present situation, wouldn't there be a temptation to ask Catholics who would like to have the liturgy according to the present Roman rite to "be extremely tolerant" with regard to their pastors who still refuse their request?

7. When priests who enjoy this indult to use the previous forms nevertheless celebrate publicly in churches on behalf of communities which follow the forms currently in force, they must use the current books, faithfully following the rules of the current Roman Rite.[31]

8. The competence, and indeed the authority of the Holy See in the case of those communities which enjoy the indult to follow the previous forms of the Roman Rite, belongs to the Pontifical Commission *Ecclesia Dei*. But the relations of these communities with particular Churches, so far as liturgical celebrations are concerned, are subject to the competence of the Congregation of Divine Worship and Sacramental Discipline, other interested jurisdictions having the right to be heard.

9 . . .

10. This clarification is issued and made a matter of public law after consultation with and with the approval of the Pontifical Commission *Ecclesia Dei*.[32]

As the reader will have noted, the Church considers that the Roman liturgy is the one that, after a long and often eventful history, is celebrated today according to the norms and definitions contained in the Roman Missal compiled following Vatican II and promulgated by Paul VI on April 3, 1969.[33]

It is always legitimate to discuss the good qualities and failings of such a missal, but care must be taken that these discussions do not have the effect of disturbing the order of the present Roman rite: in the celebration of the faith, indeed, the viewpoints of such-and-such a theologian, or this historian, or that pastor, cannot replace the authority of the Successor of Peter. It is evident that, for a Catholic, the opinions of various schools of thought cannot be placed on the same level as a council or decrees ratified by the Supreme Pontiff.[34]

---

[31] We must note that there is every reason to be astonished that the Holy See is so demanding with the "traditionalist" priests in requiring them to "observe carefully the prescriptions of the Roman rite", when at the same time so many other diocesan priests never observe this rite themselves.

[32] The document is signed by Cardinal Jorge Medina Estévez, [former] Prefect of the Congregation of Divine Worship and the Sacraments.

[33] Since it appeared, the missal has been supplemented by other liturgical works, for instance, the *Ceremonial for Bishops*. We will not begin to examine them here.

[34] Already in the nineteenth century, Dom Guéranger criticized those who placed themselves under the authority of this cardinal or of that prelate in order to go against a decision of the Supreme Pontiff.

25

THE NEW "GENERAL INSTRUCTION ON THE ROMAN MISSAL"

The history of the liturgy does not dwell on the quarrels that set Catholics against each other when they are obliged to participate in liturgical celebrations that seem to be completely out of control: the true prayer life of the Church goes on, beyond the strife engendered by these feelings or those pastoral decisions.

This is demonstrated by the publication of the revised text of the "General Instruction on the Roman Missal" (abbreviated "GIRM"; in Latin, *Institutio Generalis Missalis Romani*). This new version of the document, which specifies the form that the Roman rite should have today, was approved by Pope John Paul II on Good Friday of the year 2000 and replaces the old one that dated back to 1975.

According to the Canon Law presently in force in the Church, the GIRM will be printed at the beginning of every missal used by a priest who celebrates the Eucharist.

It is important to understand that this revised "General Instruction" is not, in itself, something new; it continues along the lines of both the Vatican II Constitution *Sacrosanctum Concilium* and the 1975 GIRM. Moreover the new text perfectly illustrates the continuity of the liturgical tradition of the Church. Consequently, it is necessary to study it in order to understand how the Church intends her official prayer to be conducted—the prayer in which the faithful have the right to participate.

THE VARIOUS CHAPTERS OF THE "GENERAL INSTRUCTION"

Note, in the first place, the importance of the Preamble of the new GIRM; it sets forth teaching that is theological and at the same time spiritual; this shows that the new document promulgated by the Congregation for Divine Worship is the result of an organic development of the liturgical renewal called for by the whole Church at the time of Vatican II, a renewal that is situated within the larger movement of the history of the liturgy.

This Preamble is followed by eight major chapters. Just as in the first version of the GIRM, the first chapter insists on "The Importance and Dignity of the Eucharistic Celebration"; the second chapter deals with "The Structure of the Mass, Its Elements and Its Parts"; the third chapter, which addresses the question of "The Duties and Ministries in the Mass", is divided into three sections concerning (1) ordained ministers, (2) the people of God, and (3) extraordinary ministers.

Note that, although these first three sections summarily reiterate what was already found in the old version of the "General Instruction", a fourth section has been added in the new edition: it deals with the distribution of duties among the participants in the liturgy and the preparations for the celebration.

The fourth chapter ("The Different Forms of Celebrating Mass") has been revised considerably. The first section, which concerns the Eucharist celebrated in the presence of a congregation, is now divided into two subsections: (1) "Mass without a Deacon" (this section previously bore the title "Typical Form of the Liturgy"), and (2) "Mass with a Deacon" (the section previously entitled "The Duties of the Deacon").

The duties of the acolyte and of the lector are likewise discussed in greater detail.

A third section of this same fourth chapter, which was formerly called "Mass in the Absence of a Congregation", is now entitled "Mass at Which Only One Minister Participates". This section recalls that a priest may not celebrate the Eucharist alone except for a truly extraordinary reason.

Chapter 5, which concerns "The Arrangement and Furnishing of Churches for the Celebration of the Eucharist", has now been subdivided into three sections:

I. General principles,

II. The arrangement of the sanctuary for the Sacred Synaxis (Eucharistic assembly),

III. The arrangement of the church.

Chapters 6, 7, and 8 are practically unchanged. As for chapter 9, we will return to it later on.

In perusing the new document, the reader will also note that in many places the word "sacred" has been combined with certain terms such as, for example, "minister", "vestments", "celebration". This modification makes it possible to insist on the fact that the beauty and nobility of the objects employed in Eucharistic celebrations should "evoke sacred use, avoiding thereby anything unbecoming" (no. 344).

Recall here that Paul VI, in his day, had warned the faithful many times—clergy and laity—against a veritable desacralization that had seized the Roman liturgy following Vatican II.

Elsewhere the reader will note that the term "liturgical" is used to describe more precisely the dignity and the meaning of the congregation.

Several rather significant modifications have been introduced in the discussion of the following subjects:

- the bishop, the priest, and the deacon;
- the lay ministers;
- the rites;
- sacred objects;
- possible adaptations.

We will examine these different points.

THE BISHOP, THE PRIEST, AND THE DEACON

A new introduction (no. 91) has been added to chapter 3, which deals with the ministers of the sacred liturgy. The "General Instruction" takes this opportunity to recall that the Eucharistic celebration is first of all the work of Christ and of his Church, "the people united and ordered under the bishop"; consequently, the Mass is not so much a private action as a good belonging to the whole Church.

Since the celebration of the Eucharist manifests the Mystical Body of Christ and at the same time influences it, every member of this Body is affected by the Eucharistic celebration in a personal way that depends on his rank, his duty, and his degree of participation in the liturgy.

It is by participating in the liturgy that the people of God, "a chosen race, a royal priesthood, a holy nation", manifests its internal cohesion and its hierarchical structure. Consequently, everyone of Christ's faithful, whether an ordained minister or a layman, must perform his liturgical duty by doing all and only that which he can do and actually has to do.

In the liturgy not everybody does everything; everyone ought to be at the "right" place to perform his specific duty (see SC 28).

1. The bishop

At the center of every Eucharistic celebration is the diocesan bishop (GIRM no. 22). The Masses that he celebrates with his clergy and his people show forth the mystery of the Church and ought to be the model for all the liturgies celebrated in the diocese.

The bishop, therefore, must be prominent as the true guardian and the authentic promoter of the whole liturgical life in the diocese of which he is in charge.

The new version of the "General Instruction on the Roman Missal" presents two new rites for Mass celebrated by a bishop:

- after the Gospel is proclaimed, the bishop can bless the congregation with the Book of the Gospels (no. 175);
- the opportunity is provided, during the Eucharistic Prayer, to pray expressly for the co-adjutor bishop and the auxiliary bishops. The other bishops who may be present during the Mass are not mentioned.

2. The priest

Celebrating the Eucharist remains the most important act for every priest. That is why it is required that, if at all possible, every priest should celebrate a daily Mass (no. 19).

It is specified, however, that Mass can be celebrated by a priest alone (that is, without a congregation or acolyte) only for a just and reasonable cause (no. 114). In that case, the celebrant omits the greetings and the final blessing (no. 254).

The GIRM recalls an important point that is found in the conciliar Constitution on the Liturgy: during a Eucharistic celebration, the celebrant is not permitted to add, omit, or modify anything whatsoever in the liturgy.

Although it is certainly legitimate for the priest to make certain choices provided for by the liturgy, he must also remember that he has the delicate task of conducting the celebration in a correct fashion (no. 111). This point resonates like an echo of what John Paul II wrote in his Apostolic Letter for the twenty-fifth anniversary of the conciliar Constitution on the Sacred Liturgy: "Since liturgical celebrations are not private acts, ... it is not permitted to anyone, even the priest, or any group, to subtract or change anything whatsoever on their own initiative." [1]

Thus, by choosing among the options proposed in the missal for liturgical chants, prayers, and gestures—those that best correspond to the level of preparation and the mentality of a given congregation (no. 24)—the priest-celebrant must always remember that the spiritual good to which the people of God are entitled is more important than his own choices or his personal preferences (no. 352).

The GIRM states precisely how the celebrant should understand the liturgical "adaptations" that are permitted: these are mainly concerned with commentary on the Mass, and their sole purpose is to make more accessible to the faithful certain explanations that are given in the course of a liturgy.

Nevertheless, the priest must always follow the instructions contained in the liturgical books and must keep any explanations very brief (no. 31) and limit them to clearly determined moments: at the beginning of the Mass of the day, during the Liturgy of the Word, at the beginning of the Eucharistic Prayer, and before dismissing the congregation.

The introductory rites of the Mass

There is no denying that great confusion prevails today in the penitential rite that opens every Eucharistic celebration; many

[1] *Vicesimus quintus annus*, 10 (December 4, 1988).

celebrants—including bishops—have popularized the idea that the *Kyrie eleison* in and of itself can serve as the act of penitence.

The "General Instruction" specifies once more the rules that are to be followed (no. 51): there is a selection of formulas that can be used for the act of penitence at the beginning of Mass, but it may not be omitted.

The Liturgy of the Word

After recalling the norms to be followed in proclaiming the Gospel (no. 212), the GIRM makes several clarifications concerning the homily. In no case may it be given by a layman (no. 66); it must be a "living commentary on the Word of God" that forms an integral part of the Eucharistic celebration (no. 29).

The homily, which is given from the chair or at the ambo—or at any other convenient place—(no. 136) by the priest, standing, may not be omitted on Sundays or feast days without a serious reason (no. 66).

Following the Creed, the intercessory prayers of the faithful are offered. They are introduced by the celebrant, standing at his chair with his hands joined.

They are concluded by the celebrant, who extends his hands to say the prayer (no. 138).

The Liturgy of the Eucharist

During the offertory, the celebrant says the liturgical prayers in a loud voice, unless a song is sung or organ music is played (no. 142).

The priest, by virtue of his ordination, is the one who should recite the Eucharistic Prayer.

The faithful unite themselves to the celebrant by a silence that expresses their faith and their interior assent, or by responding with the various acclamations: the Preface dialogue, the *Sanctus*, the acclamation following the Consecration, and the Amen that concludes the final doxology (no. 147).

Other acclamations can be recited, provided that they have been approved by the Holy See.

It is strongly encouraged that the celebrant sing the Eucharistic Prayer; however, it must not be improvised, but should follow the ad hoc divisions that have been approved (no. 147).

In the new "General Instruction", the sign of peace is described in great detail.

Has anyone failed to notice that, in many churches, the gesture that underscores the exchange of the peace of Christ is quite chaotic—more a source of distraction than of recollection?

Therefore it is recalled, in the first place, that the sign of peace is the rite whereby "the Church asks for peace and unity for herself and for the whole human family, and the faithful express to each other their ecclesial communion and mutual charity before communicating in the Sacrament" (no. 82).

So as not to interrupt the harmony and the momentum of the Eucharistic ceremony, the celebrant must exchange the sign of peace only with the ministers who are present in the sanctuary and nearby; movements of the priest in the nave, among the faithful, are forbidden (no. 154).

The faithful, for their part, are invited to exchange a sign of peace only with those immediately to their right and left, and to do so in a dignified manner (no. 82). The one who offers the sign of peace says, "May the Peace of the Lord be with you always." The one who receives the sign of Peace responds, "Amen" (no. 154).

The bishops' conferences are invited to find the gesture for the sign of peace that is best suited to the mentalities of their respective cultures.

Before distributing Communion, the consecrated Bread is broken by the celebrant, with the help of the deacon, if one is serving.

The laymen designated as extraordinary ministers of the Eucharist must not be at the altar at that moment and may not participate in this rite of the "the fraction or breaking of bread" (no. 83).

In order to present to the faithful the Body of Christ at the moment when he says the words, *"Ecce Agnus Dei ..."* ("Behold the Lamb of God ..."), the celebrant can choose between two gestures:

- he either raises the Host over the paten, or
- he raises the Host over the chalice containing the Precious Blood.

The final blessing

In the new "General Instruction", the manner of giving the final blessing, also, is described in greater detail so as to help the celebrants make gestures that are truly dignified.

After the *Dominus vobiscum* ["The Lord be with you"] and the response by the congregation, the priest joins his hands, begins the formula of the blessing, then places his left hand on his chest while raising his right hand to make the Sign of the Cross over the faithful (no. 167).

3. The deacon

A new section [IV.1.B.] has been added to the GIRM to define more precisely the ministry of the deacon at Mass.

When he carries the Book of the Gospels during the entrance procession, the deacon should hold the book at a moderate height (no. 172) so as to avoid any misplaced grandeur.

Once he arrives in the sanctuary, he does not bow, but immediately places the Book of the Gospels on the altar. He then kisses the altar at the same time as the celebrant.

If the Book of the Gospels is not carried, the deacon bows in front of the altar and venerates it in the usual manner (no. 173).

It is the deacon's duty to proclaim the Gospel, to read the intercessions at the prayer of the faithful, to prepare the altar before the offertory, to clear the altar after Communion, to serve at the altar in general, and to distribute Communion.

On certain occasions, he can also give the homily. Furthermore, he is responsible for showing the congregation what gestures to make and what postures to assume (no. 94).

When he is at the altar, the deacon stands at the celebrant's side and somewhat further back (no. 215); he thereby signifies that, in virtue of his ordination, he ranks first after the priest in the liturgy (no. 94). The dalmatic is the liturgical vestment that the deacon should wear over the alb and the stole; it can, however, be omitted for a good reason or if the Mass is not festive (no. 338).

During the Eucharistic Prayer, in keeping with an ancient tradition, the deacon kneels from the epiclesis until the elevation of the chalice (no. 179). However, during the elevation, he can also incense the Host and the chalice. In that case, he prepares the censer, kneels in front of the altar, and incenses the Blessed Sacrament (no. 179).

In the absence of a deacon, another minister (the thurifer) performs this rite (no. 150).

At the kiss of peace, the deacon, with hands joined, is the one who invites the members of the congregation to exchange a sign of peace.

After receiving the kiss of peace from the celebrant, the deacon offers the peace of Christ to the ministers who are on either side of him.

At the end of Mass, if there is a solemn blessing, the deacon invites the faithful to bow their heads; then, after the blessing has been given, the deacon, with hands joined, sings the *Ite missa est* ("The Mass is ended, go in peace") to a melody that from now on is to be used exclusively—except during certain Masses of the Easter season (no. 185).

THE LAY MINISTERS

The new "General Instruction" clarifies the role played by the lay ministers in the course of the Eucharistic celebration.

Selected by the rector of the cathedral or the pastor of the parish, these ministers are confirmed in their temporary duty by a blessing (no. 107).

In order to perform their liturgical duties, they must put on an alb and a cincture or another vestment (not a free-flowing gown) approved by the Conference of Bishops (no. 339).

1. The extraordinary ministers of the Eucharist

An extraordinary minister of the Eucharist can be designated only if, during the Mass, there are not enough priests and deacons present (no. 162).

To designate this minister, the following preferential order should be followed: first, the *instituted* acolyte, then the *instituted* extraordinary minister of the Eucharist, and lastly the occasional extraordinary minister (no. 162).

The new GIRM describes in detail the manner in which this minister should perform his duty: during Mass he does not approach the altar until after the priest himself has received Communion (no. 162). He then receives from the celebrant the sacred vessels containing the Sacred Species.

After Communion, the Precious Blood that remains in the chalice is consumed by the deacon or, in his absence, by the celebrant himself.

The priest or the deacon, or else an *instituted* acolyte, purifies the sacred vessels immediately after Mass. It is not permissible for the sacred vessels to be purified by an extraordinary minister of the Eucharist who has not been instituted (no. 279) [although a special indult permits this in the United States "for grave pastoral reasons"; this is a three-year indult—ED.].

2. The lectors

The role of the *instituted* lectors is clearly defined as well (no. 99).

In the absence of *instituted* lectors, a qualified person who has had suitable preparation can proclaim the sacred texts, except for the Gospel (no. 101). The reason why the duty of lector has been extended in this way to any Catholic is because the proclamation of the biblical texts (other than the Gospel) is dependent on a ministerial duty and not on the duty of presiding (no. 59).

In order to perform his function during a Eucharistic celebration in which there is no deacon, the lector, wearing the prescribed liturgical vestment, carries the Book of the Gospels during the entrance procession (no. 194). Upon arriving in the sanctuary, he places the book upon the altar and takes the place that is reserved for him (no. 120).[2]

The "General Instruction" specifies also the duties of the master of ceremonies (no. 106), the musicians in general (no. 103), the

---

[2] The Lectionary is never carried in procession (no. 120).

sacristan (no. 105), the liturgical "animator" (no. 105),[3] the ushers, and those who are in charge of greeting the faithful as they arrive (no. 105).[4]

3. The acolytes

The instituted ministry of acolyte involves particular duties (nos. 187–93) that may be distributed among several acolytes. Some of these should be performed by the deacon instead, when there is one; this is the case with the incensing of the celebrant and the congregation, with the preparation of the gifts on the altar (no. 190), and with administering the chalice during Communion (no. 191).

In the absence of instituted acolytes, laymen can serve at the altar and help the priest and the deacon as well: they are called to carry the cross, the candles, the censer, the bread, and the wine, as well as the water. With due regard for the liturgical norms, they can also be called to serve as extraordinary ministers of the Eucharist (no. 100).

It is the prerogative of the bishop to establish norms concerning what service at the altar the acolytes should provide (no. 107).

4. The assembly of the faithful

The new GIRM devotes a few lines to the subject of the gestures that the faithful should make and the postures that they should assume during Mass.

It is clearly stated that the faithful must conform to the liturgical rules and to the traditions of the Roman rite rather than seek to make themselves conspicuous. The harmony created by uniformity in gestures and postures is the sign of the unity of the faithful and also, especially in the eyes of nonbelievers who may have occasion to attend a celebration of the Eucharist, the witness of a common spiritual attitude.

---

[3] Actually, the GIRM does not speak of an "animator" but rather of a "commentator": his role is to give, if necessary, some brief, well-prepared explanations so that the faithful can better grasp the sense of certain liturgical rites.

[4] In any case, the celebrant himself is not the one responsible for this welcome.

As in the old version of the "General Instruction", the postures that the faithful should assume at Mass are described in detail.

However, in the new text, several additional clarifications are given. Thus, it is required that the faithful stand up at the beginning of the *Orate fratres* ("Pray, brethren, that our sacrifice ..."), whereas in many cases they are accustomed to remain seated until the Preface dialogue begins (no. 43).

The new GIRM insists also on the fact that kneeling during the Consecration is to be encouraged (no. 43),[5] while recognizing that certain persons can remain seated or standing for health reasons. Those who choose to remain standing are asked to make a profound bow at the moment when the priest genuflects after the Consecration (no. 43).

Two paragraphs are devoted to the "basic" liturgical gestures: genuflection and bowing. Genuflection, performed by lowering the right knee to the ground, signifies adoration. It is reserved for the Blessed Sacrament in general and for the veneration of the Cross from the service on Good Friday until the Easter Vigil (no. 274). The servers who carry the processional cross or candles should bow instead of genuflecting: bowing is an expression of the reverence due to persons or to exterior signs that represent those same persons (no. 275).

The new "General Instruction" retains only two sorts of bows: the "profound" bow [made from the waist] and the simple bow of the head.

MODIFICATIONS MADE TO CERTAIN RITES

1. The Liturgy of the Word

The GIRM begins by recalling that no nonbiblical reading may replace a text from Scripture that is designated by the liturgy (no. 57).

---

[5] Unfortunately it must be noted that in the majority of parishes [in France] the faithful are prevented from kneeling.

On the other hand, except for the reading or chanting of the Passion during Holy Week, it is not permitted to divide among several lectors in dialogue form the sacred texts that are to be proclaimed during a Mass (no. 109).

Finally, it is specified that during a Mass that is celebrated with a congregation, the readings must always be proclaimed from the ambo (no. 58). As for the prayer of the faithful, the intentions must be sober, discreet, and brief, always expressing the needs of the assembly that is reunited in the name of the whole Church (no. 71).

2. Silence

The GIRM gets around to mentioning the need for silence. Liturgical silence—which is not an interruption of noise but rather a quiet expression of prayer—should be observed not only during the celebration, but also before and after it, both in the church proper as well as in the sacristy and in other areas near the sanctuary (no. 45).

Since the purpose of proclaiming the Word of God is to foster meditation, it is also important in the liturgy to avoid anything that would resemble impatience or any sort of haste, and to encourage stretches of silence so that the listeners may take the divine teaching to heart (no. 56).

3. Music

Following the conciliar teaching, the GIRM recalls the important role of music, chiefly in Masses celebrated on Sundays and holy days (no. 40).

The importance of Gregorian chant is affirmed once more: it is "proper to the Roman liturgy" and should hold pride of place.

Other musical styles are not excluded, provided that the melodies and the words are fully in keeping with the liturgical action and foster the piety of the faithful (no. 41).

The new directives emphasize furthermore that it is preferable that the liturgy be sung in its entirety. At the same time, they recall that the sung prayers of the Ordinary of the Mass (*Gloria, Credo,*

Sanctus, Pater noster, Agnus Dei) cannot be replaced by songs or hymns with words other than those of the liturgy (no. 366).[6]

As for the organ, it must be used as discreetly as possible during Advent and Lent and should be limited to accompanying the singing (no. 313).

4. The Liturgy of the Eucharist

It is preferable that Communion be distributed from the Sacred Species that were consecrated during the same Mass that the faithful have attended (no. 85). During the Communion procession, the people sing the appropriate antiphon or, if that is not possible, they recite it (no. 87).

The celebrant should likewise make sure to bring the Eucharist to the members of the schola cantorum (choir) who wish to receive Communion (no. 86).

The local bishop is responsible for establishing norms concerning the distribution of Communion under both Species, with a view to avoiding any danger of profaning the Blessed Sacrament. These norms will not be in force until they have been approved by the Apostolic See (no. 283).

5. The purification of the sacred vessels

The new "General Instruction" introduces several changes in the manner of purifying the sacred vessels: after the Precious Blood has been consumed at the altar by the priest, the deacon, or an *instituted* acolyte, the sacred vessels are placed on a credence table and covered with a corporal. They are purified immediately after the Mass (nos. 163, 279).

However, since there is ordinarily neither a deacon nor an instituted acolyte in the parishes, it is usual for the celebrant to purify the sacred vessels after Communion.

---

[6] For example, the "Lamb of God" litany with the words "Jesus, Lamb of God, . . . Jesus, Bread of Life, . . . Jesus, Word made flesh". [TRANSLATOR'S NOTE TO EDITOR: This footnote is an adaptation for North American, English-speaking readers. A literal translation of Crouan's note 398 follows: "For example, the song, *I believe in God who sings* . . . instead of the Creed, or *Peace will be you and me* . . . instead of the Lamb of God."]

There are more detailed instructions concerning the bread to be used in celebrating the Eucharist (no. 284c), the distribution of Communion (no. 285b), and the place (i.e., the sacristy) where the sacred vessels should be kept and in some cases purified (no. 334).

THE FURNISHINGS AND SACRED OBJECTS

The "General Instruction" begins by clarifying what is meant by "the sanctuary". This is the space where the altar is located, where the Word of God is proclaimed, and where the priest and the deacon stand, as well as the other ministers who perform a specific liturgical duty (no. 295).

1. The altar

The rule states that every church should be furnished with a single consecrated altar, which manifests that there is one Christ and one Eucharist and symbolizes Christ the living Cornerstone (no. 303).

Allowances can be made, nevertheless, for an old altar of artistic value that cannot be moved, and if celebrating at that altar really interferes with the participation of the faithful, a new fixed altar that is more suitable may be set up. In that case, the old altar must no longer be decorated and it must not be used anymore to celebrate Mass (no. 303).

A new directive specifies that, except for what is necessary for the celebration of the Eucharist, nothing should be placed directly upon the mensa of the altar (no. 306). Floral arrangements must always be used with moderation; they should be arranged near the altar but never on it (no. 305).

During Lent—except for *Laetare* Sunday—the sanctuary should not be decorated with flowers. In contrast, during Advent a few floral arrangements in keeping with the character of the season can be introduced; care should be taken so that their lavishness does not anticipate the joy that should burst forth when the Nativity of the Lord is celebrated (no. 306).

2. The altar cross

The new GIRM specifies that the altar cross must bear the image of Christ Crucified (no. 308) and should be placed either upon the altar or near to it, in such a way that it can easily be seen by the whole congregation.

The cross should remain in the sanctuary even when Mass is not being celebrated; it is a reminder to all that the Passion of the Lord is what is celebrated upon the altar.

3. The ambo

The ambo must be a worthy place [as to its location and furnishings, i.e., "not simply a movable lectern"]. Only the minister who is designated to proclaim the Word of God has access to it (no. 309).

4. The seats reserved for those who participate in the liturgy

Repeating the directives from 1975, the new "General Instruction" recalls that the apse (or the back of the sanctuary) is the best place for the celebrant's chair (no. 310).

This arrangement is not feasible, however, if the tabernacle is located at that same place. In that case another harmonious solution should be devised, that allows each minister to carry out his liturgical duty while emphasizing the distinction between the members of the clergy and the faithful who are not clerics (no. 310).

5. The tabernacle

The tabernacle must be fixed, solid, under lock and key, and fashioned of a noble material that is not transparent. Its placement is determined according to the directives given in the Instruction *Eucharisticum Mysterium*, while taking into account the judgment of the diocesan bishop (no. 315). The tabernacle can be placed either in the sanctuary or else in a chapel that is reserved for adoration and private prayer by the faithful.

The Blessed Sacrament present in the tabernacle is honored by a lamp (no. 316).

6. The sacred vessels

They must be easily distinguishable from objects used in everyday life (no. 332). These vessels have an important place in the celebration of the Eucharist; furthermore it is necessary that they be fashioned of a precious metal (no. 328) that does not rust [or they should be gilded on the inside].

The different conferences of bishops are to make proposals concerning the fashioning of the sacred vessels; these proposals can be adopted locally after they are approved by the Apostolic See (no. 329).

7. Sacred images

A new paragraph has been added in the GIRM to deal with the question of sacred images. These have always had a place in the liturgy: representations of the Lord, the Virgin Mary, and the saints are so many means of fostering among the faithful a spirit of adoration or of veneration and of drawing them further into the spirit of the liturgy (no. 318).

Prudence should be exercised, however, so as to avoid the multiplication of images or an arrangement that puts them in unsuitable places in the church building (no. 318).

8. The Eucharistic bread

The hosts that are to be used in celebrating the Eucharist must be prepared in accordance with the rules given in the Code of Canon Law;[7] Eucharistic bread is made exclusively from pure wheaten flour and must be recently baked (no. 320).

9. Incense

Several lines are devoted to the role that incense plays in the liturgy; the new text explains that, "as Scriptures show, incense is an expression of respect and at the same time a sign of prayer."

[7] Canon 924.

After placing incense in the censer, the celebrant blesses it by making the Sign of the Cross without saying anything; he bows before and after incensing persons or objects (no. 277).

10. The blessing of sacred objects

The new GIRM is very insistent about the dignity and the beauty that all sacred liturgical objects should have, and also about the respect that one should have for them (no. 350).

According to a traditional custom, the tabernacle, the organ, the ambo, the celebrant's chair, the liturgical vestments of the priest and the deacon, and the sacred vessels must be blessed before being used in Eucharistic worship (nos. 309–10, 333, 335).

POSSIBLE ADAPTATIONS IN THE LITURGY

Certain adaptations of the liturgy are in the spirit of the Second Vatican Council, if they foster a greater participation of the faithful in the celebration. But in this particular area, it is necessary to distinguish what is within the jurisdiction of the diocesan bishop and what is within the province of the bishops' conferences.

The role of the diocesan bishop is clearly restated: he is the principal promoter and guardian of the liturgy in his diocese (no. 387). With him lies the responsibility of

- regulating the discipline that is to be observed in concelebrating Masses,
- establishing norms for serving the priest at the altar,
- establishing norms for distributing Communion under both Species,
- establishing norms for the construction and ordering of church buildings.

It is up to the conference of bishops

- to prepare a complete edition of the Roman Missal in the vernacular language(s) and to submit it for the approval of the Holy See before publishing it (no. 389),

- to define possible adaptations of the Roman Missal and to submit these likewise for the approval of the Holy See,[8]
- to provide translations of the biblical texts used in the liturgy (no. 391),
- to prepare high-quality translations of the liturgical texts, making sure that they are indeed faithful "translations" of the original Latin and not "adaptations" (no. 392),
- to approve the musical settings that are to be used during Mass (no. 393),
- to draw up a calendar for the local liturgical feasts (no. 394),
- to propose variants in the rites that, after being approved by the Apostolic See, can eventually be used to promote greater participation of the faithful in the liturgy of the Church (nos. 395–96).

In any case, care should be taken that these possible adaptations do not strengthen the autonomy of the particular churches to the detriment of their communion in the one Church of the Lord: the doctrine of the faith must be preserved, as well as the sacramental signs and the customs handed down by the unbroken liturgical tradition.

The new "General Instruction" concludes with a warning against those who would go so far as to injure the faith of believers by depriving them of the treasures contained in the Roman liturgy when it is celebrated in its integrity, that is, as defined in the Roman Missal (no. 399).

CONCLUSION

Unity, dignity, and recollection: these are the aims of the new "General Instruction on the Roman Missal". Christ's faithful who respect the Roman liturgy, the Church's patrimony, cannot help but rejoice to see that the Congregation for Divine Worship has reaffirmed these distinctive marks of Christian worship.

---

[8] The text of the GIRM gives a list of possible adaptations.

To be sure, some will be disappointed to discover that the Holy See has not taken into account the more or less felicitous customs that have been allowed to creep into the liturgy because they were thought to be more pastorally effective. Others will express their bitterness at finding that the Holy See has not followed up on their demands for a return to the pre-Vatican II liturgy. But should we not see in this a sign that Rome works in genuine freedom, without giving in to pressures of any sort, thus guaranteeing the complete objectivity of the liturgy?

CONCLUSION

"Nisi Dominus aedificaverit domum,
in vanum laboraverunt qui aedificant eam."

"Unless the Lord builds the house,
those who build it labor in vain."
(Psalm 126)

Never in the course of its history has the implementation of the Roman rite been the cause of so many difficulties and so many divisions as it has been since the Second Vatican Council.[1] Why is this? For two principal and obvious reasons:

- first, because a false concept of the liturgy has taken hold in the Western world: in the name of individual liberties, many have wanted to make the liturgy a place where everyone must be able to express himself freely so as to try to "fulfill himself" without any reference to the Absolute;
- then, because the episcopate in several countries—especially in France—is incapable of appreciating the liturgical disaster that is unfolding right before the eyes of the faithful and quite incapable also of taking clear and effective measures to remedy the situation. On this point, all the testimonies agree perfectly.[2]

[1] Studies dealing with the "liturgical crisis", or more simply with the liturgy, appear regularly. For the record we mention a few titles: Claude Barthe, *Reconstruire la liturgie* [Reconstructing the liturgy] (Paris: Éd. F. X. de Guibert, 1997); Alain Bandelier, *Simples questions sur la messe et la liturgie* [Simple questions about the Mass and the liturgy] (Tours: Éd. C.L.D., 1999); Lionel de Thorey, *Histoire de la Messe, de Grégoire-le-Grand à nos jours* [History of the Mass, from Gregory the Great to the present] (Paris: Éd. Perrin, 1994); Aidan Nichols, *Looking at the Liturgy* (San Francisco: Ignatius Press, 1996).

[2] Renée Casin, *Du rôle des évêques dans la restauration du tissu Chrétien* (Éd. Résiac, Monsûrs in Mayennes).

By their persistent silence, the diocesan authorities have made themselves accomplices; meanwhile Masses have been turned into "celebrations" during which the know-how (or the pretense of *savoir-faire*) of the participants has become more important than the true meaning of the Eucharist, a meaning bestowed by the liturgy itself. This slippery sense of the liturgy can be observed every Sunday in many, many parishes, where the cleverness of the celebrant (who has changed into a liturgical "animator") matters more than the commission that has been entrusted to him.

As a result of this new situation (even if one is not clearly aware of it at first), a merely human power has been substituted for the commission that the priest has received from the Church; the individual has arrogated to himself an arbitrary authority that replaces the power that had been conferred upon him and for which he has to render an account.

This is how the *exousia*-structure [authority-structure] of the liturgy has been abandoned more and more, and this is also how the essential character of liturgical worship has been lost: nowadays the rite is nothing more than an instrument that everyone is free to utilize as he wishes, that each celebrant can modify at a moment's notice, something that merely manifests his own commitment, his altruism, his philanthropy, his sympathy, his refined manners, his desire to please, his ambition to be involved in society. But the liturgical rite that has been modified in this way—subverted, rather—no longer transmits any of the Church's faith.

As a result of being immersed constantly in "liturgy lite" [*a-liturgie*], Catholics—and many priests in the first place—have completely lost sight of the fact that the important thing in celebrating the faith is not that worship be organized in a sympathetic way by sympathetic people; for the essential thing about the Church is not that she is made up of sympathetic people (which is still something very much to be desired, it is true), but rather that the liturgy can speak words of salvation and perform saving acts that man always needs and that he will always be incapable of providing for himself, as if it were something that came from within him.[3]

---

[3] This is paraphrasing Cardinal Ratzinger from *A New Song for the Lord: Faith in Christ and Liturgy Today*, trans. Martha M. Matesich (New York: Crossroad Publishing, 1997), pp. 75–76.

Yes, the essential thing about the liturgy is that it performs acts of which man has need.[4] And it can do this only if it is not bartered away [*aliénée*] by those who have received from the Church the mandate to implement it:

> The Sunday liturgy ... will come off badly if it [tries to compete with] show business. A pastor is not an emcee, and the liturgy is not a variety show. It will also come off badly if it wants to be a sort of engaging circle of friends. That can perhaps develop subsequent to the liturgy and out of encounters that have evolved there. But the liturgy itself must be more. It must become clear that a dimension of existence opens up here that we are all secretly seeking: the presence of that which cannot be made—theophany, mystery, and in it the approval of God, [who says that all is good and] reigns over being and is alone capable of making it good, so that it can be accepted by us in the midst of all the tensions and suffering.
>
> We have to find the happy medium between a ritualism in which the liturgical action is performed in an unintelligible and nonrelational manner by the priest and a craze for understandability which in the end dissolves the whole into the work of human beings and robs it of its Catholic dimension and of the objectivity of mystery. Through the community that believes and[, in believing,] understands, the liturgy must have its own luminosity which then becomes a call and hope for those who do not believe and therefore do not understand.[5]

In order to do this, it is urgent—no, it is imperative to put an end to the "calculated confusion" that has invaded the Mass, the result of which is that any ditty is considered to have the same value as a Gregorian chant, that any piece written for the occasion is as good as a piece by Bach or Couperin, that anything said by a celebrant or a liturgical commentator is worth as much as an official prayer of the Church, that anything the extraordinary ministers of the Eucharist may happen to do is the equivalent of a rite recognized by tradition.

---

[4] The essential thing is not that we should declare valid and legitimate the liturgy that we like, but rather that we learn to love the liturgy that the Church considers valid and lawful. From this perspective it would be necessary to reevaluate the position presently adopted by many charismatic movements who "design" their own liturgies and thus participate, willy-nilly, in the break-up of the Roman liturgy approved by the Church.

[5] Cardinal Ratzinger, *New Song*, p. 77.

For the true liturgical values handed down by tradition have been authenticated by the Magisterium, and wherever they are ignored, scoffed at, or distorted, it causes the faithful to forget how to prioritize and cherish what is worthwhile. And so, it all ends up being interchangeable, and Beauty as well as Truth are diluted by makeshift and temporary arrangements and become no more than subjective preferences, incapable of building up anything other than a subjective, individualistic faith that can support nothing but emotions.[6]

Now, only the liturgy as carried out according to the will of the Church can be an "open sesame" for an understanding of the faith, an antidote to boredom as well as to the doctrinal relativism that, as we now know, is the source of so many aberrations and confusions in the world today.

The liturgical question is most assuredly at the heart of the problems that confront the Church today. Consequently, the Roman

---

[6] "Prayer that is composed exclusively of words taken from the liturgy and carefully selected from among the most expressive passages, accustoms the child to model his own prayer on the prayer of the Church; it impresses upon his mind, at an early age, strong, sober formulas that are laden with meaning, founded squarely upon the Christian mysteries, and suited to inspire an aversion, both to that spiritual chattering, the *multiloquium* that the Incarnate Word forbade his disciples to indulge in [Mt 6:7], and also to an excess of emotion and sentiment in prayer.

"I do not hesitate to say that this latter danger is very great and very formidable. Why are so many Christians less pious as adults than in their childhood? One of the reasons, and not the least important, is that the manner in which they have been accustomed to pray has left them convinced that prayer is emotion and effusiveness. When they find, as they get bigger, that they are less capable of this emotion and effusiveness, they conclude that piety is not for them, that they are not geared for devotion. There are some who have the stubborn idea that the piety of priests and nuns depends on the fact that they have remained or become capable (by who knows what sorcery) of experiencing, every day and every hour of the day, the same emotions that they had at their First Holy Communion. One even encounters very saintly souls who are very close to God, but are desolate about not being 'pious', because a faulty education has imbued them with this same error. It is as though, at the age of thirty, someone regretted not having his baby teeth any more.

"Experience shows that this confusion between piety and emotion may well be denied a thousand times, but once implanted it is practically impossible to uproot; we must, then, prevent it from taking root, and the best, perhaps the only way of preventing it is liturgical education." V. A. Berto, *Le cénacle et le jardin* [The upper room and the garden] (Bouère: Éd. DMM, 2000).

liturgy, the history and importance of which we have examined, can no longer continue to present itself as something ephemeral that is constantly being revamped, constantly being pulled this way and that by groups of Catholics who endlessly declare whatever they please on the subject, since they have not studied it systematically.[7]

It is of the utmost urgency that the Roman liturgy become once more the durable luggage that lasts a lifetime; therefore it can no longer afford to be dissipated in the various sorts of "pastoral modifications" that it has been subjected to, but should instead concentrate on what is essential to it. For a liturgy that ceaselessly tries to please will always be a liturgy that is sure to lose its way among the mirages of Modernism and to establish nothing but an anarchy in worship that will result in ignorance, instability, disorder, and division.

What we need so urgently to rediscover today, therefore, is not so much an "invariable" liturgy as a "stable" liturgy: one that is stable in its orderly progression, in its dignity, in its expressiveness, in its prayers, in its singing, in the comportment of its participants, and chiefly in the attitudes of the celebrants.

For the priest is the one who, in "presiding" at the liturgy, sets the tone for the celebration. Now a priest who celebrates according to his mood, according to his tastes, according to the latest "fad" in local pastoral practice is not necessarily in tune with what the liturgy means for the Church, that is, for the people of God. We must therefore rediscover a liturgy that, as long as it lasts, obliges the priests and those who assist him to give up their subjectivity, so that the only thing that is manifested, in the fullness of truth, is the mystery of Christ.

Catholics who are described as "progressives" and who, with the complicity of the diocesan bureaucracies, have taken over Masses in the parishes almost everywhere, have ended up turning the liturgy into an inhibition-free zone [*un espace de libre-expression*].

This is a very serious mistake, and everyone knows very well—even if no one wants to say so officially—that it is the principal reason that the churches are presently deserted.

---

[7] Cf. SC 16.

As for the "conservatives", they can be found in places where the preconciliar liturgy is celebrated, precisely because they feel this need to have a stable liturgy; understandably, they cannot abide the hijacking of the rites by the "progressives", and so they blame the "Mass of Paul VI" for being a liturgical form that is inimical to the formality of worship. For them, everything in the current Mass is "optional", and we are dealing with an "evolving Mass" designed according to the good pleasure of the celebrant and his "liturgical teams", who choose what they want from the missal to devise a sort of liturgical synthesis. And this is unbearable to them, inasmuch as it involves a confiscation of what is sacred.

This last criticism leveled at the present Roman rite by the "conservatives" is no more on track than the manner in which the "progressives" currently treat the liturgy.

Indeed, you need only to open the Roman Missal in order to verify that it does not authorize any and all options. It simply authorizes, more than the old missal did, certain adaptations that may facilitate the task of those priests who perform their ministry under especially difficult conditions. The parish priest who has to celebrate a Mass in a hamlet deep in the Cordilleras of the Andes Mountains and notices that he has forgotten to bring his chasuble is not obliged to send an e-mail to his bishop to ask his permission (an indult) to celebrate the Eucharist anyway. But it goes without saying that this particular case is not at all commensurate with the case of many priests in our parishes who refuse to wear the prescribed liturgical vestments.[8]

---

[8] "This subordination of the minister, of the celebrant, to the *mysterium* which has been entrusted to him by the Church for the good of the whole People of God, should also find expression in the observance of the liturgical requirements concerning the celebration of the holy Sacrifice. These refer, for example, to dress, in particular to the vestments worn by the celebrant. Circumstances have of course existed and continue to exist in which the prescriptions do not oblige. We have been greatly moved when reading books written by priests who had been prisoners in extermination camps, with descriptions of Eucharistic Celebrations without the above-mentioned rules, that is to say, without an altar and without vestments. But although in those conditions this was a proof of heroism and deserved profound admiration, nevertheless in *normal conditions* to ignore the liturgical directives can be interpreted as a lack of respect towards the Eucharist, dictated perhaps by individualism or by an absence of a critical sense concerning current opinions, or by "*a certain lack of a*

It is therefore untrue to say that the present Roman liturgy demands that the celebrant "designs" his Mass or that he "works out" the form of his Eucharistic Celebration. Exactly the contrary is demanded by the entire history of the Roman liturgy, of which the last Council is yet a further stage.

That is why it is necessary to learn to implement the Roman liturgy in the spirit of tradition: a spirit of stability and continuity that is opposed to a spirit of immobility and sclerosis as well as to a spirit of fluctuation and rupture:

> The priest as minister, as celebrant, as the one who presides over the eucharistic assembly of the faithful, should have a special sense of the common good of the Church, which he represents through his ministry, but to which he must also be subordinate, according to a correct discipline of faith. He cannot consider himself a "proprietor" who can make free use of the liturgical text and of the sacred rite as if it were his own property, in such a way as to stamp it with his own arbitrary personal style. At times this latter might seem more effective, and it may better correspond to subjective piety; nevertheless, objectively it is always a betrayal of that union which should find its proper expression in the sacrament of unity.
>
> Every priest who offers the holy Sacrifice should recall that during this Sacrifice it is not *only* he with his community that is praying but the whole Church, which is thus expressing in this sacrament her spiritual unity, among other ways by the use of the approved liturgical text. To call this position "mere insistence on uniformity" would only show ignorance of the objective requirements of authentic unity, and would be a symptom of harmful individualism.[9]

The whole history of the Roman rite shows us that the great problems that have shaken the Church over the course of the centuries have always arisen when "individualism", in one form or another, had succeeded in infiltrating the liturgy. Now we are in an age when individualism has never been so pronounced, so powerful, so widespread.

---

spirit of faith" (John Paul II, *Letter to all the Bishops of the Church on the Mystery and Worship of the Holy Eucharist*, February 20, 1980, *Dominicae Cenae*).

[9] John Paul II, *On the Mystery and Worship of the Eucharist*, no. 12.

In any case, it should be understood that in a society that has a thirst for the absolute but that too often has lost its bearings, our Roman liturgy, faithful to the spirit that has enabled it to be established and consolidated throughout its history, must be vigilant so as to avoid individualism, if it wants to stop being like sand and become marble again (cf. Mt 7:24–27).[10]

---

[10] See also the *Instruction on Prayers for Obtaining Healing from God*, issued by the Congregation for the Doctrine of the Faith, November 23, 2000 [available in the library archives of www.ewtn.com].

APPENDIX I

WHAT IS THE "RITE OF SAINT PIUS V"?

Ever since Vatican II, some Catholics who are usually called "traditionalists" have been attached to a form of the Roman liturgy that was in more or less regular use from the sixteenth century—after the Council of Trent—up until Vatican II in the twentieth century.

This form of the liturgy conforms to the rules contained in a missal that was composed at the behest of Pope Saint Pius V; that is why, in "traditionalist" circles, the Roman Mass prior to the liturgical renewal following Vatican II is called the "Mass of Saint Pius V". The groups and movements that reject the present form of the liturgy claim the right to use regularly the form of the Roman rite that was described in the missal that was in use until 1972.

The problem is that this older form of the Roman liturgy—the one defined by the missal "of Saint Pius V"—is often described as "traditional". And so, misled by the frequent use of this term, which is actually unsuitable, many Catholics end up thinking that the "liturgical tradition" is to be identified exclusively with what was done before Vatican II, and consequently that the renewal of the Roman liturgy called for by the last Council was a betrayal of this "tradition" or else a break with it—a break that is unique in the entire history of the Church's liturgy.

For many people, therefore, defending the "Mass of Saint Pius V" has become a synonym for "defending the liturgical tradition" and what is most authentic in it.

However, a lot of them, in their defense of the old rites, forget

- that the rites exist in order to engage us, to seize us, to direct, and to change us; they are there to make us transmitters of what the liturgy signifies, and not simply custodians of the latest version of the Mass;
- that there is always a close and organic connection uniting the Church and her liturgy. Indeed, the Church can never have a

clear view of herself unless, at the same time, she takes a new look at the way in which she celebrates and manifests her faith. For, as John Paul II reiterated in his Letter *Dominicae Cenae* and then in his Letter *Vicesimus quintus annus* on the occasion of the twenty-fifth anniversary of the Constitution *Sacrosanctum Concilium*, "The Church not only acts but also expresses herself in the Liturgy and draws from the Liturgy the strength for her life." Now the view that the Church had of herself in the sixteenth century, which determined the main lines of her pastoral activity then, cannot be the same as in the twentieth century. We should consider that in 1570, when Saint Pius V decided on a printed edition of the Roman Missal, the Church had just been confronted with the Protestant Reformation, which disturbed a great part of Christian Europe; consider that at the moment when the Council of Trent was convening, the New World was still only a vague idea for many people. But we should also consider the fact that when Vatican II opened, the Church was obliged to take a stance vis-à-vis a world that was won over by the errors of modern ideologies and shaken by totalitarian regimes that enslaved entire populations. The manner in which the Church celebrated and witnessed to her faith through the liturgy could not, therefore, be the same in the twentieth century as in the sixteenth;

▪ that the rites codified in the sixteenth century had been appreciably subverted by being immersed, throughout the nineteenth century, in the currents that arose from Romanticism. It is well known that by aggravating the cult of the "self" and of personal feelings, which were more or less tinged with a Jansenist pessimism, Romanticism created a religion made up of sincere piety but devoid of any solid theological basis; it also fostered a theatrical manner of treating the liturgy, which was totally foreign to the sixteenth century. Now some of these defects would still be very much present in the twentieth century when, in most diocesan seminaries, future priests were trained in a manner of celebrating Mass that was more "juridical" than genuinely "traditional".[1]

---

[1] We must have the courage to ask ourselves whether the requests of many priests for laicization after Vatican II were a result of the conciliar *aggiornamento*, or whether they were not instead the legacy of the nineteenth century.

How did that missal come about which today is improperly said to be "of Saint Pius V"?

As part of a colloquium sponsored by the *Centre International d'Études Liturgiques* [the International Center for Liturgical Studies],[2] Dom Jean-Marie Pommarès, a monk of Flavigny (Diocese of Dijon) and member of the Congregation for Divine Worship and Sacramental Discipline, gave a conference on "The Origin of the Roman Missal in the Reform of Saint Pius V". We will take up again here several points of his presentation, in order to show what our Roman liturgy looked like before the appearance of the first printed missals.

How was a missal "designed" before the advent of printing?

This is the first question that one might ask; it is also the question that Dom Pommarès answers.

In order to meet the specific need of a cathedral, a parish, or a monastery, one called on a copyist to transcribe again by hand all the formulas necessary to celebrate Mass. How did he select the prayers that were to be recopied? Simply on the basis of local custom and the needs of that particular place.

There was a real freedom, therefore, in liturgical matters; but it was a regulated freedom, that is to say, it could be exercised validly and legitimately only within the framework of observance of the customary law.[3]

The copyist, therefore, copied out a model that he had available—not necessarily the best version, but the one that he judged to be the most practical—and interpolated into it, under the supervision of the competent ecclesiastical authority, the local customs that were deemed necessary. Then this new missal—a unique copy—was taken to the sanctuary for which it was made.

---

[2] C.I.E.L., *Actes du Colloque de Versailles*, novembre 1999 (84, avenue Aristide Briand, F92120 Montrouge).

[3] Dom Pommarès remarks: "Consulting collections of church laws and conciliar decrees brings to light only a small number of rules (a dozen or so over more than a thousand years!) dealing with particulars, and no regulations at all concerning the compilation of liturgical books."

Therefore it was not a matter of vigilantly guarding, in the first place, a single form of the Roman liturgy, just as it was not a matter of allowing the liturgy to fall into anarchy. The customary law, in effect, kept the liturgy on track.

Nor was it a matter of comparing missals with one another; if two works were found that differed on certain points, they were regarded indulgently, taking into account their respective destinations, the use that was made of them, and the difficulties in producing them.

The first printed Roman Missals

With the advent of printing, the manner of "making" a Roman Missal would change. The first Roman Missal was published, it seems, around 1470 in Constance, in southern Germany. Soon after that, other works began to be circulated.

It should be noted that these printed missals display a certain number of variants: although they are minimal in the "Roman Canon"—the one Eucharistic Prayer in the Roman liturgy of that period—they are more numerous in the readings and in the offertory and communion prayers.

Still, a desire for a greater unity was felt; in response there would be a decree of the Lateran Council in 1515. Pope Julius II determined that books dealing with faith and morals would have to be approved by the bishop before being published. The Roman Missal, therefore, had to be approved officially before it could be employed in celebrating Mass.

In 1539 a Roman Missal was published in Paris: it was officially approved by Archbishop Jean du Bellay—proof that the episcopal prerogative in liturgical matters was beginning to be asserted clearly.

The Council of Trent

At the time when the Council of Trent was convened, in 1545, few diocesan bishops actually made it a point to verify the contents of the missals that they used; a certain "pluralism" remained, therefore. It would not be until 1562 that the Council Fathers decided to make a list of the "abuses" that they found in the liturgy. Among them were additions made to the *Gloria*, unworthy or dubious manners of celebrating Mass, differences in rites from one place to the next, some prefaces of suspicious origin, and the fact that during the offertory the not-yet-consecrated bread was called *"hostia sancta et immaculata"*.[4]

In September 1562, a plan for unifying the liturgy was approved, but there was no talk of revising the Roman Missal. The matter was placed in the hands of the Supreme Pontiff: the Council of Trent thus recognized the supreme power of the Pope in matters of liturgical legislation, a recognition that would furthermore be reaffirmed clearly in the Constitution *Sacrosanctum Concilium* of the Second Vatican Council.[5]

The work of Saint Pius V

A Dominican friar, Fr. Michele Ghislieri, became pope in 1565 and took the name of Pius V. The new Pontiff appointed experts to work on compiling a single Roman Missal.

It is known that these experts worked essentially on the basis of various missals that were preserved in the Vatican Library.

They succeeded in compiling a Roman Missal that would be published in 1570, accompanied by the Bull promulgating it,[6] dated July 14 of the same year.

As Rev. Fr. Dom Pommarès has clearly shown in his study, the liturgy codified in the Roman Missal of 1570—a liturgy that the "traditionalist" movements call "Tridentine" or "traditional", or even "the Mass of Saint Pius V"—is, at least in certain respects, more a liturgy of the thirteenth century ornamented with sixteenth-century pomps than it is a "traditional" liturgy, that is to say, a liturgy with a form approximating the original liturgy of the early Church.

The "new" Roman Missal, as published by Pius V, plainly reflects the concerns of that period:

---

[4] Traces of this way of describing the host would be found in the liturgy celebrated before Vatican II; in the prayer beginning *Suscipe* that begins the offertory ritual, the celebrant used to say, *"Hanc immaculatam hostiam"* [This spotless host/victim].

[5] See SC 22.

[6] The Bull is entitled *Quo primum tempore*.

- promoting liturgical unity in the Christian West,
- guarding the faithful from errors that might creep into the official prayer of the Church from the currents of thought originating in Protestantism or Anglicanism,
- affirming the authority of the Supreme Pontiff in matters concerning the organization of rites connected with the celebration of a sacrament.

The Roman Missal promulgated by Pius V is a response to a very precise historical situation—a "Western" turn of events, rather—that saw the emergence of modern thought but did not foresee the new questions that would be raised by the spread of Christianity in the newly discovered territories.

Was the missal promulgated by Pius V used in the dioceses?

It is wrong to think that the Roman liturgy, as codified in the missal promulgated by Pius V, was followed faithfully everywhere. The study of Dom Pommarès testifies that many dioceses took no notice of the "Tridentine Missal".

The example of Paris, on this point, is eloquent: a missal published in 1648 (less than a century, then, after the appearance of the Roman Missal promulgated by Pius V) bears the title of *Missalis parisiensis cum missali romano ex decreto sacrosancti concilii tridentini restituto* [Parisian missal, revised according to the Roman missal by decree of the sacred Tridentine Council]. We actually have here a "Parisian Missal" supplemented by the "Roman Missal" as revised by Trent. With regard to the liturgy in Paris, seventeenth-century Catholics proved to be Parisian first—and then eventually Roman.

In 1654, again in the Diocese of Paris, a new missal was published. This time it really was a "Parisian Missal" corrected according to the "Tridentine Missal".

The appearance of such a work demonstrates that the diocesan authority, after having bowed to the Roman directives concerning the liturgy, asserted later on its power and independence.

In the eighteenth century, each diocese published its own liturgical books, in complete insubordination with regard to the Holy

See; as a result some liturgies were more or less tainted with Jansenism.

The church in France would have to wait for the coming of Dom Prosper Guéranger [1805–1875] and the publication of his studies on the liturgy to witness the end of the anarchy that prevailed in the Roman rite.

Conclusion

The history of the Roman liturgy—if one is at all willing to study it with a certain objectivity—demonstrates what the work of the Council of Trent, and then of Pope Pius V, consisted of.

The volume that is referred to as "the missal of Saint Pius V" defines all the elements that go into celebrating the Eucharist according to the Roman rite; it is indeed a "Roman Missal". But is this missal "traditional"? Is the liturgy that it defined more "traditional" than some other?

The project of Saint Pius V never was to issue a "traditional missal", but rather to bring about a unification of the liturgy, given the numerous variations found in the Roman rite[7] before the discovery of printing.

---

[7] Among these variants of the primitive Roman rite, we might mention the rite of Aquileia, which disappeared in 1596. This rite was in use at Milan as well until the sixteenth century. At that time, the parishes of this diocese that had refused to adopt the Milanese liturgy were "authorized" by Rome to use the missal published by Saint Pius V; cf. Arcdale A. King, *Liturgies anciennes* (Tours: Éditions Mame, 1961).

APPENDIX II

BLAME THE COUNCIL?[1]

The first form of the Eucharistic liturgy that I can remember is the one that is referred to nowadays as "the Mass of Saint Pius V". Before the Second Vatican Council, nobody could have imagined that this form would ever change. For the "people in the pew", as they say, the manner of celebrating the Eucharist seemed as untouchable as the Bible itself. Scripture was sacred, so was the liturgy of the Mass—to the point where many imagined that the rites that they saw performed in church on Sunday had never varied over the course of the centuries.

Then came the Second Vatican Council. At that time I was organist in my parish.

The conciliar texts on the liturgy? I don't remember that any priest took the trouble to bring them to the attention of the faithful. On the contrary, I remember that one Sunday, just before beginning the "High Mass", the pastor of the parish came up to the choir loft and, in front of the singers who were assembled and ready to sing the *Asperges me*, said to me: "As of this Sunday, we won't sing the *Credo* in Latin any more. Furthermore, we will have new songs in French [i.e., the vernacular] so that everybody can understand them. Here are a few of the pieces that you will have to know for next Sunday."

That was the rather abrupt fashion in which the "Council's liturgical renewal" got started in many a parish.

Nothing really shocking, at first. The musical compositions that were introduced into the liturgy sometimes seemed odd, that's all. It was something new: well, why not?

[1] This essay was written at the request of Fr. Héry, a priest at the parish of Saint-Nicolas-du-Chardonnet in Paris.

However, after a few weeks, the proliferation of songs that no one knew was followed by innovations in the manner of celebrating that were more disastrous: the altar was replaced by a table that was brought forward to the Communion rail, while the latter was ruthlessly removed.

As for the celebrant, he felt that he was invested with a new authority: he was in charge of implementing the liturgical "reform" and explaining it. In his hands, the microphone became the most important thing in the worship service.

All of these changes were introduced with drum rolls and flourishes as part of a general euphoria that is expressed in the bishops' statements of that period: "before", everything was rigid; "now", everything was going to come to life. Enthusiastic Catholics were going to fill the churches, and the Sunday duty would become a universal cause for joy.[2]

Now, the result of these modifications that took place in the liturgy, which were imposed with military efficiency, was gradually to give the impression to the faithful that the Mass had been handed over to a team of iconoclasts: the recollection, stability, and seriousness of the celebrations were replaced with agitation, contingencies, and entertainment. Before the eyes of the helpless parishioners, the general atmosphere of the liturgy was debased.

Like anyone else, I began to ask myself a few questions: Did all these innovations that were being introduced into the liturgy by way of "clerical" authority make any sense? Did they have a purpose? If so, what? It was not difficult to admit that certain "adjustments" in the liturgy were called for; but still, was it necessary to go so far as to eliminate expressions of the sacred that over the centuries had become, so to speak, the patrimony of the Catholic Church?

I noticed that the Masses celebrated in the neighboring parishes were all suffering from the same malady of change, which allowed me to conclude that orders were coming from "higher up" to put a new face on the liturgy. Now, what was being done everywhere "in the name of the Council" seemed more like pottering around than like the implementation of a carefully considered program.

---

[2] *La réforme liturgique: décisions et directives d'application* [The liturgical reform: decisions and practical directives] (Paris: Éditions du Centurion, 1964).

I also verified that the feelings that I experienced with regard to the "new look" of the liturgy being imposed by the priests—especially by the young assistants—were shared by other Catholics: from one Sunday to the next, in the parish churches, the congregations were becoming more and more sparse.

By sheer coincidence, my studies led me one day to the Abbey of Solesmes. There, the liturgy that I was privileged to participate in (for one can participate in the liturgy even by silence) made me discover a completely different world: a world of reverence, recollection, and beauty—a world that I knew I could no longer find in most rural and urban parishes.

Surely, the Benedictines of Solesmes must have rejected the Council so as to be able to preserve the solemnity of their monastic liturgy. Well, that wasn't the case at all! I inquired and learned that the monks were applying the Council to the letter: the Mass as it was celebrated at Solesmes was quite in conformity with what the Church had asked for through the official documents of Vatican II.

So I had to face up to the evidence: the same conciliar Constitution on the Liturgy and the same Roman Missal that had been revised following Vatican II were giving rise to different interpretations and contrary applications. Here, they continued to celebrate in Latin and to sing Gregorian chant, to use incense and the liturgical vestments. There, they gladly omitted (or even forbade!) these elements, which conferred upon the Roman rite its dignity and specific character. Here, they were preserving what the Church was asking us to preserve; there, they were selling off monstrances.

I decided, therefore, to study the official documents concerning the liturgy: the Constitution *Sacrosanctum Concilium* and the "General Introduction on the Roman Missal". After reading these texts, only one conclusion was possible: at the heart of the Church, certain individuals, claiming the authority of a Council whose documents they surely had never studied, were acting—whether deliberately or not—to ruin the Roman liturgy and to scatter the faithful.

To be sure, the Constitution on the Liturgy could give rise to various interpretations, depending on the particular conditions that the Church met with throughout the world. But was it not the responsibility of the diocesan pastors in the first place to indicate clearly to the priests and to the faithful what was the "right" way of interpreting and applying the conciliar directives? Well, there was a deafening silence.

The revised Roman Missal itself described in the clearest way how the Eucharist should be celebrated: a whole chapter set forth in detail the "typical form" of the liturgy.[3] Now, this form was never observed in parishes; it seems that it was never even wanted by the bishops who still do not observe it today, inasmuch as they are unacquainted with it.

At about the same time when so many novelties, unintended by the Council, were being introduced into the liturgy, a conference took place in Strasbourg: a meeting of the "Silent of the Church", led by Pierre Debray. There was a crowd and, in a peaceful manner, many voices were raised to deplore the erroneous fashion in which the conciliar liturgy had been implemented.

The same impetus produced several associations of Catholics. Among them was Una Voce,[4] the original purpose of which was to work for the preservation and promotion of the Latin Mass, Gregorian chant, and sacred art.

We should note that there was no question then of returning to the form of the Roman liturgy that had been in use before Vatican II. What the faithful wanted, quite simply, was that someone should put a stop to the orchestrated deviations and the desacralization that were threatening the integrity of the liturgy: what the faithful demanded, was that the bishops take responsibility and truly carry out their mission as "guardians and promoters" of the liturgy.[5] Well, these grievances scarcely received a hearing, and the response to the just demands of the faithful (if there was any response at all) came in a dilatory fashion.[6]

What was going on during that time in the diocesan seminaries, where, according to the Council, instruction on the liturgy was

---

[3] See the "General Instruction on the Roman Missal," chapter 4, A, articles 82–141.

[4] Una Voce is located at 3, rue Lamandé, Paris XVIIe, France.

[5] See the Dogmatic Constitution *Lumen Gentium*, art. "25" [*sic*; that article is about infallibility; actually the reference is to articles 26–27].

[6] Jacques de Ricaumont, *Visites à messieurs les curés de Paris* [Visits to the Reverend Fathers of Paris] (Paris: Éditions de la Table Ronde, 1981).

supposed to be a priority?[7] In a book entitled *La blessure* [The wound],[8] Jean-Pierre Dickès has given a thoroughgoing account of what was done in the seminary of Issy-les-Moulineaux. Unfortunately, this was not an isolated case: what happened at Issy happened also in practically all the major seminaries in France.[9]

In the immediate aftermath of the Council, it must be said, the seminaries were the centers in which the disintegration of the Roman liturgy was organized, whether officiously or officially. The old rite (called "the Mass of Saint Pius V") was forbidden there. So be it. But so was the revised Roman rite! From then on it was expected of the seminarians to form "teams" responsible for taking turns "preparing" the Mass, which meant, in reality, introducing new songs of a socio-political tinge,[10] inventing new prayers and even composing Eucharistic Prayers.[11]

The seminarian who wanted the Mass to be celebrated worthily and as it ought to be was immediately accused of not having "an open mind", of being "old-fashioned", and, to put it bluntly, of being a "fundamentalist" [*"intégriste"*]. Well, when this last [politically charged] word was hurled at him, the seminarian had only one recourse: leave the seminary so as not to lose his faith and his health. For he knew that, from then on, he would not be admitted to Holy Orders.

It was by acting in this way in the parishes and the seminaries that most of the priests who were appointed to key positions by the bishops swelled the ranks of those who were disappointed in Vatican II in the 1970s.[12] Isn't it painful to find out that, during that time, not one bishop spoke up to denounce officially a process

[7] Cf. SC 16, 17, 18.

[8] Éditions Clovis, 1998.

[9] Patrick Chalmel, *Écône ou Rome: le choix de Pierre* [Écône (Switzerland) or Rome: the choice of Peter] (Paris: Éditions Fayard, 1990).

[10] *Cercle Jean XXIII de Nantes* [John XXIII Association of the city of Nantes, France], Jean and Colette Guichard, *Liturgie et lutte des classes, symbolique et politique* [Liturgy and class struggle: symbolism and politics] (Paris: Éditions de L'Harmattan, 1976). This work includes an interesting bibliography.

[11] Pierre Lassieur, *Les curés rouges: les prêtres et la politique* [The Red pastors: priests and politics] (Paris: Éditions Grancher, 1997).

[12] Cf. Jean Bourdarias, *Les évêques de France et le Marxisme: histoire d'une connivence* [The bishops of France and Marxism: history of connivance] (Paris: Éditions Fayard, 1991).

that was leading to what Paul VI called "the self-destruction of the Church"?[13]

It is said today that the bishops could not speak because they were in the grasp of very powerful diocesan structures. It is true that the situation was difficult, but, given a modicum of courage, some bishops could have and should have not only spoken, but also acted[14]—acted by systematically refusing to appoint to important positions in their dioceses those priests who had a reputation for being the most "progressive" and the most "anti-Roman" among the local clergy.[15]

How many Catholic laymen who had the courage to speak up and denounce the liturgical and catechetical abuses that they had witnessed or suffered were reduced to silence by the very ones who ought to have listened to them and responded to their legitimate demands? Yet, in the postconciliar situation, the diocesan authorities "courageously" preferred to lay the blame on those who were sounding the alarm to avert the liturgical disaster, instead of on those who were setting the fires.

After the Council, many Catholics did not reject the renewal of the Roman liturgy: they only rejected the proliferation of haphazard celebrations that were offered "in the spirit of Vatican II", but that were in reality nothing but falsifications of the liturgy defined in the revised Roman Missal.[16]

Amid this collapse of the liturgy, Archbishop Marcel Lefebvre appeared to many people at that time as the sole bishop capable of resisting what seemed more and more like a universal devastation.

Nevertheless, I have reason to believe that his battle, which was completely justified at the time, eventually went awry; his error would be to lead Catholics to "take refuge" in the so-called "Tridentine" liturgy, instead of offering them the chance to participate

---

[13] Paul Vigneron, *Histoire des crises du clergé français contemporain* [History of the contemporary crises of the French clergy] (Paris: Éditions Téqui, 1976).

[14] André Frossard, *Le parti de Dieu: lettre aux évêques* [God's party: a letter to the bishops] (Paris: Éditions Fayard, 1992).

[15] François-Georges Dreyfus, *Des évêques contre le pape* [Some bishops against the Pope] (Paris: Éditions Grasset, 1985).

[16] Maurice Angibaud, *Fidèle ou infidèle au Concile* [Faithful or unfaithful to the Council] (Hauteville, CH: Éditions du Parvis, 1976).

in the current liturgy celebrated in a fully "traditional" form, with the Latin language and Gregorian chant.

Why was this an "error"? For five reasons, at least:

1. The "Tridentine" liturgy, strictly speaking, is no more specifically "traditional" than any other. It resulted from a compilation of several missals that were influenced as much by the Gallican rites as by the rite that was in use at Rome; hence it constitutes only one stage of the Roman rite, which includes answers to the problems that the Church had to resolve in the sixteenth century.

2. The decorum with which the rite "of Saint Pius V" was celebrated until the Council was derived more from a religious sentimentality inherited mainly from the nineteenth century—at least in France—than from the authentic Roman tradition.[17]

3. Numerous elements of the "Tridentine" liturgy that are supposed to be "traditional" date back to more recent periods (the fourteenth, fifteenth, and nineteenth centuries) in which the accent had been on a personal or subjective piety.

4. When celebrated in its solemn form, the "Tridentine" liturgy appears to be the result of an artificial combination of the part that is read by the celebrant and the part that is sung by the schola and the congregation.

5. The Roman rite, as revised following the Council of Trent, developed in a context that led, especially from the eighteenth century on, to a view of the liturgy that was often more "juridical" than truly "traditional".

For these reasons it is possible today to adhere to the idea that the renewal of the Roman liturgy called for by Vatican II was necessary.

To affirm this, however, is not the same as admitting that what is done today in practically all parishes—at least in France—is right and legitimate.[18]

If, immediately after Vatican II, care had been taken to treat the liturgy as the Council really wanted it to be treated, then surely the

---

[17] Cf. Dom Cuthbert Johnson, *Prosper Guéranger (1805–1875), a Liturgical Theologian: An Introduction to His Liturgical Writings and Work* (Rome: Pontificio Ateneo S. Anselmo, 1984).

[18] Denis Crouan, *The Liturgy Betrayed* (San Francisco: Ignatius Press, 2000) and *The Liturgy after Vatican II* (Ignatius Press, 2001).

problems would have been less serious: the renewal of the Roman rite would have been accepted by most Catholics. It would have been accepted all the more easily, given the fact that, when the "current" Mass is celebrated in the "traditional" way—that is, in Latin; that is, on a real altar and not on the sorts of crates that have been installed in many churches; that is, with reverence and recollection; that is, by priests wearing genuine liturgical vestments and not some kind of formless shift (which one famous theologian used to call a "pre-natal alb");[19] that is, with a tasteful amount of pomp and splendor (why not?)—few Catholics would be able to tell the difference between the preconciliar Roman rite and the postconciliar Roman rite.

There's just one thing: to my knowledge, no bishop in France ever sought to promote this "traditional" form of the current Mass. All requests for this kind of liturgy ran up against staunch refusals in the name of a certain "pastoral approach", which today often produces *kitsch*, after having criticized "triumphalism" during the 1970s.

Instead of acting like genuine guardians of the Church's liturgy, the bishops undeniably have yielded the powers and responsibilities that they had in matters of divine worship to pressure groups—publishing houses, liturgical planning committees, "involved" lay people—who transform the liturgy according to their whims, without paying the least bit of attention to what is clearly prescribed by the Roman Missal.

Let us not disguise the truth: presently, in France at the very least, it is no longer those in charge of the Church who direct and supervise the liturgy, but rather certain publishing houses, working in tandem with groups of Catholics selected in the dioceses to be promoters of the haphazard celebrations that are imposed on parishes across the board.[20]

[19] Louis Bouyer, *Le métier de théologien: entretiens avec Georges Daix* [The theologian's calling: conversations with Georges Daix] (Paris: Éditions France-Empire, 1979).

[20] The Sunday Masses broadcast on [French] national television are revealing and suggest that there has been a "Gallic-French" rereading of the conciliar documents. Living in Alsace, I am that much more aware of it, since on Sundays I can turn on the Swiss and German channels to see how they treat the current liturgy in those countries: absolutely nothing in common with the French "miserabilism" [a *faux*-poverty in religious matters], which, furthermore, extends far beyond the liturgical realm!

The crisis that the liturgy has been going through since the end of the last Council cannot be resolved, therefore, until those in high places decide to provide serious liturgical formation in the seminaries; until they put a stop to the spread of the "liturgical planning magazines" that are invading the sacristies and the rectories, to the point where they have more influence on the priests than the missal itself; and until the pressure groups accept the fact that the Latin and Gregorian form of the current liturgy can have its rightful place in the parishes.

Does it have to be said? As a theologian and as president of an international association created to promote the precise application of the principles contained in the liturgical Constitution *Sacrosanctum Concilium*, I wrote in 1999 to the Assembly of the Bishops of France to request that concrete steps be taken to foster the current liturgy in its Latin and Gregorian form. Eventually, I received the reply that such a demand could not be considered, since the Latin and Gregorian Mass should be viewed only as an exception in the present situation.

It is clear, therefore, that in high places no one wants to implement the Council: no one is seeking to provide for Catholics the liturgical form to which they are entitled. It is quite clear, also, that under these circumstances, the "old" Roman liturgy is the only thing left that can guarantee the solemnity, the dignity, and the objectivity of a Eucharistic celebration: qualities that a growing number of Catholics are yearning for.

Under these circumstances, one must admit that the divisions at the heart of the Church over questions of rite still have some great days ahead. These divisions cannot be settled, at any rate, by parsimoniously granting, in a few dioceses, an indult to celebrate according to the "old" rite, by virtue of the Motu Proprio *Ecclesia Dei adflicta*, while at the same time authorizing all sorts of capricious variations on the "new" rite.[21]

---

[21] In a letter dated May 12, 2000, to the President of the Association *Pro Liturgia*, Bishop Bernard Lagoutte, Secretary General of the French Bishops' Conference, writes, "Although it is true, for example, that few congregations nowadays are in a position to celebrate the Mass in Latin with Gregorian chant, there are nonetheless some churches where the Ordo of Paul VI is strictly followed."

The present problem, therefore, is not so much concerned with the form that the Roman rite should have, as with the meaning that should be given to the liturgy (inasmuch as it is the celebration of the mysteries of the faith) and, at the same time, with the importance that is assigned to the preserving of the sacred, which is the basis for our relationship with God.

The rite is not the liturgical celebration itself. A celebration can be equivocal, even when the rite is followed perfectly, and, in some cases, a celebration can be perfect, even though it is not possible to follow the rite perfectly. Surely Archbishop Lefebvre would not have been one to contradict this statement, since he knew, as Archbishop of Dakar, that the missionaries were often obliged to take some liberties with the rites when it was a question of making sure that the faithful would have their celebration of the Eucharist in the middle of the African wilderness.

The difficulties that have been encountered over the last forty years in implementing the liturgical renewal called for by Vatican II must not make us lose sight of the fact that, ultimately, the goal remains fidelity to the revised Roman Missal. Why?

First, because the liturgy is the Church's affair, and not the private reserve of our feelings, our memories, and our personal preferences.[22] In the twentieth century, the Church judged it necessary to revise the Roman liturgy once more; we must conform to this decision. It is a question of trust, of fidelity, and, in a word, of "catholicity".

Then, because we have no reason to hold the current liturgy responsible for the errors committed by those who were in charge of implementing this same liturgy, we should always carefully distinguish what Vatican II called for, and what the current missal prescribes, from what certain individuals have wanted to make out of the Council and the Roman Missal: it is enough to open the current Roman Missal and study the rules that it gives for celebrating Mass to see that what the Church is asking for is simply incommensurate with what one ordinarily sees in the parishes—not to mention the Eucharistic celebrations broadcast on Sunday by TV, which in most cases are only simulations of the liturgy.

---

[22] This was taught very clearly by Fr. Victor-Alain Berto, who in 1963 was the theologian for Archbishop Marcel Lefebvre for the second session of the Second Vatican Council.

Finally, because we must remember that no earthly liturgy is perfect: not one that is celebrated according to the Roman Missal published during the pontificate of Saint Pius V, any more than one that is celebrated according to the Roman Missal published under the pontificate of Paul VI. If one finds defects in the current Roman liturgy—and there are some—one can find just as many in the liturgy that was in use before the Second Vatican Council.

In conclusion, with your permission, I would like to make two requests. One is addressed to the Catholics who are called "traditionalists", the other to the diocesan bishops.

I would ask the first group not to consider the "rite of Saint Pius V" as the sole bearer of the liturgical tradition: with the liturgy, the authentic "tradition" cannot be reduced to a previous state of the liturgy within the memory of the most elderly believers.

I would ask the second group to become once more the true guardians and promoters of the Church's liturgy. I would ask them to have the courage to admit that the vast majority of the liturgies that are presently carried out in the parishes in the dioceses for which they are responsible do not conform to what was called for by Vatican II. Indeed, what official document says that the Church has done away with liturgical vestments? The possibility of kneeling? Latin? Gregorian chant? Incense? Reverence? Recollection? Which official text mentions an obligation to celebrate "facing the people"? Where do we read that "liturgical committees" can impose upon entire parishes the whims suggested by "liturgical planning" magazines? Where do we read that the celebrant has the right to add, to omit, or to modify anything whatsoever in the liturgy?[23] Nowhere.

And yet that is what is happening. Worse still, this has become a habit, a "norm". Now we know that these bad habits, the results of disobedience as well as of a certain lack of formation, are at the root of the falsification of the current liturgy; and this widespread falsification is what has provoked a reaction among the faithful, causing them to reject the liturgy called for by the last Council.

Allow me, in conclusion, to quote an excerpt from the preface of a recent work published by Cardinal Ratzinger, which is dedicated to the liturgy:

[23] SC 22.

In 1918, the year that Guardini published his book, the liturgy was rather like a fresco. It had been preserved from damage, but it had been almost completely overlaid with whitewash by later generations. In the Missal from which the priest celebrated, the form of the liturgy that had grown from its earliest beginnings was still present, but, as far as the faithful were concerned, it was largely concealed beneath instructions for and forms of private prayer.

The fresco was laid bare by the Liturgical Movement and, in a definitive way, by the Second Vatican Council. For a moment its colors and figures fascinated us.

But since then the fresco has been endangered by climatic conditions as well as by various restorations and reconstructions. In fact, it is threatened with destruction, if the necessary steps are not taken to stop these damaging influences.

Of course, there must be no question of its being covered with whitewash again, but what is imperative is a new reverence in the way we treat it, a new understanding of its message and its reality, so that rediscovery does not become the first stage of irreparable loss.[24]

[24] Cardinal Joseph Ratzinger, *The Spirit of the Liturgy* (San Francisco: Ignatius Press, 2000), pp. 7–8.

APPENDIX III

GREGORIAN CHANT IN TODAY'S LITURGY

A talk given at the International Colloquium
on Gregorian Chant in Brussels

(November 25, 2000)

Your Eminence,
Reverend Fathers and Sisters,
Ladies and Gentlemen,
Dear Friends of Gregorian chant,

More than thirty years ago, the Second Vatican Council officially gave pride of place to Gregorian chant in liturgical functions.[1]

The reason that we are gathered today in Brussels is to study
how, in circumstances that are not always favorable, we can give to
Gregorian chant this place of honor that the Church wishes it to
have in the present Roman liturgy.

To do this, we will examine two major themes:

1. The liturgical renewal called for by Vatican II, and
2. Gregorian chant in the context of today's liturgy.

I. The liturgical renewal called for by Vatican II

Those who lived through the experience of Vatican II can testify:
this Council, convened by John XXIII, then continued and completed by Paul VI, raised high hopes. For the Council Fathers who

---

[1] SC 116.

were gathered at Saint Peter's in Rome, it was a matter of assessing a quickly spreading crisis that was convulsing the Church.[2]

For all Catholic believers, it was a matter of taking a stance with regard to a crisis in the modern world, a crisis that had its roots in the late Middle Ages, the fruits of which matured during the Renaissance and were gathered and tasted during the seventeenth and eighteenth centuries.

Paradoxically, as the Second Vatican Council opened, this crisis was still unnoticed by the great majority of Catholics. Indeed, everything in the Church at that time gave the impression that it was running smoothly. The liturgy, especially, could fool you: well-regulated ceremonies, as orderly as music paper, never deviated from the prescribed rituals and unfolded—at least in France—in a setting of pomp and splendor that still answered to the demands of religious sentiments inherited from the nineteenth century.[3]

But another reality had given cause for alarm: the number of vocations. We will simply cite two statistics: from 1963 to 1971, in France, the number of seminarians declined from 732 to 77 (a decrease of 89 percent), while the number of priestly ordinations fell from 573 to 237 (a decrease of 59 percent). And during the same time, many of the clergy were asking to be laicized.[4]

The Church was forced to realize, therefore, that things were no longer going as well as one might have thought or pretended: although external appearances might suggest that the institution was running well, thanks to a clergy that was seemingly disciplined and motivated, within ecclesiastical circles one could infer that there were increasingly severe tensions, sometimes even outright feuds.

By organizing the Council, therefore, John XXIII was asking Catholics, both clergy and lay people, to open their eyes: it was no longer a matter of ignoring the reality; it was necessary to oblige the Church, confronted as she was with modernity, to take a good look at herself, whether or not that was pleasant, whether or not it was easy.

---

[2] *La réforme liturgique: decisions et directives d'application* (Paris: Éditions du Centurion, 1964).

[3] Cardinal Joseph Ratzinger, *The Spirit of the Liturgy* (San Francisco: Ignatius Press, 2000).

[4] Georges Suffert, *Tu es Pierre* [You are Peter] (Paris: Éditions de Fallois, 2000).

The primary role of Vatican II, therefore, would be to study how to chart a better course for the Church's involvement, so that she might respond to the great challenges of the contemporary world, without ceasing, however, to manifest her fidelity to Christ and without diluting her identity.

It is within this difficult context of *aggiornamento* that we must situate the principle of restoring the liturgy. Indeed, the renewal of the Roman rite called for by Vatican II can be understood only if one considers the close and organic connection that unites the Church and her liturgy. At the opening of the Council, the Church therefore could not hope to take a good, clear look at herself unless, at the same time, she took a new look at the way in which she was celebrating and manifesting her faith.[5]

It was from this perspective, then, that the Council Fathers were invited to lay the foundations for a renewal of the Roman liturgy that would be obligatory for all as soon as the official books could be published that would allow the principles to be implemented.

As a preliminary to any reworking of the Roman rites, the Council Fathers recalled that

- the liturgy must not be susceptible to manipulation by the faithful, whether clerics or laymen;[6]
- in carrying out the sacred rites, each participant must know how to perform his own duties, doing only what he has to do and all that he has to do;[7]
- in the liturgy, changes can be made only if they are legitimate and truly helpful;[8]
- in the Roman rite, the Latin language must be preserved and Gregorian chant must have pride of place.[9]

---

[5] As Pope John Paul II has reminded us in his Letter *Dominicae Cenae* [art. 13] and then in his Letter *Vicesimus quintus annus* [art. 4] on the twenty-fifth anniversary of the Constitution *Sacrosanctum Concilium*, "The Church not only acts but also expresses herself in the Liturgy and draws from the Liturgy the strength for her life".

[6] SC 22.

[7] SC 28.

[8] SC 23.

[9] SC 36; 114–17.

Now, once Vatican II was over, these principles would often be forgotten or ignored, inasmuch as they seem to contradict the surrounding culture in the West,[10] which exalts the omnicompetence of each individual to the point of glorifying reason and deifying man.

That is to say that such a culture is hostile to every form of liturgy that places faith on a higher plane than mere reason[11] and sets God above the individual.[12]

Consequently, the liturgical renewal envisaged by Vatican II ran into a barricade [*une fin de non-recevoir*, an estoppel]. In 1966, Pope Paul VI was obliged to warn Catholics against a widespread process of desacralization that was aimed right at the liturgy. He called for an end to unauthorized liturgical experiments and demanded the preservation of everything in the Mass that expresses the sacred. Nothing more should interfere with the implementation of the rites defined in the official liturgical works that would appear after the Council.[13]

But the Pope already seemed like a "voice crying in the wilderness": his appeals were scarcely heeded, since those were the days when everybody was inventing liturgies, which above all else were supposed to be attractive, congenial, convivial, and entertaining; worship was degraded, then, to the point of being nothing more than "a bad show that was not worth going to".[14] Those were the days when many Catholics felt like they were attending a garage sale of the treasures of the Roman liturgy.[15]

By the 1970s, many Catholics seem to have forgotten already that, although the Church envisaged a new harmonious arrangement of the Roman rituals, it was so as to remind us that the liturgy exists in order to engage us, to direct and change us; it exists in order to make us the conveyors of what it signifies, and not the custodians of the last form that it has assumed.

---

[10] This is a culture inherited from the Enlightenment philosophers and grafted onto seventeenth-century religious currents that were hardly favorable to the Church.

[11] Cf. SC 10.

[12] Georges Suffert, *Tu es Pierre*.

[13] Address to the *Consilium ad exsequendam Constitutionem de Sacra Liturgia* [the "Concilium" charged with carrying out the directives of the Constitution on the Sacred Liturgy], October 13, 1966.

[14] Cardinal Godfried Danneels.

[15] Cf. Cardinal Joseph Ratzinger, *The Feast of Faith* (San Francisco: Ignatius Press, 1986).

Although the Council intended to return to simpler forms of celebrating Mass and the sacraments, it was not in order to impoverish the liturgy but rather so as to make it more intelligible, that is to say, less theatrical than it had been since the nineteenth century. The Church hoped in this way to make us understand that it is more important to grasp the fact that God is present and speaking to us, than it is to tire ourselves out in staging complex ceremonies in which we end up losing sight of the essential message that the symbols preserved by the Church's living tradition are supposed to communicate to us.

The nineteenth century handed down to us a manner of celebrating the liturgy that was surely more "juridical" than truly "traditional", and Romanticism had left its mark on the ceremonies, to the point of imparting to them a tinge of Jansenist pessimism.[16] It was therefore of capital importance that the Second Vatican Council should recall that no ceremony developed solely to meet needs of a psychological or an emotional order can boast of being truly "liturgical" in the sense in which the Church understands it.

As Cardinal Danneels has emphasized:

> We are not the creators, but rather the guardians of the Mysteries. We are neither their proprietors nor their authors. The fundamental attitude of the *homo liturgicus* [liturgical man] must therefore be an attitude of receptivity, ... of self-giving and of resignation [to the will of God]. ... The *homo liturgicus* does not seek to manipulate the liturgy in order to express or fulfill himself in it. He is turned toward God, in thanksgiving, adoration, and praise.[17]

II. Gregorian chant in the context of today's liturgy

How, indeed, can we speak of Gregorian chant in circumstances that, at first glance, are so unfavorable to it? How can we speak of a chant designed for praise, silence, beauty, adoration, when we live in a world of noise, agitation, and the search for immediate satisfaction? How can we speak of a chant designed for contemplation when many of our liturgies have been devised according to

---

[16] To verify this, one would do well to study the words of the hymns from this period.
[17] Cardinal Godfried Danneels, op. cit.

pastoral criteria, that is to say, according to an exclusively pragmatic view of things? Finally, how do we speak of a chant that,
after years of being abandoned by many parishes and even excluded
from the churches, is now unknown by most Catholics? To answer
these questions, I suggest considering the question of Gregorian
chant from three different perspectives.

1. *The perspective of the Church*

If we consult the great documents that address the question of liturgical singing,[18] we see that the Church always views liturgical singing as part of the way in which the Mysteries are celebrated, and
not as entertainment or simply as a way of embellishing worship.
To be sure, singing makes the liturgy more beautiful. But that is
not its primary role. Its essential mission is to make liturgy more
"effective" because it is thereby carried out in its most complete
form, the form closest to perfection. "The role of music", says
Saint Pius X, "is to clothe with an appropriate melody the liturgical text being presented to the mind of the faithful."

A musical repertoire, therefore, is not "liturgical" when it presents
melodies that seem beautiful to the ears of the faithful, but rather
when it consists of melodies that are "appropriate" to the liturgy.
There is a big difference.[19]

Following Saint Pius X, Pius XI recalls that "the proper end of
sacred music is to render the text itself more efficacious."

Here again, the particular role of liturgical singing is perfectly
defined: it is conceivable only in terms of a sacred text. Consequently, one must recognize that not just any text and not just any
music is suitable for use in the liturgy; just because a song is about
Jesus, or charity, or even love, does not necessarily guarantee that it

[18] The Motu Proprio *Tra le sollecitudini* of Saint Pius X (November 22, 1903), the Apostolic Constitution *Divini Cultus* of Pius XI (December 20, 1928), and the Encyclical *Musi-
cae sacrae Disciplina* of Pius XII (December 25, 1955).

[19] The beauty of a musical work intended for use in the liturgy, therefore, can be the
natural result, so to speak, only of the fact that the composer has managed to devise, based
on profound meditation, melodies that are perfectly adapted to the prayers and readings of
the liturgy, words that are themselves the reflection of the Eternal Beauty, inasmuch as they
are the utterance of Divine Truth, transmitted by the Church's liturgy.

has a place in worship and can be described as "liturgical singing". Just because the congregation likes a musical number doesn't mean that it is apt to nourish the faith and to express correctly the true prayer of the Church. Just because a song is rhythmic does not mean that it is capable of "inspiring" Mass-goers in the way the Church understands the expression.[20]

In reality, singing is liturgical only to the extent that it pursues the same objective as the liturgy: glorifying God in an "orthodox" manner and sanctifying the faithful.[21]

Only when singing is considered in its close connection with the liturgy can it contribute to the authentic beauty of worship. Singing then enhances all the intrinsic beauty of the liturgy, and at the same time it safeguards the ceremonies from anything that appears either paltry or, on the contrary, pompous, mannered, and artificial.

Indeed, in the liturgy, the chief quality of true beauty must be propriety: the beauty that is suited to the liturgy is the kind that begins by forgetting itself so as to go unnoticed and blend completely into the sacred action. The beauty required by liturgical singing is therefore the kind that is careful not to place its own decorum [i.e., rules and demands] ahead of the sacred service.[22]

Is it necessary to explain here that Gregorian chant is the kind of music that is most in keeping with all the principles that we have just enumerated?

It is the kind of music that is best suited to worship, inasmuch as it never is just music that is added on to the liturgy: it is the liturgy itself in musical form.

---

[20] Fr. Alain Bandelier, *Simples questions sur la messe et la liturgie* [Simple questions on the Mass and the liturgy] (Tours: Éditions C.L.D., 1999).

[21] Thus, in order for a type of singing to be described as "liturgical", it must above all be possible to perceive it as an expressive extension of the liturgy, that is, as an enhancement of the sacred texts and the rites. Such singing will become, then, a meditation on what the liturgy expresses and, at the same time, the due praise that the whole Church gives to the Father through the voices of the faithful. It is evident that this is just the opposite of all the kinds of superficial music that are brought into the liturgy for merely esthetic or sentimental reasons.

[22] A Benedictine monk, *Quatre bienfaits de la liturgie* [Four benefits provided by the liturgy] (Le Barroux: Éditions Sainte-Madeleine, 1995).

Although Gregorian chant contributes to the beauty of worship, it never does so by making itself the center of attention: Gregorian chant remains humble and discreet, because its sole reason for existing is to serve the sacred services reverently. Every piece in the Gregorian repertoire blends in with a precise moment of the liturgical action in order to highlight its meaning. For this reason, we can say that Gregorian chant is not so much a sort of music to be incorporated into the liturgy as it is music that enables us to understand the universality of the liturgy by interiorizing it more and more.

Let us look now at what the text of the conciliar Constitution on the Liturgy says. All of chapter 6 is dedicated to the subject of sacred music.

Article 112 underscores the inestimable value of the musical treasure that the Church has acquired over the centuries and recalls once more that "sacred music is to be considered the more holy, the more closely connected it is with the liturgical action."

Articles 114 and 115 state that the treasury of sacred music is to be preserved with great care and that great importance is to be attached to the teaching of music in seminaries and religious communities.

Finally, articles 116 and 117 address more particularly the subject of Gregorian chant. "The Church recognizes Gregorian chant", says the Council document, "as being specially suited to the Roman liturgy." Article 116 goes on to say that this kind of chant should have pride of place, inasmuch as it is an essential part of our Roman rite. And the Church understands this preeminence, the rightful place of chant in the liturgy, in such a way that she insists that editions of chant books be made available to the faithful, including those in smaller parishes, who will then be able to sing the less difficult Gregorian melodies with the help of a *Graduale simplex*.

2. *The perspective of the practicing Catholic*

It seems pointless to list here the qualities of Gregorian chant: others have done a better job of it than we could. Instead, I will mention a few of its advantages.

Let us say, first, that since Gregorian chant originated in the liturgy in order to serve the liturgy, it is so closely connected with the sacred actions that it seeks constantly to bring us face-to-face with God, just as they do.

How does it bring about this encounter? Very simply—by getting rid of two obstacles for us: the artist and ourselves.

Gregorian chant frees us first from artists—from the composer as well as from the performers, that is to say, from those who are often tempted to use the liturgy for personal ends by subordinating it to their own interests, such as money, glory, and setting a mood.

Gregorian chant then frees us from ourselves. It liberates us from our merely sociological or psychological preoccupations, which all too often creep into the liturgy without our noticing it, transforming our celebrations into safe havens where nothing is left but the inadequate good will of this group and that.

Gregorian chant therefore keeps us from "privatizing" the liturgy,[23] that is, from making the liturgy a purely personal matter that is more or less subject to the ambiguities of our human make-up.

In thus safeguarding the objectivity of the celebrations, Gregorian chant helps the liturgy itself to become, increasingly, our prayer, instead of the actions that we perform with the best intentions.[24] Gregorian chant safeguards us against any sort of celebration that would allow egotism to thrive in those who participate in the liturgy.

Gregorian chant, therefore, is the sort of music that opens souls to the prayer of the Church. And in opening souls, it makes them "susceptible to Beauty", which, in liturgical celebrations, must always be the reflections of the Absolute.

This Beauty does not depend on us; it is not the result of what our ingenuity might add to the liturgy to make it more attractive or popular. This Beauty emanates from the liturgy itself, inasmuch as it is the product of the correct performance of the rites handed down by tradition.

The Beauty that emanates from the liturgy forms an integral part of the liturgy. That is why it must not only be preserved and protected, but also be expressed. For although this Beauty is not essen-

[23] Cf. John Paul II, Letter *Vicesimus quintus annus*.
[24] Cf. Saint Pius X, *Tra le sollecitudini*.

tial, it is nonetheless necessary. This is so for two reasons: first, it honors the Divine Majesty, and then it impels us to contemplate God.[25]

Nowadays it seems that we have often lost the sense of this liturgical "Beauty". And so, when we need to make a service more solemn, we think first of making some sort of music that is "pleasant" instead of singing the music that is "appropriate". First place is reserved for Gregorian chant, but we give it over to kitschy songs or to pompous musical numbers that too often make our celebrations artificial or just plain miserable.

Now, if there is any sort of music that can steer us clear of these antiliturgical reefs, it is once again Gregorian chant. For Gregorian chant itself is incompatible with either a grandiose style or theatricality; it loves the Truth alone. Although it is the enemy of liturgical casualness, it is also completely opposed to that striving for musical effect that some performers resort to in order to arouse superficial, sometimes ambiguous feelings, or else to aggravate feelings that have little to do with an authentic faith.

Gregorian chant remains, in a way, the guarantee of the "noble simplicity" that is one of the characteristic qualities of the Roman rite, and that the Second Vatican Council wished to bring to light again by means of a liturgical renewal, properly understood and correctly implemented.

Gregorian chant possesses another virtue: by opening us to the Light of God, it enables us to discern our specific vocation. Gregorian chant makes us discover what we are really made for and invites us to take a part that is commensurate with our nature. In a way, Gregorian chant puts every believer in his true place, where he can play a role that is neither arrogated nor artificial.

Let us recall what article 28 of the Constitution on the Liturgy says: "In liturgical celebrations, each person, minister, or layman who has a service to perform, should carry out all and only those parts which pertain to his office by the nature of the rite and the norms of the liturgy."

Gregorian chant lends itself to the demands of various liturgical functions: the repertoire of the celebrant is not the same as that of

[25] Cf. Joseph Samson's speech given at the Congress of Versailles in 1957.

the schola [choir], and what the schola sings is not meant to be sung by the congregation.... Thus the roles are distributed evenly; in making us play them, the Gregorian liturgy educates us; it clarifies our personal vocations, which complement one another. The balance and the harmony that are thus brought about in this microcosm (which the liturgy is) then resonate beneficially in the macrocosm of our societies.

This synergy between the liturgy and life at the heart of the world is spelled out perfectly in the introduction of the Constitution on the Liturgy.[26] This passage, in which our liturgy is considered under the aspect of the relation that it has with Christ, enables us to understand better what a singular role Gregorian chant plays in contemporary liturgical celebrations: it opens a vista onto invisible realities while remaining a profoundly human form of song; it fosters contemplation without falling into the trap of fleeing from worldly realities; it places our actions in the full flood of the Divine Light, so that we might better grasp the fact that what Christ is accomplishing invisibly upon the altar is more efficacious than what we do visibly around the altar; it reminds us that our earthly celebrations can be only the reflection of the eternal liturgy that is going on in heaven.

Being the song of humility and the interior life, Gregorian chant elicits in us an attitude similar to that of the Publican as he prayed: unlike the Pharisee, who used prayer only to display the confidence that he had in himself, the Publican acknowledges above all the greatness of God while confessing his own twofold human nature—a creature who is at the same time redeemed and sinful.[27] Gregorian chant is like the prayer of the Publican: it expresses perfectly the attitude of the religious man who thinks of prayer first of

---

[26] "For it is the liturgy through which ... 'the work of our redemption is accomplished,' and it is through the liturgy, especially, that the faithful are enabled to express in their lives and manifest to others the mystery of Christ and the real nature of the true Church. The Church is essentially both human and divine, visible but endowed with invisible realities, zealous in action and dedicated to contemplation, present in the world, but as a pilgrim, so constituted that in her the human is directed toward and subordinated to the divine, the visible to the invisible, action to contemplation, and this present world to that city yet to come, the object of our quest" (SC 2).

[27] Cf. Dom Paul Delatte, *L'Évangile* [The Gospel] (Éditions de l'abbaye de Solesmes).

all as an act of trust and freely offered praise that is addressed to God.

3. *The perspective of the musician at the service of the Church*

How can a musician who places his talent at the service of the Church's prayer restore Gregorian chant to the place that it should have in the liturgy?

We have all heard the arguments of those who do not favor the use of Gregorian chant in liturgical actions. While acknowledging the musical and expressive value of Gregorian chant, they see in it certain defects that, in their opinion, make it unusable in a contemporary pastoral program for the liturgy. What are these alleged defects? Let us recall four of them:

- Gregorian chant is sung in Latin, and nobody understands Latin anymore;
- Gregorian chant does not promote the "active participation" called for by the Council;
- Gregorian chant is difficult to sing; it is suitable for monks, but not for the simple lay people in our parishes;
- Gregorian chant no longer interests young people.

Is the Latin language really an obstacle?

Let us return to Vatican II. The Constitution *Sacrosanctum Concilium* mentioned the possibility of using vernacular languages in liturgical celebrations. In doing so, the Council never ordered that Latin be replaced by the vernacular languages; it simply gave modern languages the status of liturgical languages, a status that until then, at least in the Roman rite, had been the sole possession of Latin. Hence it ought to be possible today to attend Masses celebrated in Latin in the current rite as well as Masses celebrated in vernacular languages. Now we know that this possibility, in practice, scarcely exists.[28]

---

[28] Indeed, it is officially forbidden by the bishops of France.

Those who went further than what the Council allowed (for it was certainly only a permission!) and thought that replacing Latin and Gregorian chant with prayers and songs in modern languages would solve all the problems by making the liturgy comprehensible seem to have lost sight of one essential thing: they forgot that a language used within the framework of a liturgical rite enjoys a special status that is not the same as that of the common utterances ordinarily used to exchange information.[29]

Yes, vernacular languages foster one type of understanding. But what does "understanding" mean in the liturgy? What does it mean "to understand" a rite? "To understand" a celebration? "To understand" a mystery?

Since our modern-day mindset is immersed in a context where the only important words are "profitability", "communication", and "information", we have lost sight of the fact that the liturgy is neither profitable, nor communicable, nor reducible to an exchange of information.

In the liturgy, the mode of understanding is not exclusively of the rational order; it takes place especially through the performance of the gestures and the singing of the ritual formulas that allow the participants to enter into a symbolic structure that must be situated in the existential sphere rather than simply on the intellectual level; outside of this sphere, any celebration loses a great part of its meaning.

One can also say that the liturgy is not so much something to be understood as a means of understanding. As for Gregorian chant, in this perspective it becomes an invaluable aid to fathoming and penetrating the meaning and import of the mystery being celebrated.

I declare emphatically that, over the course of many Gregorian chant-training sessions that I have conducted and many Gregorian services that I have accompanied at the organ, the use of Latin has never seemed to be an insurmountable obstacle. On the contrary, after more or less of an adjustment period, the participants in the chant-training sessions or in the Gregorian services become more

---

[29] "In the liturgy, we do not comprehend only in a rational way, as when one understands a course, but in a complex way, with all our senses" (statement of Cardinal Joseph Ratzinger).

and more familiar with the Latin text of the Gregorian melodies and see in it an invitation to participate in the Church's prayer in a more *deliberate* way, which is therefore more recollected, more interior.

Does Gregorian chant prevent the active participation of the faithful?

Allow me to say first a few words about the notion of "active participation". I think that I will surprise some people by stating here that the Second Vatican Council never spoke about "active participation".

The expression used in the Constitution *Sacrosanctum Concilium* is *"participatio actuosa"* and not *"participatio activa"*. Vatican II called for an "effective" participation in the liturgy, that is to say, a participation that is in contrast to a "passive participation" as well as to an "activist participation".

The true and only participation that the Church wants is the kind that results from an interior attitude that places us in a state of receptivity for the liturgy.

In this, too, it is obvious that the virtues of Gregorian chant shield us against a sort of participation in the liturgy that is too dependent upon contemporary mindsets and would end up being no more than a sterile activism.

Gregorian chant safeguards us against that ceaseless agitation that seems to have taken over a great number of contemporary Masses and that ends up making the liturgical space a sort of experimental laboratory run exclusively by those who mistake the Church for an "international volunteer association".[30]

The experience of recent years clearly demonstrates that replacing Gregorian chants by a repertoire of songs in the vernacular languages has not necessarily improved the quality of our participation in liturgical prayer.

Today, at Sunday Mass, it is quite possible for me to sing the words of the *Our Father* in my native language while thinking about the forms that the tax collector has just sent me.

---

[30] This is an expression used by a bishop during the Synod of the Bishops of Europe that was held at the Vatican in 1999.

*Is it true that Gregorian chant is too difficult to sing and
therefore is not popular music?*

Once again, I cite my experience as a choirmaster, and I answer:
no, Gregorian chant is not difficult.[31]

Let me explain.

Let us remember first of all that for almost eight centuries the
repertoire of liturgical music that was the source of what we now
call "Gregorian chant" was created, handed down, and preserved
without the aid of musical notation and scores.

Doesn't this prove that, at the origins of Gregorian chant, there
are fundamental elements of a "popular" character? Doesn't it indicate that the Gregorian repertoire is rooted in a "popular" tradition, in the noblest sense of the word?

I can already hear the objections: How can certain ornate, mel-
ismatic pieces, which are difficult to sing, be "popular"?

The answer is simple: it all depends on what you mean by "popular". "Popular" does not mean "which everybody must be able to
sing", but rather, "which can be appreciated by all" or, if you prefer, "which is meaningful for everyone".[32]

Every time that I direct a training course in Gregorian chant, I
notice that the beginners are not in the least disconcerted by the
more ornate pieces; even when they don't learn to sing them correctly by themselves, they get carried away by the more experienced singers who are invited to sing the more complex melodies.
In a way, one can say that the beginners get a taste of the repertoire by listening to those who know how to sing it easily and by
being completely with them "in spirit".

Now, isn't "being completely with others in spirit" an essential
form of participation in the liturgy that we should aim for in our
congregations? Gregorian chant, therefore, is perfectly well suited
to our parish liturgies, provided, of course, that all are willing to
abide by the essential principle stated in article 28 of the Consti-

---

[31] Gregorian chant has been made "difficult" since the nineteenth century, when it was
locked into musical theories that most often were foreign to it.

[32] The accordion is often described as a "popular" instrument; that does not mean that
everybody plays the accordion.

tution *Sacrosanctum Concilium*, which we have already discussed: in the liturgy everybody does not do everything.

I am well aware that in mentioning this, I am going completely against the ideas that are generally accepted today and against certain practices that have become habitual.

Is Gregorian chant no longer of interest to young people?

As a teacher, I can say that young people have nothing, in principle, against either Gregorian chant or against a Gregorian liturgy. It all depends on the way in which you present things to them. Someone who presents the Gregorian liturgy as a "step backward" is really only seeking to deceive young people and to provoke a negative reaction.

Similarly, if we present Gregorian chant to young people as something fixed and restricted, we will obviously have little chance of arousing their overwhelming enthusiasm. If we speak to them about the Gregorian liturgy with a quavering voice and say, "It was so beautiful back then", they will have every right to look at us as though we were the last survivors of some "liturgical Jurassic Park".

But if we present Gregorian chant to them as music that is truly living, dynamic, relevant, that allows them to transcend themselves, if we show them how Gregorian chant is capable of conveying a genuine interior freedom and inspiring a real joy, then we can quickly get young people interested. There is no lack of examples of this, and we know very well that young people are not always completely impervious to what is true, solid, authentic, expressive. And Gregorian chant is all of that!

We should also emphasize the problem posed by the attitude of young people toward Gregorian chant: the problem of handing on permanent values.

We know that the idea of *traditio*, "handing on", is essential in the liturgy. Now in order for this handing on to take place, there has to be some stability: stability in the rites, but also stability in the musical repertoire that forms an integral part of the ritual action.

Now this stability is lacking today to such a degree, from one region to another, from one generation to another, from one parish to another, that there is no longer any connection: during liturgical celebrations they sing nothing but ephemeral songs. The Gregorian repertoire has been replaced by songs that go out of style as soon as they are replaced by new compositions. Thereby the whole idea of the "liturgical cycle" crumbles, since from one year to the next, instead of reencountering the melodies that evoke the major milestones along our Christian way, there is a ceaseless effort to create brand new music—which is most often flimsy and superficial and which turns out to be incapable of leaving any trace in our memories.

At present, we observe that the absence of Gregorian chant in our liturgies has resulted in a sort of amnesia among the faithful: among them, the younger generations are the ones most affected, inasmuch as they make up the contingents that have been deprived, sometimes by demagoguery, of something that constitutes a treasure of the Roman liturgy.

III. Conclusion

Sprung from contemplation in order to lead us into contemplation, Gregorian chant infinitely transcends the contingencies of an age or of an artist's subjectivity; it is first and foremost the product of a humble submission: the submission of the musical art to the prayer of the Church at its highest degree of expression.

Even more: Gregorian chant is the fruit of the participation of the musical art in a unique history: the history of the salvation of mankind. The Church never tires of singing about this history, of praising it, so that we ourselves might be able to contemplate it in the depths of its mystery, by repeating with the psalmist: *ad te levavi animam meam, in te confido: non erubescam."* [33] ["To thee, O LORD, I lift up my soul. In thee I trust, let me not be put to shame" Ps. 25 (24):1–2].

Let us not be ashamed to love Gregorian chant so much that we want to restore it to its place in our liturgies, for whenever we sing it, we lift up our souls to God and we are then assured of drawing other souls along in this movement.

---

[33] Introit of the First Sunday of Advent.

APPENDIX IV

ORGAN AND SONG IN THE LITURGY

The introduction of the organ into Christian liturgy

If historians are to be believed, the first records mentioning the Christian liturgy and organ music together go back to the seventh century. At that time Pope Vitalian (d. 672) sanctioned the accompaniment of sacred song.

What did this "accompaniment" consist of? It is certain that the design of the organs in that remote period did not allow for the sort of accompaniment that we know today. The keyboard was made up of a series of reglets that allowed the player to open or close the channel by which the air reached a given pipe. This system, of course, left no scope for real virtuosity; at the most, one could give the pitch for the liturgical melodies or sustain notes, over which the singers would elaborate their chant.

For a long time the organ remained an instrument of very modest size, as one can see depicted on certain old tapestries (for example, the Unicorn Tapestries in Paris). The organ, therefore was placed upon a table, in the midst of the musicians, hence its name, "positive" [*positif*].

Another peculiarity of this early instrument comes from the fact that its timbre is not homogeneous: in the lower notes, it produces a sound reminiscent of string instruments, whereas the higher up on the keyboard you play, the more it sounds like a flute.

This phenomenon is due to the fact that craftsmen had not yet discovered the principle of maintaining the same proportion between the length of a pipe and its diameter: at that time, all the pipes, from the lowest in pitch (the longest) to the highest (the shortest), had the same diameter (which was approximately the diameter of a pigeon's egg, as some manuscripts specify).

This peculiarity would be significant: it meant that the lower tones produced rich harmonics[1] that, when amplified by the particular acoustic of some sanctuaries, can give the illusion of a discreet polyphony.

The organ in the late Middle Ages

The medieval period provides the organ with a mechanism that is now more complex: "trackers" allow the movement of each key on the keyboard to be transmitted to valves that control the passage of air (organ builders use the term "wind" rather than "air") in the different pipes.

The instrument thus becomes more weighty: it has not only keyboards, bellows, and pipes, but also an elaborate mechanism. All of this will be housed in an "organ case" [*"buffet"*].

The organ, which is now bigger and more powerful, is then placed either on a small rostrum usually located near the choir [i.e., the chancel] or else in a loft suspended along a side wall.[2]

At the end of the Middle Ages, organ builders had not really discovered the principle of employing various stops with sonorities that can complement and enhance each other. The instrument was thought of, rather, as one, big *organum plenum* [*"pleinjeu"*], that is, as an instrument that can increase volume by adding new ranks of pipes. These ranks form a whole: in northern countries they usually cannot be divided, and so they form what would be called a *Blockwerk*; arranged so as to be divisible in Italy and in nearby lands, they would form what is called the *ripieno*.

[1] Harmonics or "overtones" are the secondary tones that make up one fundamental note. For example, if I play *do*, I find that this fundamental note contains several harmonic tones that the ear perceives more or less distinctly: the first harmonic is the *do* an octave higher than the fundamental note, the second harmonic is the *sol* (fifth), the third harmonic is another *do* an octave above the first harmonic, the fourth harmonic is a *mi* (third), and so on. To have a more exact idea of what a harmonic is, you need to listen to a bell toll: you hear the fundamental tone that results from the clapper striking against the inside surface of the bell, then, above that tone, you hear something like a murmur or a resonance; this is one of the harmonics produced by the metal of the bell that begins vibrating.

[2] See, for example, the organ of the Cathedral of Metz, which has an organ case dating in part from 1537, or the organ in the church of Valère à Sion in Switzerland.

In the fifteenth and sixteenth centuries

Organ building had made considerable progress and, at the dawn of the Renaissance, the organ had become a complex instrument with a wealth of possibilities. A new role was then assigned to it, mirroring the role that was played in that same period by sophisticated polyphony that had become detached from its Gregorian source. The organ therefore either had to dialogue with the singers or the choirs, or else play solo.

Nevertheless, even though it had become a prestigious instrument, the organ was still subordinate to the liturgical service. Furthermore, pieces for the organ were always composed in a manner that imitated vocal works, and their style remained more or less related to that of Gregorian chant.

During this same period, which witnessed the increasing assertion of national identities, organ building adapted to the demands of local tastes. As a result, the organs of Europe acquired a style that one could describe as "national": the French organ,[3] the Italian organ,[4] the Germanic organ,[5] and the Iberian organ[6] are so

[3] To get an idea of the sonorities of the French organ (of the seventeenth and eighteenth centuries), we suggest the following CD's: *Livre d'orgue de Louis-Claude d'Aquin*, performed by Pierre Bardon on the organ of Saint-Maximin-de-Provence (PV 783122); *Livre d'orgue de Jacques Boyvin*, performed by Aude Heurtematte on the organ of Cliquot de Souvigny (TEM 316004); *Les Hymnes de Nicolas de Grigny*, performed by Bernard Couturier on the organ of Cintegabelle (BNL 112813); volume 4 of the series "La route des orgues", *Oeuvres de François Couperin et de Guilain*, performed by Laurent Beyhurst on the organ of Seurre; *Oeuvres pour orgue de Louis Couperin*, performed by Jan Willem Jansen on the organ of Saint-Michel-en-Thierache (WM 334592291).

[4] To get an idea of the sonorities of the Italian organ, we suggest the following CD: *L'oeuvre de G. Frescobaldi à l'orgue de Brescia*.

[5] For the Germanic organ we suggest *Bernard Couturier à l'orgue Arp Schnitger de Norden* [B.C. performing works by Scheidemann] (BNL 212869); *L'orgue baroque en Allemagne du nord; oeuvre de Bruhns et de Hanff*, performed by Bernard Couturier on the organ in Norden (BNL 112754); *Oeuvres de Böhm et Buxtehude*, performed by W. Zerer on the organ in Leens (ISRC 92088); *Oeuvres d'orgue de J. H. Buttstett*, performed by Helga Schauerte on the organs of Römhild and Rötha (SYR 141334).

[6] For the Iberian organ we suggest *El organo castellano*, with Francis Chapelet performing on the organs of Albarca de Campos and Frechilla (V 4653); *La escuela de Zaragoza* [The Saragossa school], with Lionel Rogg performing on the organs of Daroca and Sabada

many different ways of designing instruments and of giving them particular timbres adapted to a style of music that is just as particular.

Since the instrument is always expected to be in dialogue with the voices, it is situated as close as possible to the place where the vocal sonorities originate; it has to be an instrument that is clearly audible. But at the same time, since the imposing organ case (the exterior cabinet work) has become a veritable work of art, the organ must also be an instrument that is admired.

To be heard clearly and to be seen readily: these are the considerations that will determine the placement of these instruments. In a parallel development, the technical advances achieved by the organ builders enable organ music to become more and more sophisticated, to the point of developing a special repertoire allowing the organist to highlight the different sonorities and the variety of timbres of the instruments.

Then composers appeared who truly wrote for the organ: Andrea Gabrielli (1520–1586) and his nephew Giovanni (1557–1612), Girolamo Frescobaldi (1583–1643), Jehan Titelouze (1563–1633), and so forth.

The works of these old masters, which are essentially at home in the Catholic Church, consequently bear the hallmarks of genuine liturgical music: brevity of form, unity of composition, subordination to the text that is chanted or amplified polyphonically, and a technique that is characteristic of the organ.

One can say that the organists of this period were masters in the art of adapting the musical language perfectly to the requirements of the liturgy.

However, the sixteenth century is also the century of the Protestant Reformation.

After ridding themselves of the constraints of the Catholic liturgy, the reformed churches could allow more freedom to sacred music. Now, at that same time, secular music had reached the height of polyphonic composition.

New and more sophisticated musical forms found then, in the services of the reformed churches, a freedom that they could not

---

(V 4648); *Tientos y glosas en Iberia*, with Jesus Martin Moro performing on the organ of Saõ Vincente de Lisbon with the Gilles Binchois ensemble (TEM 316014).

have in the Catholic liturgy. It was in the Germanic world, which had been won over to the ideas of Protestantism, that the first great organ virtuosos appeared: Franz Tünder [1614–1667], Hieronymus Praetorius (1560–1629), Michael Praetorius (1571–1621), and Samuel Scheidt (1587–1654).[7]

It should be noted that the works of these composers are still marked by a certain liturgical spirit that, it is true, is not lacking during that period in the worship of the reformed churches. Thus we find, in many pieces for the organ, themes that are authentically Gregorian: *Christ lag in Todesbanden* (Christ lay in the bonds of death) is a generally moderate paraphrase of the Latin hymn *Victimae pascali laudes*, and *Nun komm der Heiden Heiland* (Now come, O Savior of the Gentiles) is a reprise of the *Veni Redemptor Gentium*, to cite only two examples.

The seventeenth and eighteenth centuries:
The triumph of the Baroque style

While in many Southern lands, the organ remains the heir of the medieval period and keeps its place in the chancel [choir] of the church, in the countries of the North that were affected by the Reformation, the organ finds a new place better suited to its size, which has become imposing: it is placed either in a transept, or else in a loft constructed over the western door [main entrance]. This new arrangement also allows choirs or an orchestra to join the organ if necessary to perform grand works such as cantatas.[8]

Yet, at the same time, this distancing from the chancel presents an opportunity for the organ and organ music to declare a certain autonomy.

---

[7] Cf. the following CD's: *North German Music*, played by Gustav Leonhardt on the organs of Norden (D) and of Roskilde (DK) (SK 53371); *Psaumes et chorals de Jan Pieterszoon Sweelinck*, performed by the ensemble Sagittarius, with Freddy Eichelberger playing the organ (built in 1627) of Saint-Martin-de-Bocherville (TEM 316006).

[8] Limiting ourselves to the Catholic repertoire, we suggest the CD *Te Deum (et autres oeuvres de Marc-Antoine Charpentier)* performed by Les Arts Florissants under the direction of William Christie (HMC 901298). Baroque music has been popularized in recent years by the sound tracks of [French] films such as *Tous les matins* or *Farinelli*.

During the seventeenth century and the first half of the eighteenth century, Pachelbel (1653–1706), Buxtehude (1637–1707), and Bach (1685–1750) were still writing works that were inspired directly by the liturgy, in which it is not uncommon to discover traces of psalmody (in the fugues on the *Magnificat*, for example), or of Gregorian melodies (think of the *Orgelbüchlein* of Bach).

One can also say that, from the introduction of the organ into the Catholic liturgy until the eighteenth century, organ music remains essentially under the rubric of Christian liturgy, if not in its precise form, then at least in its spirit.

1750: The death of Johann-Sebastian Bach

Curiously, the death of Johann-Sebastian Bach in 1750 coincided with the start of a decline associated with a crisis that all of Christian Europe would go through, whether Catholic or Reformed.

The new ideas that sprang from the "Enlightenment", and led to a deification of human reason, made it seem that submission to the liturgy had had its day; from now on music—and art in general—would have to be crafted, not in keeping with a higher value, but rather in terms of the subjective emotions of the soul.[9] The compositions of the sons of Bach (Wilhelm-Friedemann and Johann-Christian), of Josef Haydn (1732–1809), or of W. A. Mozart (1756–1791) already contribute to a great extent to this pre-Romantic movement, which is fond of ascending and descending by halftones and using the aptly named "leading" note.

This new concept of art produces innovative musical forms, the most notable examples of which are the symphony and the sonata.

These are the forms that would serve, chiefly in German-speaking lands, as guidelines for the development of the *Singmesse*, which is nothing other than a sort of concert against the background of the Mass.

---

[9] Several motets by Mondonville, for example, already suggest something of these subjective emotions in their striving for effect. Cf. the CD *Grands motets de Jean-Joseph Cassanéa de Mondonville*, performed by the Baroque Ensemble of Limoges under the direction of Christophe Coin (AS 128614).

The nineteenth century: Romanticism

The subjectivism inherited from Romanticism made it necessary to build organs that could perform music that was intended above all as the expression of human feelings.

Therefore larger and larger multipurpose organs were built in the churches: they would play solo to emphasize the pomp of a liturgy that had often become theatrical, accompany soloists who came to sing an opera aria on "important occasions",[10] and help the congregational singing, but they would always heighten or express, through the music, the feelings of a sort of piety that was often sincere but certainly lacking a solid theological basis.

During the Romantic period, the manufacture of Cavaillé-Coll organs provided extremely massive instruments, equipped with stops that are capable of producing multiple colorings over the entire range of sound.[11] In parishes that were already furnished with an older organ, restorations were made allowing the sonorities of the old stops to be attuned to the current tastes: some pipes were reshaped in order to make their tones sweeter, less mordant. More often than not, entire ranks would disappear: thus the forthright sonorities possessed by seventeenth- and eighteenth-century organs were replaced by modulated timbres, making possible "a sweet music, suitable for enrapturing pious souls". The names of these new stops, furthermore, evoke a spiritual state: "Aeolian", *"Voix céleste"* ["celestial voice"], "Dulciane" [suggests "sweetheart"].

---

[10] Far from being a thing of the past, this practice is still with us today. On the occasion of the death of François Mitterrand, for example, during the funeral Mass at Notre-Dame in Paris they performed the *Pie Jesu* from the Fauré Requiem. We might emphasize, in passing, that this text, which is taken from the final verses of the sequence *Dies irae, dies illa*, no longer has a place in the conciliar liturgy.

[11] Cf. the CD *Pièces pour orgue de César Franck*, performed by Jacques Amade on the Cavaillé-Coll organ in the abbey church of Saint-Ouen in Rouen (CHCD 5626); *Louis Vierne (Messe pour deux orgues et choeurs) et Charles-Marie Widor (10e symphonie romane)*, performed by Michel Bouvard on the Cavaillé-Coll organ of Saint-Sernin in Toulouse and by the vocal ensemble "Les Éléments" (TEM 316008); *Fauré, Vierne, et Séverac*, performed by the Oxford Schola Cantorum under the direction of Nicholas Ward (Naxos 8550765); *Oeuvres de Vierne*, performed by Marie-Thérèse Jehan on the Debierre organ of the Cathedral of Nantes (ELCD 007).

Besides this, in order to be able to portray nature, of which the Romantics were so fond (as Beethoven does in his Pastoral Symphony), they also added (at least on the larger instruments) stops and mechanisms capable of imitating, for example, a clap of thunder during a tumultuous storm.

With these instruments, which were designed to rival a symphonic orchestra, appear the works of César Franck (1822–1890), Max Reger (1873–1916), or Josef Gabriel Rheinberger.

The hallmark of the compositions of these masters, what differentiates them fundamentally from the works written before the mid-eighteenth century, is the especially subjective and personal style to which they give expression.

Thus the compositions of the nineteenth century no longer seek to adapt to the liturgy; they are free-form works, emancipated from the Church's ceremonies, even though they often show signs of a real mystical-religious sensibility.

We can say, therefore, that in the late nineteenth century the prevailing climate in many churches, largely due to the organ music, is an atmosphere supersaturated with sentimentality and sensitivity.

Nevertheless, we must not forget that the nineteenth century is also the period when the Roman liturgy and Gregorian chant were "rediscovered". In the larger churches, beside the grand symphonic instruments, they would therefore build also organs of more modest dimensions that they would place, as they did before the Renaissance, in the sanctuary, not far from the altar, often within the woodwork of the choir stalls reserved for the canons [clergy praying in community].

This was the appearance of the "choir organ"; its chief role would be to accompany the Gregorian chant, which was being restored at that time and which many people were then just discovering. Recall that it was in November of 1829, in the Church of Saint-Étienne-du-Mont in Paris, that a choir organ for the first time accompanied the Gregorian chant melodies for the Dedication: *Terribilis es locus iste.*

Consequently, the grand organ was expected, above all, to create a "sonorous ceremonial", which combined with the visual ceremonial of the liturgy or sometimes even replaced it, since the liturgy in cathedrals unfolds far from the view of the faithful. Furthermore, since the congregation did not hear what the celebrant was saying (churches at that time had no sound systems), it was expected that the organist would "accompany the ceremony" [*"meubler la cérémonie"*], that is, play softly while the priest at the altar said the prayers of the Mass in a low voice.

Gradually the taste for Romanticism placed the Roman liturgy, as handed down by the Council of Trent, in a sort of context that was governed by the sensibility of the nineteenth century: a sensibility that was often marked by a sort of *kitsch* or by a fondness for theatricality.

The twentieth century

The Second Vatican Council, which was the defining event for the Church in the twentieth century, affirms, "The pipe organ is to be held in high esteem in the Latin Church, for it is the traditional musical instrument, the sound of which can add a wonderful splendor to the Church's ceremonies and powerfully lifts up men's minds to God and higher things" (SC 120).

However, at the moment when the Church was recalling this principle, neither organ building nor organ music was at its height.

Organ building had not yet extricated itself from the requirements that originated in the nineteenth century,[12] even though there began to be in certain localities an interest in the instruments that had come down from the seventeenth and eighteenth centuries; these remaining specimens had escaped the overhauls that were demanded by nineteenth-century tastes.[13]

---

[12] See vol. 5 of the series "La route des orgues", *L'orgue Callinet de Dannemarie en Alsace*, with works by François Boely, Johannes Brahms, Felix Mendelssohn-Bartholdy, Louis-James Alfred Lefébure-Wely, Charles Gounod—performed by Olivier Vernet (LIDI 0104084-99).

[13] Bernard Sonaillon, *L'orgue: instruments et musiciens* (Paris: Éditions Vilo, 1984); Jean Guillou, *L'orgue: souvenir et avenir* [Organ: remembrance and future] (Paris: Éditions Buchet et Chastel, 1978); Fr. Meyer-Siat, *Les Callinet, facteurs d'orgues à Rouffach et leur oeuvre en Alsace* [The Callinet family, organ builders from R. and their work in A.] (Paris: Éditions Istra, 1965); Meyer-Siat, *Valentin Rinkenbach, François-Ignace Hérisé et les fils Wetzel, facteurs d'orgues* [VR, F-IH and the Wetzel sons, organ builders] (Strasbourg: Éditions Istra, 1979); Norbert Dufourcq, *Le livre de l'orgue Français* [Book of the French organ], vols. 1 through 5 (Paris: Éditions Picard, 1969); Claude Noisette de Crauzat, *L'orgue dans la société Française* [The organ in French society] (Paris: Éditions Champion, 1979).

As for the music played in the parishes, in large measure it proved to be attached still to Romanticism, as though feelings trumped everything: many songs owe their popularity with the faithful more to what they suggest than to what they say. Do you want proof of this? Just look at the sort of music that people ask organists to play for wedding and funeral Masses. Just consider that, for many of them, a "real" midnight Mass is a Mass during which someone sings "O, Holy Night", which, it is said, was composed by Adolphe Adam as a stunt as the result of a bet.

Conclusion

Liturgical chant had its origins in the contemplation, reverence, and humility of those who were willing to be self-effacing so as better to serve the sacred rites. At the origins of organ music there was reverence and admiration for liturgical chant: a chant that the musician could freely ornament or expand on, but never betray.

At the end of the Baroque period and with the birth of Romanticism, the values that governed liturgical music gradually disappeared, only to be replaced by the affirmation of the individual "self".

But it is interesting to note that during the twentieth century the individual "self" very quickly found itself encompassed within a larger idea: that of "the people".

On the eve of Vatican II, this very notion of "the people of God" drifted more and more toward a new meaning that is conveyed in certain triumphalist tunes. Then, in this new context, the saying of Jesus, "When two or three are gathered in my name" (Mt 18:20)—quite innocent and traditional at first blush—is used to set the gathering of a few individuals in opposition to the "institutional" Church.

During the time when the directives of Vatican II were being applied, a whole liberal theology took advantage of the collective feeling that had asserted itself by means of tendentious songs, to declare that the Church no longer had priority over the group, but rather the group consisting of a few persons had priority over the Church. One often heard it said, "We are Church" [*"Il faut faire l'Église"* = "We must make Church"].

Consequently, the liturgy should no longer proceed according to a preestablished "rite", handed down by the living tradition, but rather according to the consensus and the choices made by the group members.

As a result, the trend in music that had started with Romanticism found its ultimate development: it convinces Catholics today that the Church's music must in the first place demonstrate that the "people of God" (in reality, the local group) can discover and establish its true identity only by singing its own musical creations.

Well, then, the music that is made during the liturgy—which is never the same from one Mass to the next, from one parish to the next—becomes the distinguishing feature of the community. And the music quickly becomes poor, destitute, being nothing more than the reflection of the states of our own souls.

As for the quality of the liturgical celebration itself, this is no longer measured in terms of respect for the rites determined by the Church, but rather according to the "expertise" of the "liturgical planners", who all too often choose only the kind of songs and music that suits the sensibility of the group that has gathered to celebrate.

"What is sung" and "who gets to sing" become more important that "what should be sung". We are witnessing, therefore, an inversion of the essential criteria of the liturgy: each celebration is then stereotyped to the point where it is possible to distinguish a parish Mass from the Mass of a charismatic community, a Mass for scouts from a Mass in a monastery, or a Mass of traditionalist Catholics from a Mass organized for a diocesan conference.

Of course, in every age there were differences, and the style of a monastery was just not the same as that of a parish deep in the heart of rural France. Nevertheless, before such variations existed from one place to the other, the Catholic who, on occasion, left his rural parish to go to Mass at a monastery would not lose his liturgical bearings; he recognized all the chants there and all the texts that he was used to hearing in his village church.

At the very most he might agree that the Mass at the monastery was perhaps better prepared and sung than in his parish.

That is not how it is today: often the different communities are so beholden to a particular musical repertoire, so compartmentalized, that they end up being self-enclosed, without even noticing it.

Someone who attends Mass somewhere other than in his parish, where he knows the habits of the priest and the repertoire of the local choir, often finds himself incapable of joining "the local welcoming community": besides the unfamiliar songs and music that he hears, the whole liturgical atmosphere seems strange to him.

Isn't that proof that the choice of the music that one makes in church is never a neutral decision? When the style of the music that is made during a liturgical celebration is no longer capable of uniting hearts and souls in the same prayer, that one can be sure is the prayer of Church, then very quickly these celebrations become occasions for setting up barriers and partitions among groups of Christians, and eventually they close or blockade the communities in on themselves.

History teaches us that the Church has always taken care to provide guidelines for the music that is to be used in worship. This guidance is clearly indicated by the liturgical texts that the Church herself has selected to celebrate her faith: it is clear, therefore, that liturgical music, in its inmost character, must correspond to the demands of these same liturgical texts.

This correspondence is essential; isn't that what Pius XI was emphasizing when he taught that "the proper end of sacred music is to give greater efficacy to the text itself"?

This does not mean that all we need to do is "adapt" melodies to the words of the texts. Such a task resembles something that a conservatory student could do, but it would not be sufficient for the purpose of creating a repertoire that is worthy of being called "liturgical".

We have to go still farther: the music must first find in these sacred texts, which themselves are situated within the context of the Church's liturgical prayer, the line that it should follow in order to bring to the fore their own expressive capabilities.[14]

The bottom line is: authentic liturgical music can be identified by the fact that it is like true liturgy; it is cosmic and does not take its measure from a group. Being cosmic, it frees us from other people's ways of acting and thinking. And so, once it manages to restore silence and interior peace to us, it draws us to contemplate the mysteries celebrated in an "orthodox" manner.

---

[14] Jean Brun, *Essence et histoire de la musique* (Geneva: Éditions Ad Solem, 1999).

APPENDIX V

PEDAGOGY, CATECHESIS, AND LITURGY

I. [French] pedagogy today

Ever since the French Enlightenment philosopher Condorcet, at the latest, the hope of continual progress, combined with the idea of democracy, has been the justification for the notion of intellectual effort that has been inculcated in the younger generations, with a view to making them future participants in a social movement aimed at bringing humanity out of the "darkness of superstition".

Were schoolteachers during the Third Republic in France [1870–1940] disciples of Condorcet? In any case, no one will dispute the fact that they made it a point of honor to educate their pupils according to a system that has been described on occasion as a "meritocracy".

Besides, the school wars that have lasted for over a century in France must not cause us to overlook the important role played by the brothers and the nuns; they managed to compete with the "black hussars of the Republic" [i.e., secular educators] in encouraging the promotion of the most gifted students and in eradicating illiteracy. It would take either a very clever or a very biased umpire to award a prize for the best patriotic values and "striving for excellence"—things that were taught, at the cost of some self-denial, both in the public schools and in religious educational institutions, at least until the Fourth Republic [1946–1958]. For later on it was remarked, parodying the poet, "Times change, and with them change the teaching methods."

Ever since the 1960s, most educators have changed to the point where, in their view, the notions of "duties", "authority", or "morality" have become old-fashioned, indeed, should be regarded as revolutionary. The slogan "It is forbidden to forbid", which was popularized by the student protestors of May 1968, seems to have been taken up again by those who appear to be the first and only beneficiaries of the consumer society. Well, scholarly institutions have not been spared the influence of these hedonist theories that reject the "categorization [*embrigadement*] of the individual" denounced by Sartre.

In a work entitled "School or civil war",[1] Philippe Mérieu, Director of the National Institute of Pedagogical Research, is not content to denounce the school [of pedagogical thought] of Jules Ferry, allegedly because it is "a myth that has never succeeded in creating genuine social mobility". This proponent of the theory of *"pédagogisme"* [in some ways resembling "outcome-based education"] goes on to demand that the transmission of knowledge be replaced by an "apprenticeship in citizenship".

Thus, according to Mérieu, "the job of the school is not so much to impose truths on children as it is to create the conditions whereby they can find them for themselves once they are adults"; in this way they become "capable of inventing the society in which they want to live".

By doing this, are the ideological proponents of *"pédagogisme"* guiding children "toward a totalitarian school", to cite the title of a book by Liliane Lurçat,[2] who denounces this as an attempt to indoctrinate students?[3]

Thierry Desjardin[4] says, "Yes!" In a scathing indictment, well supported by documentation and official statistics, he shows that "the leading lights in our [French] National Department of Education are Marxists who want nothing to do with our society and dream of making another one out of it by means of the school system.... The revolution could not be carried out in broad daylight, and so, for want of a better strategy, they play at being ter-

---

[1] Philippe Mérieu, *L'école ou la guerre civile* (Paris: Éditions Plon, 1996).

[2] Liliane Lurçat, *Vers une école totalitaire* [Toward a totalitarian school] (Paris: Éditions F. X. de Guibert, 1998).

[3] The docile instructors who follow the curricular programs and new so-called "pedagogical" methods are not always aware of this.

[4] Thierry Desjardin, *Le scandale de l'éducation nationale* (Paris: Éditions Robert Laffont, 1998).

mites and gnaw at the structural beams of the society that they were unable to destroy."[5]

But rather than inquire into the thoughts and second thoughts of the theoreticians of the new pedagogy, let us look instead at the results of their teaching methods: "By dint of saying, year after year, that the school must be open to society," an unnamed source of Jean-Pierre Chevènement remarks, "they have brought in, not the knowledge and skills, but the problems of the neighborhood, the behavior and the values of the street, and therefore violence."[6]

This violence in the schools has contributed to delinquency, drug-dealing, and a number of sexual assaults, to say nothing of the development of illiteracy, an incomprehensible blot on the record of a nation that once could boast that it had one of the best educational systems in the world. In addition, this disastrous pedagogical theory has not only consolidated the "law-free zones" in those urban areas where French is becoming a foreign language; it has also contaminated the teaching of catechism.

II. A failure of catechesis

"Senior citizens" remember receiving instruction in the Christian faith based on a manual that summed up, in question-and-answer form, "the truths that are to be believed and the virtues that are to be practiced". Now, this sort of catechesis has been deemed old-fashioned, and it, too, has been relegated to the dust heaps of history.

Beginning in 1954 with Canon Colomb, an experimental project, the "progressive catechism" was developed. Brand new at the time, this method was not content to question the value of learning by heart, a method dear to the traditional catechism. Influenced by

---

[5] This calls to mind the distributors of contraceptives who are invited to gym classes; the authorization of school nurses to administer the "morning-after" pill to students; the formation of "high school councils" (modeled on the Soviet system?); the inability of teachers to make a student repeat a year, even though his scholastic achievements are abysmal, or to expel a student whose behavior is corrupting an entire class; test answers for sale; and inflated grades that make it possible for any candidate to get a diploma.

[6] *Le Point*, no. 1340, 23 mai 1998.

the studies of Piaget,[7] it proposed "allowing the student to discover the Christian message subjectively and inductively ... in a progressive manner".[8] This was an excuse to put off until "later" the presentation of dogmas that were supposed to be too abstract. In 1957, although Rome demanded that this experiment in progressive catechesis be stopped, it was wasted effort. Not only was this method not abandoned, it was cordially promoted by Bishop Elchinger of Strasbourg and popularized, in large measure thanks to the Institute for Religious Instruction of the Strasbourg Faculty of Theology.

It does no good to lament today that this "catechetical method" contributed to "the religious illiteracy of the younger generations".[9] It would be more helpful to understand the dialectic of the new catechesis, which cannot be separated from the similar disruptive efforts that we observe in the area of liturgy.

When, in the years to come, historians try to understand the postconciliar crisis of the Church, they must not forget to study, above all, the influential lobby of so-called "Modernist" exegetes.

If these exegetes are to be believed, the Gospels are documents that were composed in the "religious turbulence of the second and third centuries".[10] The boldest among them even claim that the Gospels were "retrieved" and "codified" by a clerical hierarchy that, while not "reactionary", was already all too conservative. Starting from this hypothesis, which is debatable at best, the modernist exegetes conclude that in order to know the true message of Jesus, the New Testament must be "demythologized"[11] so as to recover the "kerygma"[12] of the earliest Christian communities.

---

[7] Jean Piaget, Swiss psychologist; his studies on child psychology were authoritative in the postwar period.

[8] This is a pedagogy defended in a little book entitled *Plaie ouverte au sein de l'Église* [An open wound at the heart of the Church].

[9] This is according to Cardinal de Lubac.

[10] These are theories defended by Fr. Émile Boismard, a member of the [Dominican-run] *École Biblique de Saint Étienne* (St. Stephen's Bible School) in Jerusalem, and uncritically adopted by practically all of the professors in charge of the formation of future priests in the seminaries and religious institutes.

[11] This is according to the principles articulated by the Protestant theologian Bultmann.

[12] Theologians apply the Greek word *kerygma* (meaning the announcement made by a town crier) to the summary formula with which the early Christians proclaimed their faith. It was a sort of primitive Creed.

The importance of the kerygma—in other words, the fundamental message proclaiming the Resurrection of Christ, which illumines the entire Christian mystery—must not be minimized, of course. But does that mean that we must allow it to be distorted by a hermeneutic that is all the more seductive for many scholars because it is reductive?

Catechists are often blamed for allowing the prestige of using learned words like "kerygma", "hermeneutic", and "demythologize" go to their heads too quickly when they are dealing with the ignorance of the poor rural parishioner. But aren't the ones really responsible for this giddiness to be found instead among the "mandarins" of modern catechesis, who force teachers to use books "stuffed full of sugar-coated truths" [13], when they are not proposing a "deliberately inverted chronology as a framework for truncated texts" [14] for the purpose of encouraging the faithful to invent creative liturgies inspired by the alleged model of the first Christian communities? [15]

III. From the failure of catechesis to the destabilization of the liturgy

Taking advantage of the weary resignation of millions of Catholics who have become dyslexic, as it were, in their Christian faith, the pedagogy of free expression and the emphasis on creative liturgy (to the detriment of ritual observance) are imposed even more easily, inasmuch as catechists are generally the co-workers of the liturgical planners (when they are not the same persons). Besides, catechist and liturgy planner are interchangeable roles in most parishes, and it is quite easy—just visit the parishes in France—to verify that the *pédagogisme* that has infiltrated catechesis is no stranger to that liturgical "creativity", which is so impoverished as to defy description.

[13] Bulletin *Fidélité et Ouverture* [Fidelity and openness], 36000 Châteauroux, France.

[14] Ibid.

[15] The contents of the catechetical manual *Pierres Vivantes* [Living stones]—published by the authority of the French Bishops and made obligatory for all catechists—is enlightening on this subject.

In this church we have "Gospel-sharing sessions", punctuated by processions around the altar to express openness to others. In that church we have banners with naïve slogans (usually full of spelling errors!), inviting us to "journey together" on the basis of our "lived experience".

But what really takes the cake, in my opinion, is the Mass that I attended recently where, at the end of the Eucharistic Prayer, a ravishing beauty intoned at the microphone: "Although the word 'father' is a term fraught [*piégé*] with conservative connotations, we, relying on Jesus, our liberator, say together: Our Father in light; liberation be your name; may your love for our struggles be our hope ... etc." [16]

Why should we have any scruples at all in pastoral or liturgical matters, given that the soft focus through which the exegetes view the origins of Christian structures allows them to declare any "do-it-yourself liturgy" [17] to be "catholic" and "apostolic", as long as it bears the stamp of approval from a "demythologizer"?

The pretensions of what it has become customary to call a "parallel magisterium" are all the more inadmissible, given the fact that although exegesis can be considered a science, it could never be mistaken for an exact science. It is derived, rather, from the human sciences, which are dependent upon the state of our knowledge about a given era, and which devise interpretations that are always liable to be called into question again when new information is discovered.

Christians, therefore, have good reason to dread the influence wielded by certain professors of biblical exegesis, who continue to indoctrinate diocesan seminarians, while other independent exegetes conclude that, as of the early second century, the Gospels were proclaimed within communities that were very well structured.

---

[16] Bulletin no. 85 of the Association *Pro Liturgia* alluded to this strange *Our Father*, taken from *Prières et chants du peuple de Dieu* [Prayers and songs of the people of God], Édition Tardy CMR, 1992. I personally witnessed the use of this *Our Father* during a Mass celebrated in the Diocese of Amiens. And what can be said about those songs that have managed to replace the *Creed* during Mass in almost all parishes?

[17] This is an expression used by Cardinal Ratzinger (in the French edition of the journal *Communio*, novembre 1977, p. 42).

"What do you know about it," the "demythologizing" exegetes will ask, "given that the oldest surviving manuscripts of the New Testament go back only to the fourth century?"

To be sure, fragments of papyrus older than that have been found, but they are written in Greek and therefore are foreign to the earliest Judeo-Christian community.[18] Critics who have dared to insinuate that the "demythologizing" exegetes end up having the same attitude toward Judaism as did certain German philosophers, such as Kant or Hegel, have been vilified. Furthermore it is high time to present to the public at large the conclusions of independent exegetes, whose studies are often passed over in silence.[19]

In complete disagreement with the teaching that has become official, some philologists have noted that the Greek Gospels of Matthew and Mark follow the rules of Hebrew grammar and syntax.

The rationalist "demythologizers" have completely neglected this fact, which was already glimpsed by Erasmus of Rotterdam in the sixteenth century.[20]

Aren't the Gospels, then, translations of Semitic texts that are no longer extant today? To get to the heart of the matter, some experts in textual criticism tried to translate the Gospels, which are said to be composed in Greek, back into Hebrew. It was astonishingly easy to accomplish, and the work convinced Abbot Jean Carmignac[21] that the writings of Matthew and Mark are "faithful translations of Semitic originals. As for the Gospel of Luke, it was composed in Greek, but on the basis of very literally translated Semitic texts

---

[18] The first Christian community was composed of Jews praying in Hebrew.

[19] See *Le Christ Hébreu: la langue et l'age des Evangiles* [The Hebrew Christ] by Claude Tresmontant (Paris: Éditions F. X. de Guibert, 1983). Claude Tresmontant died in 1997.

[20] According to their theory, the Gospels had borrowed certain myths from the culture of their time. The purpose of "demythologizing", then, is to extricate from this miraculous mythical material the "primitive kernel" of the genuine message of Jesus. According to these exegetes, the kerygma expresses the sole message of Christ.

[21] Abbot Jean Carmignac was an incomparable Hebrew scholar. In order to become better acquainted with his work, you could read *La naissance des Évangiles synoptiques* [The origin of the Synoptic Gospels] (Paris: Éditions F. X. de Guibert) or *Recherche sur le Notre Père* [Research on the Our Father] (Paris: Éditions Letouzay). The writings of Abbot Carmignac (which could be considered embarrassing for modern exegesis) are sequestered at the *Institut Catholique de Paris*. It has become possible, however, to consult them today, and it is hoped that a specialist can have them published in the near future.

which he incorporated into his own edition, sometimes retouching them, and sometimes preserving their rough form."

The Hebrew substratum of these Gospels proves their antiquity, at least if one is willing to recall the horrible drama of the year A.D. 70. Accused of rebelling against the Roman authority, the city of Jerusalem was razed, its inhabitants massacred, and the populations of Judea were deported by legions under the command of Titus. No historian will be able to maintain that a Hebrew literary corpus could have been written in the second century, that is to say, in the midst of a vanished civilization. You might as well imagine Holocaust survivors composing a body of literary work in Yiddish around the year 2000, Claude Tremontant remarked in jest.

Thank God—say it now or never—sophisticated investigative techniques make it possible to declare with certainty that several fragments of the Gospel that have come down to us were written during the decade A.D. 120–130. Now, as the erudite Fr. Hamman tells us, "the writer in antiquity rarely writes. He dictates." [22] The long work of preparing the inks and the papyri, as well as making copies, not to mention the vicissitudes of their distribution, force us to admit that "the Gospels are reports [of a preexisting oral tradition], notwithstanding the opinions of some".[23]

Rather like some *nouveaux riches* who invent a flattering genealogy for themselves, some catechists and pastoral planners will perhaps refute the discoveries of the independent exegetes by retorting, as a proof of their position, that the early Christians loved one another as brothers in their feverish expectation of Christ's imminent return (the "parousia"). This view of things is based on the testimony of the Acts of the Apostles, where it says that the brethren, attending the Temple together,

> devoted themselves to the apostles' teaching and fellowship, to the breaking of bread and the prayers.... And all who believed were together

---

[22] Father A. G. Hamman, *L'épopée du livre, du scribe à l'imprimerie* [The epic of bookmaking, from scribe to printing], in the series "Pour l'Histoire" (Paris: Éditions Perrin, 1985).

[23] Marie-Christine Ceruti-Cendrier, *Les Évangiles sont des reportages, n'en déplaise à certains* [The Gospels are reports, notwithstanding the opinions of some] (Paris: Éditions P. Téqui).

and had all things in common; and they sold their possessions and goods and distributed them to all, as any had need. [Acts 2:42, 44–45]

Some preachers who galvanize the faithful by means of this description—probably embellished to serve as an edifying example to the catechumens—forget that it applies only to the Judeo-Christian community in Jerusalem. And these same preachers pass over in silence another verse from the Acts of the Apostles that makes no mystery of the failure of this community, which was hybrid at least.

Assuredly, the failure of the Christian "kibbutz" of Jerusalem was not due solely to a few haughty members who refused to work on the assumption that the return of the Lord was near. Inevitably, there are plenty of gate-crashers in this sort of utopian view of things. That is also why the Church is right to be prudent with regard to certain new communities of the "charismatic" type: as soon as it is applied on a large scale, the "communism" that the first Christians meant to put into practice brings with it a paralyzing bureaucracy, which makes the initiative fruitless but which is sometimes claimed to be a necessary evil, a defense against the ever-present danger of drifting off-course.

Although the variety of possible approaches to the Gospels sometimes presents contrasting images of Jesus, most recent exegetical studies agree in saying that Christian worship was ritualized very early on.[24] A process of codifying worship seemed natural to catechumens in the cities of antiquity, which were accustomed to seeing a "liturgy" assigned to commemorate an official festival.

Furthermore, it is significant that the Christian vocabulary adopted the term "liturgy" to designate worship. The etymology of the Greek word *leiturgia* is *laos* ("people") and *ergon* ("work"). Taken in its original sense, "liturgy" means "duty", "sacred office", "public ministry". In ancient Greece, the liturgist was the citizen who acted in the name of the city as patron for a performance of a chorus in honor of the gods, for example, the chorus of *The Persians* in which Aeschylus celebrates the victory at Salamis. The liturgist could also

---

[24] Cf. on this subject the works of the Swedish exegetes Riesenfeld and Geharson, which confirm the conclusions of Tresmontant, Carmignac, and Robinson.

be responsible for organizing a public service, for example, games or an oracle.

Obviously, it would never have been permissible for the "liturgical planner" in antiquity to substitute the product of his own creativity for the practically immutable order of the ceremonial. In a society where anyone with a stentorian voice could stir up the crowds or even start a riot, the community sponsoring the event would have excluded the liturgist from the celebration as being guilty of sacrilege.

The manner in which the Greek term *ekklesia* was "rehabilitated" tends to strengthen our argument that the earliest Christian worship was strictly codified. *Ekklesia* in the Greek cities meant the statutory assembly of the people. The choice of this term in Christian vocabulary was most likely guided by the assonance with the Hebrew word *quahal*, which means "convocation".

At the risk of setting off another round of protests by the partisans of liturgical creativity, who suppose that constraints are inimical to freedom, we should recall here that gathering for the Holy Mysteries according to a rigorously set plan was indispensable in order to assure the survival of the early Christian community. Let us not forget that Christians in antiquity did not have the day off and ring church bells on Sunday; recall, too, that the assembly for the Sunday Eucharist was held at irregular intervals from the perspective of the Roman calendar, which was not divided into seven-day weeks.

It should be added that heathen celebrations, presided over by seductive prophetesses who managed to take advantage of isolated baptized individuals who lacked sociocultural bearings, took place also. Competition of this sort with the Church at large was nothing extraordinary at that time, if we are to believe Saint Irenaeus of Lyons, who wrote at the end of the second century, "Sects claiming the Gospel as their own come out of the earth like moles."

Was the arcane discipline a factor in strengthening the credibility of the hierarchic worship of the newborn Church as opposed to the more or less anarchic forms of worship found in the sects? Let us first define "arcane", a notion that is so dear to those who love what is esoteric.

Disciplina arcani: the disciplinary rule whereby the clergy and the lay faithful must not reveal the rites of worship to the uninitiated [*profanes*]. That is what the *Dictionnaire de Théologie catholique* says.[25] The secret of the arcane—which has stirred up the fervid imaginations of so many misguided writers—was necessarily adapted to the needs of each community. Few historians today dispute the fact that it was this arcane discipline—or at least a set of traditions observed by each Christian assembly—that made it possible to transmit unfailingly the New Testament writings as well as the magisterial teaching of the first colleges of bishops.

The experience of the "Eastern lung"[26] of contemporary Christianity shows that such a way of running things is effective. How many times have I heard those in authority in Eastern-rite Churches—Armenians, Byzantines, or Copts—declare that adherence to a consensus of traditions (something as indispensable for them as the genetic code is for a living organism) had been a decisive factor in the survival of their respective communities when faced with the recent vicissitudes of history. And a rabbi confided to me that a Jew cannot help coming to an agreement with this way of running the Eastern churches, provided that "tradition" is not equated with "routine ritualism".

Rather than speak of "tradition", this rabbi preferred to speak of a "collective memory" that would include both ritual matters and the cultural patrimony, so as to solidify the identity of a community and enable it to withstand outside pressures.

"Tradition" or "collective memory"? What does it matter which expression you choose? There is evidence for this notion of cultural and cultic bearings in too wide a range of religions for it to be merely fortuitous. The Muslims, whose religious expansion is undeniable, despite (or because of) the great reverence that they have for their ways and customs, would not contradict the rabbi who was quoted earlier.

Thus, if the reliability of an organization is measured in terms of its ability to withstand crises, one can admire likewise only the functioning of the "Eastern lung" of Christianity. Far from "drifting

---

[25] Paris: Édition Letouzey et Ané.

[26] Pope Paul VI was fond of repeating that the Church breathes with both lungs: the Eastern lung and the Western lung. This image was adopted by Pope John Paul II in his apostolic Letter *Orientale Lumen*.

down a long, calm river", the Eastern Catholics have not been spared schisms, massacres, and persecutions. But our Fathers in faith did not really panic because of these endless misfortunes that have sprung up over the course of time and greatly contributed to the unavoidable tension between the institutional and the prophetic aspects of the Church.

And why didn't they panic? In past ages, every society had its own system in which good and evil, truth and error were identified, explained, and codified. Then too, although the blows were bloody, they did not shake the convictions of either camp; even when the Pope or the bishops failed, the Christian people braced themselves by relying on the liturgy and its yearly cycle, knowing that this privileged bearer of tradition professed the "deposit of faith" unambiguously. The conciseness of the famous adage *"lex orandi, lex credendi"*, which could be translated as "that which is celebrated is the law of faith", ultimately sums up a *modus operandi* that has lasted for two millennia and is practically universal, if we are to believe the anthropologists.

I was just speaking about societies that seem to have disappeared since the coming of modern culture, which is narcissistic, egocentric, and hedonistic, apparently having only one imperative: "be yourself".

Nowadays, confusing discipline and authoritarianism, our modern pedagogues forget that the authority is legitimate and justified, inasmuch as "it alone allows personal autonomy to develop. What frees the individual is this inevitable tyranny. . . . Freedom is not an ontological a priori of the human condition; rather it is something acquired by our integration into society. There is no freedom without apprenticeship, and no apprenticeship without authority", declares the Spanish philosopher Fernando Savater.[27]

The reader will suppose, perhaps, that we are far from our stated subject: how catechesis and the liturgy have become contaminated by *pédagogisme*. But could we be, on the contrary, at the very heart of the problem?

---

[27] Fernando Savater, *Politique à l'usage de mon fils* [Politics for my son's use] (Paris: Éditions du Seuil, 1995); *Pour l'éducation* [In favor of education] (Paris: Éditions Payot, 1997). See also the periodical *Le Point*, no. 1328, 28 octobre 1998.

Please understand me correctly: many, many of us rejoiced to see the conciliar Church get rid of the iron collar of authoritarianism. But on the other hand, how can we not deplore this apparent inability on the part of some of our clergy to explain "the inevitable tyranny of pastoral authority"?

A story about the Communion at a wedding Mass will help the reader to understand better my proposal and to see why our present-day liturgies, gone with the wind of a certain pastoral approach, no longer enable our young people to structure their religious personality, if need be by pointing out to them their transgressions.

At the Mass in question, after the *Lamb of God*, the celebrant announced, "This is the Eucharistic bread. For some, it is the Body of Christ; for others, it will be a symbol; for all, it will be a gesture of friendship in communion with the married couple."

As we were leaving the service, a student friend of mine, a young woman whom I knew to be an agnostic, whispered to me, "How do you expect me to take that busy-body seriously?"

Ah, but that is an extreme case, forbearing souls will say. Anyhow, as time goes on, the clergy are becoming more reasonable; more reasonable with age after having tried so many liturgical experiments that have turned out to be fruitless. So much the better. But we must nevertheless admit that, by dint of repeating these bad habits, one part of the clergy is "hooked" today on a sort of soft consensus that still presents a degraded image of our liturgical celebrations.[28] I cite as proof of this the group of young people, caps firmly in place on their heads, who were walking around in the Cathedral of Nantes while eating sandwiches during a Good Friday service.

The faithful were disturbed, if not shocked. As for the clergy who were present, on the contrary: they took care not to interfere, on the erroneous pretext of "welcoming young people who are seeking".

These young people have become suburban "savages"[29] who have lost their bearings for lack of training and examples. Should we be

---

[28] Cf. Luigi Giussani, *La conscience religieuse de l'homme moderne* [The religious awareness of modern man] (Paris: Éditions du Cerf, 1999). See also the excellent study based on this work by Jean Renaud, "Vancouver ou la modernité triomphante", in the periodical *L'Homme Nouveau*, no. 1241, 1 octobre 2000.

[29] [French] readers will recall that the expression "*sauvageons*" was used by J. P. Chevènement, mayor of Belfort and formerly Minister of the Interior for the Jospin government.

surprised that they no longer know how to show reverence for worship, since nobody explains to them that one does not walk around a sanctuary as if it were the lobby of a tourist center?

And what are we to say about the elegantly printed card with which Cedric and Charlene announced the marriage of their *parents*? The Puritan society of yesteryear supposed that it was the parents' duty to bestow their children's hands in marriage. In today's child-centered culture, a certain pastoral approach that strives to conform to contemporary tastes unfortunately finds it quite normal that parents and children should have interchangeable roles. Certain ecclesiastics (who have a "look" as casual as that of their liturgies) even aggravate the demotion of parents by insisting that they be called by their first names.

In a society where grandparents are still trying to look and act young, and where parents want their children to consider them as pals, all spiritual fatherhood is unfortunately perceived as enticing by young people, inasmuch as it no longer allows them to be confrontive.

Isn't it high time that all of our clergy draw the obvious conclusions from the remarks of Françoise Dolto (which are more often quoted than put into practice)? "A child who is never forbidden to do something, who is always humored, will spend his adulthood in the anguish of never knowing his limits or his identity." [30]

I was attempting to apply the observations of this famous psychoanalyst and pediatrician to the pastoral field when I rediscovered an article from the newspaper *Le Monde* that presents a more catastrophic analysis than the one that I ventured to propose:

Most of the 1,200 testimonies gathered before this Plenary Assembly (the Assembly of French Bishops in Autumn 1996—*author's note*) report the schizophrenic situation that seems to be experienced by young Christians who are active in their movements or their charitable causes, but are very critical of the institutional Church and abandon its practices, such as Sunday Mass, and do not know its dogmatic truths ... or else dispute its teaching.

---

[30] Françoise Dolto and Gérard Severin, *L'Évangile au risque de la psychanalyse*, volume 2 [The Gospel exposed to psychoanalysis] (Paris: Éditions du Seuil).

The journalist Henri Tincq concluded his article by quoting the General Secretary of the Bishops' Conference: "Young Catholics henceforth are in a minority, but they do not have the minority culture of young Jews or Protestants, who are more closely bound to their institution, to its rite and its obligations."[31]

Bravo to him for this lucid diagnosis. But why did Father Dubarle[32] immediately censor himself, not having the courage to propose to the young Catholics the "natural reflexes" that become necessary for other young people who are "in the minority"?

Do we have to reinstate the *disciplina arcani*?

This suggestion is still unrealistic for a kind of Christianity that, whatever they may say, retains a large popular base.

However, doing away with the "new catechetics" and liturgical creativity would enable the Church to check the inexorable decline toward "a pagan France",[33] to quote the title of an authoritative book.

Why not apply this survival strategy that has been used successfully in the minority religions?[34]

[31] H. Tincq, *Le Monde*, 23 avril 1997.

[32] Fr. Dubarle, who quotes *Le Monde*, was at that time Assistant Secretary of the General Secretariat of the Conference of French Bishops. He was also Secretary of the Bishops' Committee for Children and Youth.

[33] Bishop Hippolyte Simon of Clermont-Ferrand, *Vers une France païenne?* [Toward a pagan France?] (Éditions Cana, 1999).

[34] See the article by Fernand Le Nantais that appeared in the Bulletin of the Association *Pro Liturgia* in February 2001.

APPENDIX VI

ARE THE FLAT CHASUBLES USED BY PRIESTS WHO CELEBRATE MASS ACCORDING TO THE PRE-VATICAN II MISSAL "TRADITIONAL"?

During the so-called "traditional" Masses celebrated in chapels that benefit from the Indult granted by Pope John Paul II subsequent to his Motu Proprio *Ecclesia Dei adflicta*, one notices that the priests are usually vested in chasubles that are flat, stiff, and quite ornate.

As a result, many Catholics who are attached to the old rites now associate the liturgical vestment in that design with what they suppose to be the "traditional" form of the Roman liturgy.

Is that really the case?

In the nineteenth century, when the Roman rite had disappeared in France and Gallican liturgies (tinged with Jansenism) flourished, Dom Guéranger, the reformer of Benedictine monasticism in our country, wrote the *Institutions liturgiques*, an important work through which the Abbot of Solesmes intended to restore liturgical unity by means of a return to the Roman rites that were codified at the time of Saint Pius V.

Now, in his work Dom Guéranger emphasized the errors in judgment and taste in the Gallican liturgies that had been composed with the endorsement of the various diocesan authorities; such critiques, we may suspect, were not to the liking of certain bishops who felt that the criticism was aimed at them.

In a letter that is often severe in tone, the Archbishop of Toulouse then reproached Dom Guéranger for having written in the *Institutions liturgiques*,[1] among other things, that the chasubles being used at that time resembled "violin cases".

[1] Cf. volume 2, pp. 141–73.

Dom Guéranger would not be intimidated; he answered the Archbishop of Toulouse point by point with a long, cogently argued letter.

Now, what he says on the subject of wearing flat chasubles—the kind used today by adherents of the so-called "traditional" rite—is especially enlightening for our brief study:

I would say that I do indeed have the right to point out the deviations that become apparent in the form of the sacred vestments, if these deviations are real and if they have been introduced without the concurrence of any ecclesiastical authority.... Anyone who needs to be convinced that there have been deviations in the form of the sacred vestments, should simply take the trouble to look again at vestments made before 1789, which can still be found in many sacristies, of the cathedrals especially. Or do as I have often done, and consult the memories of the venerable members of the "old" [pre-Revolutionary] clergy. You will see then that the chasubles and the copes of that period were not as stiff and short [*étriquées*] as they are today, and that the surplices were pleated according to an entirely different method.... Besides, there are many paintings and many engravings from the seventeenth and eighteenth centuries depicting all of these various vestments; let the reader take the trouble to look them up, and after making the comparison, let him pronounce judgment.

In the old councils, in the old synodal decrees, in the old rituals, in the old ceremonials, I find, under the title of *mensura sacrae supellectilis*, all sorts of rules for the length, width, and height of each piece of the sacred furnishings of our churches. Who nowadays troubles himself to abide by those rules? Who will admit to being the official who inaugurated ... the choice of designs to be embroidered on the stoles, chasubles, and copes, or who introduced that ridiculous buckram[2] that forever deprives the vestments to which it is added of the character of clothing, etc.?

Certainly, no ecclesiastical authority ever sanctioned such things; all the blame should be laid at the feet of the manufacturers of *church supplies* who are ceaselessly pushing new fashions that are accepted with the same indifference with which the old ones were rejected. And as part of this trend, any aesthetic sense is progressively vanishing; there is no more guarantee for the sobriety and stability of the external forms,

---

[2] We should explain that buckram [*bougran*] was a stiff-finished, heavily sized cloth that was placed between the fabric and the lining of a vestment in order to make it less pliant.

so people stop giving any thought to them. Thus what is ugly, bizarre, and meaningless is becoming established where the beautiful, the serious, and the sublime ought to have a permanent place.

We have to get out of this predicament....

As for the *violin cases*, let us make sure that we understand each other. The comparison is a fair one, no doubt, but it is not mine. The illustrious Welby Pugin, who is highly regarded by the entire Catholic episcopacy in England and is also admired by many people on the continent, found that the front of our chasubles lent itself to this unfortunate comparison; I took the liberty of repeating it, while citing my source. If I were to retract my statement today, would it follow that this great and devout artist had never written the remark? Or would it change the chasuble fronts the least bit? Besides, as a way of distracting from the real issue, I have been accused of seconding this opinion of a foreign artist with regard to chasubles of any sort. But here are my exact words: *These chasubles that a piece of inflexible buckram in the front part has made similar to violin cases, to employ the all-too-true expression of the well-known English artist, Welby Pugin....*[3] It is quite clear, therefore, that the *inflexible buckram* is the sole cause of this untoward effect against which I am speaking out. This *buckram* that is inexplicably in vogue was unknown fifty years ago; vestments that are the least bit old never had any. Remove it, and the similarity to a *violin case* disappears with it. The vestment automatically yields; it no longer resembles a plank that has been fitted to a human being; it assumes the form of the body: in a word, it *clothes* the one who wears it.[4]

And so, as Dom Guéranger demonstrates, some features of the Mass said to be "of Saint Pius V", which many people believe to be traditional elements, actually go back only to the nineteenth century.

We have cited here the example of the chasuble. There are others: quite often, they are simply the customs of an age that have taken on such importance that people come to confuse them first with the liturgy, and then with the liturgical "tradition" itself.

---

[3] *Institutions liturgiques*, vol. 2, p. 629.

[4] *Institutions liturgiques*, vol. 4, pp. 76–79. It is well known that clothing often reveals the psychology of the one wearing it. In the nineteenth century, Dom Guéranger spoke out against the stiffness that had come over chasubles: What did this sudden "hardness" of a vestment reveal? A certain rigidity in thinking? We cannot help wondering also, What is revealed by the cordless albs that have become the standard vestment used today in practically all the liturgical celebrations in France?

Shouldn't we hope that the Catholics who, for various reasons, are attached to the "Tridentine" rites (which they describe as "traditional"), might be able some day, in the light of objective historical studies, to get rid of the entire heritage of the nineteenth century, which is often more "sentimental" than genuinely "traditional"?

We bet that a good dusting off would render an important service to the liturgy as a whole, by allowing us to move on to the constructive debates that are so much needed today.

APPENDIX VII

THE GENERAL INTERCESSIONS

The prayer of the faithful: From its beginnings to Vatican II

> First of all, then, I urge that supplications, prayers, intercessions, and thanksgivings be made for all men, for kings and all who are in high positions, that we may lead a quiet and peaceable life, godly and respectful in every way. This is good, and it is acceptable in the sight of God our Savior, who desires all men to be saved and to come to the knowledge of the truth.[1]

The foregoing is what the Apostle Paul wrote in his first letter to Timothy, a document that outlines the organization of the Christian communities in apostolic times. The prayer of the faithful appears in it as a method of carrying out God's project: bringing men to him so as to offer them eternal salvation.

The oldest descriptions of the Sunday liturgy, those written by Justin Martyr in the second century and by Hippolytus of Rome in the following century, testify that the churches were faithful to the precept of Saint Paul:

> The memoirs of the Apostles or the writings of the prophets are read. Then when the reader has finished, the Ruler [of the Brethren, i.e., presider] in a discourse instructs and exhorts to the imitation of these good things. Then we all stand up together and offer prayers.[2]
>
> ... [W]e offer prayers in common for ourselves and for the one who has been illuminated [i.e., the neophyte] and for all others everywhere, that we may be accounted worthy, having learned the truth, by our

---

[1] I Timothy 2:1–4.
[2] Justin Martyr, *First Apology*, chap. 67.

deeds also to be found good citizens and guardians of what is commanded, so that we may be saved with eternal salvation.[3]

The *Apostolic Tradition* by Hippolytus of Rome, on the other hand, presents the general intercessions as a prerogative of the faithful: the newly baptized, who had been dismissed after the Liturgy of the Word during their catechumenate, now take part in them for the first time.

This prayer of the faithful varied in form from one region to another, and it was suppressed during the fourth century: in the Leonine Sacramentary,[4] which appeared in 560, no trace of it remains. General intercessions were known in Rome under a related form that we still see in the Good Friday litanies, but on a daily basis they fell into disuse, no doubt after the *Kyrie* was introduced into the liturgy of the Mass. The latter prayer, which has been attributed to Pope Gelasius I (492–496), originally had the form of a litany as well, with the repeated response *"Domine, exaudi et miserere"* [Latin: "Lord, hear our prayer and have mercy"] or *"Kyrie eleison"* [Greek: "Lord have mercy"].

Although they had disappeared due to the ravages of time,[5] the general intercessions have taken their original place again after fourteen centuries, thanks to the liturgical renewal implemented by the Second Vatican Council:

> The "common prayer" or "prayer of the faithful" is to be restored after the gospel and homily, especially on Sundays and holy days of obligation. By this prayer in which the people are to take part, intercession will be made for holy Church, for the civil authorities, for those oppressed by various needs, for all mankind, and for the salvation of the entire world.[6]

---

[3] Ibid., chap. 65.

[4] This is a work that is considered to be an ancestor of our present missal.

[5] A form of the general intercessions, nevertheless, existed as part of some local customs. In Italy, France, England, or Germany, the celebrant invited the faithful after the homily to pray for various intentions by reciting an *Our Father* silently. Toward the end of the Middle Ages, this practice was incorporated into the "sermon", a set of instructions and miscellaneous announcements made by the priest along with the homily.

[6] SC 53.

Purpose of the general intercessions

Already considered by Hippolytus of Rome as a right belonging specifically to those who are baptized, the general intercessions that conclude the Liturgy of the Word and introduce the Liturgy of the Eucharist are the expression of the prayer of the whole assembly, hence the name "prayer of the faithful". Through the general intercessions "the people, exercising their priestly function, intercede for all humanity." [7]

> It is desirable that a deacon, cantor, or other person announce the intentions. The whole assembly gives expression to its supplication either by a response said together after each intention or by silent prayer. It belongs to the priest celebrant to direct the general intercessions, by means of a brief introduction to invite the congregation to pray, and after the intercessions to say the concluding prayer. [8]

The matter for this prayer consists of "petitions addressed to God, that he will deign to protect the Church, people all over the world, and the community gathered at that very moment to celebrate the Eucharist". [9]

In the outline specified by the "General Instruction on the Roman Missal" ([1975 edition] see no. 46)—"for the needs of the Church, for public authorities and the salvation of the world, for those oppressed by any need, and for the local community"—we find the main intentions that had already been formulated in the *Apostolic Constitutions* and the *Euchologion* or *Prayerbook of Sarapion*, two liturgical collections from the fourth century: the Church, the clergy, the catechumens, those in authority, the city, its inhabitants, the sick, those in exile, slaves, refugees, sailors, travelers, and those who persecute Christians.

The general or "universal" character of this prayer should be noted. It has the intentions of the whole world in view, and only after that come the concerns of the local community, which are of secondary importance. This was strongly emphasized in the recent

---

[7] GIRM, 1975 edition, no. 45.

[8] Ibid., no. 47.

[9] Denis Crouan, *Symboles et mystère de la messe* [The symbols and the mystery of the Mass] (Paris: Éditions Téqui).

note from the CNPL [Centre National de Pastorale Lituraique]; furthermore, Fr. Rey-Mermet was quite correct in pointing this out in lines that he wrote—more than twenty years ago![10]

Let us add, also, that these prayers, far from being the mere expression of the desires and hopes of a particular group (however legitimate they may be), have as their purpose the salvation of the world, as both Saint Paul and the Second Vatican Council have stated. In this sense, the general intercessions serve as an introduction to the Liturgy of the Eucharist, the memorial of Christ's sacrifice, which is offered "for the glory of God and the salvation of the world".[11]

---

[10] Th. Rey-Mermet, volume 2 in the series "Croire", *Vivre sa foi dans les sacrements* [Living one's faith in the sacraments] (Paris: Éditions Droguet-Ardant, 1977).

[11] This is paraphrasing Henri Treguier in the Bulletin of *Pro Liturgia* (juillet 1999).

APPENDIX VIII

BEAUTY AND HARMONY IN THE LITURGY

Liturgy and beauty

At the beginning of the Constitution on the Sacred Liturgy, the Second Vatican Council recalls that every earthly liturgy ought to be a reflection of the heavenly liturgy and that the human elements that quite naturally are found in liturgical celebrations here below are necessarily subordinate to the divine.

The whole people of God, therefore, is engaged in carrying out a liturgy that is the "icon" of the eternal liturgy; it is invited to participate in this liturgy inasmuch as it is the "image" of the life to come.

For this reason, the symbolic elements that are employed in celebrating various liturgies can acquire their full meaning only to the extent that they are used so as to reveal to the heart of man the beauty of the Kingdom of God: of that Kingdom that, as Scripture says, is not of this world.

Note that in Greek and in Hebrew the same word means both "beautiful" and "good". Therefore we must constantly make sure that the worship being rendered to God is beautiful; this is because we know that in the first place God is the one who utilizes beauty to make us more aware of his goodness. We are invited to contemplate divine truth as though it were something beautiful placed before our eyes. Moreover, this is the precise meaning of the Feast of the Transfiguration: God resplendent allows his creatures to behold him.

In order to grasp and experience these subtle realities better, it is necessary for man to become a child. Or rather: he must acquire a childlike spirit.

What is this childlike spirit? The true spirit of childhood is not something affected or sentimental; instead, it is essentially a spirit that is capable of wonder. For through wonder, we can discover that God is present and that he speaks to us in the beauty of the liturgy. Only the heart of a child, that is, a humble, simple heart, can grasp the significance of the liturgical beauty through which God reveals his Face to us in the splendor of his boundless Love.

The liturgy, therefore, should be beautiful: beautiful because of our gestures and postures, beautiful because of the words and the singing that have been bequeathed to us by tradition and that are the expression of the centuries-old experience acquired by the Church and nourished by the loving presence of God.

That is why a sense of beauty and balance—this correct proportion that Vatican II associates with "noble simplicity"—are necessary in the liturgy: aesthetics and equilibrium together form a complex of signifiers that are not addressed exclusively to the reason, but also to the heart of man. As for the expression "noble simplicity", it states perfectly what worship rendered to God should look like: "simple", which does not mean "impoverished" but rather "folded once" [from Latin: *simplex* = *semel-plico*], that is, without com-*plica*-tions and without even a hint of ambiguity.

It has been said that in the liturgy, learned considerations are not enough, nor are the "right words" [*les "bonnes paroles"*]; also and especially necessary are aesthetics and "beautiful words".

Why are aesthetics and beautiful words necessary—above all, the biblical words incorporated into the Gregorian chants? Simply because the liturgy, by its very nature, is designed to encompass the entire man. It aims, therefore, more at enlightening hearts so as to open them up to an understanding of the Christian message than at instructing the faithful directly by way of reason.

If a lesson is to be learned in the course of liturgical celebrations—and this is nonetheless desirable—it can come only at the end of a process of illumination: only a genuine enlightenment can guarantee the effectiveness of any instruction of a catechetical nature. The illumination clears the path for the handing on of what has been received [from tradition].

Thus, the Catholic who participates in the liturgical prayer of the Church does not come to church primarily to concentrate intellectually on the teaching that one celebrant or another, this or that preacher can impart to him. He comes in order to be imbued with the loveliness of the liturgy [cf. Ps. 84]; in this way he can nourish his soul, his mind, and his heart.

We must insist, therefore, on this point, which was already suggested earlier: in the liturgy we must behave like children, like little children who are open to the wonders of the world. This attitude requires, at the same time, peace, tranquility, and concentration. When the beauty and correctness of a celebration allow all this, when liturgical aesthetics are conducive to this essential disposition, then the services never seem long or boring: quite on the contrary, one no longer notices the passage of time. The celebration then appears as a moment of eternity in which we place our lives in Him-Who-is-Life, as a privileged occasion when, thanks to a certain asceticism, we are able to experience something like a suspension of time in a foretaste of the Kingdom of God. The liturgy then becomes peaceful, because everything in it breathes the silent presence of the Lord.

Liturgical aesthetics are necessary, because all liturgy is consecrated to God; indeed, every liturgical celebration is offered first of all to the Divine Majesty as a sacrifice of praise. In observing the beauty of the liturgy as it has been handed down by the Church, that is, in performing correctly and with dignity what the Church asks us to perform with faith and reverence, we enable the faithful to experience wonder at the beauty of worship: a beauty that does not depend on the manner in which the celebrant plans the liturgy, but depends instead on tradition—the tradition that fashioned the worship ceremony so as to make it an "icon" of the Kingdom in which we are even now called to find our place.

Chant and liturgical beauty

The liturgy ought to be inconceivable except as expressed in song. The normal form of our Roman liturgy is the sung form. For every feast of the liturgical year, for every moment of the liturgical ceremony, there is indeed a corresponding chant, which is the melodic and verbal expression of the celebration.

In the liturgy, chant is never something added "to make it more beautiful" or "to make it more solemn", or else in order to please the congregation. Chant is in the first place an expression of reverence and an aid to prayer. Therefore it must be an open window: not a window opening onto the choir or the congregation or the cantor or the liturgical commentator, but rather a window open to the invisible Kingdom.

That is why liturgical singing, too, must obey certain canons or rules. Just because some trend or a particular event introduces a song into the liturgy, that does not make the song "liturgical" in the full sense of the word.

A person who can compose pleasant tunes or popular songs does not *ipso facto* become a "liturgical composer"; the composers of "Silent Night" or of "O Holy Night" never were so pretentious as to call themselves "liturgical composers". Besides, can there be such a thing as a "liturgical composer", strictly speaking? Isn't the Church herself the only one capable of giving rise to the melodies that alone are capable of expressing her prayer properly?

Liturgical singing necessarily has its own aesthetics, which corresponds to the liturgical tradition which inspires it. That is why, in the first place, genuinely liturgical singing avoids anything that would make it resemble a decorative art in which the tones are more suggestive than expressive.

The principal mission of liturgical singing is to create a universe of sound capable of channeling man's thoughts and raising his mind by calming him, so that without any apparent effort he may open himself to contemplation. And so liturgical singing must never seek to take delight in human feelings or emotions, neither by its words nor by its melodies. It should be so crafted, melodically and verbally, as to draw the listener to forget his cares, so that, in a movement of self-transcendence, he may be open to the presence of God.

Gregorian chant fulfills these essential requirements perfectly: that is why the Church has made it the distinctive sacred song of our liturgy and the perfect model for all singing that is meant to be liturgical.

Gregorian chant uses only the human voice, which alone is suited to praising God. The text always has priority over the music; the latter is only an aid to the sacred text, even though in certain cases the words disappear so as to let the chant become a pure melody capable of expressing the ineffable.

Authentic liturgical singing must also be able to create a harmony of tones that is united with the harmony of rites: from this union is born the harmony of the entire "liturgical edifice". Now, in order that liturgical singing may participate in the development of this harmony, of this synthesis, it is not enough for the melody to be perfect; there has to be a perceptible rhythm as well.

Now, in liturgical chant, the rhythm is not produced exclusively by a regular succession of accented and unaccented beats, as in contemporary music. It must be based upon the succession of verbal accents, on the consonants that give structure to the words, and on the vowels that "illuminate" the sacred text that is being sung [as a copyist might illuminate a manuscript with colorful designs].

We should note here also that only Gregorian chant succeeds in creating this synthesis. It is true that the flexibility of the Latin language makes its task easier. Indeed, Latin is an accented language, rich in vowels, with a grammar that allows word order to vary, according to choices determined by the liturgy, which is understood to be "contemplated theology". The Latin text provides a perfect instrument for producing song that is suited to serving divine worship.

Finally, in genuine liturgical singing, melody and rhythm should be closely united, so as to be identified then with certain moments of the liturgy that are specified by the gestures or the postures of those who participate in the celebration. That is why an *Introit* cannot be composed in the same style as an offertory and cannot emit the same "atmosphere". That is also why the chants of the liturgy cannot be placed just anywhere; what is meant to be sung at the beginning of the celebration cannot be sung at Communion. In the liturgy, the chants are never interchangeable.

When they are at their respective places, each one of the pieces chanted during the liturgy emphasizes an important moment in the celebration; thus they create periods of transition that are necessary both for the harmonious unfolding of the liturgy and also for the reverent performance of the sacred rites. This phenomenon is quite evident during the Liturgy of the Word, for example: when the *Gradual* and *Alleluia* chants are at the right place, they perfectly fulfill their purpose as "meditative transitions" to the different Old and New Testament readings; they promote the sort of atmosphere that is conducive to experiencing the Liturgy of the Word in a more intense, more interior way—so that those who are in attendance not only hear, but also "ponder" the Word.

This essential meaning of the rhythm and melody is found also in some simple prayers, in the psalms, or even in the proclamation of the readings. Prayers, psalms, and readings must never resemble theatrical speeches accompanied by glances toward the congregation and varying vocal emphases aimed at highlighting this word or that expression. It is important that each liturgical text be declaimed in the proper manner: a manner that quite rightly enables the lector to eliminate emotions, so as to spare the congregation the discomfort of being held hostage to the moods and whims of the one who has been assigned to read.

In the liturgy, it is imperative that the participants in the liturgical celebration (celebrant, choir members, lectors) not seek to express their feelings; on the contrary, they must mask their respective personalities (the liturgical vestments are there to help them) in order to make room for the inspiration of the Holy Spirit and so as to allow God to act freely. Only God, acting through his Word and in the Sacred Species, should enter the hearts of the faithful; in order for this penetration to be possible, it is necessary to avoid interference from the personalities of those who participate in the liturgy and, even more important, to prevent the appearance of any pathological traits that they might have.

Conclusion

Beauty and harmony of worship and the self-effacing subordination of the personalities of the ministers are the three essential components of the liturgy that we should rediscover today.

If our contemporary liturgies are often at cross-purposes with the major principles that have been presented here, which are common to all the [historic] rites [of the Church], it is because they have often been deprived of the "beautiful" that manifests the "true". Then, in order to fill up the void that is felt in so many Eucharistic celebrations that have become as dull as they are ugly, they call in the liturgical committees, which sometimes don't know what else to devise in order to make the celebrations attractive.

We certainly must agree that many of the experiments in "pastoral approaches to the liturgy" that have been carried out in this way over the past thirty years have produced no results.

Well, then, why not try one last experiment, which would consist simply of implementing what is in the revised Roman Missal, while seeking as honestly as possible to carry out everything in the beauty and harmony of the traditional forms that are the heritage of our Roman liturgy?